D1254181

THE WARSAW ECONOMY IN TRANSITION

The Warsaw Economy in Transition

DAVID E. DOWALL
MARTA SADOWY
ALOJZY ZALEWSKI

Avebury

Aldershot · Brookfield USA · Hong Kong · Singapore · Sydney

© D.E. Dowall, M. Sadowy and A. Zalewski 1996

All rights reserved. No part of this publication may be reproduced, stored in a retrieval system, or transmitted in any form or by any means, electronic, mechanical, photocopying, recording or otherwise without the prior permission of the publisher.

Published by
Avebury
Ashgate Publishing Ltd
Gower House
Croft Road
Aldershot
Hants GU11 3HR
England

Ashgate Publishing Company
Old Post Road
Brookfield
Vermont 05036
USA

British Library Cataloguing in Publication Data

Dowall, David E.
    The Warsaw economy in transition
    1. Warsaw (Poland) - Economic conditions
    I. Title II. Sadowy, Marta III. Zalewski, Alojzy
    330.9'4384

    ISBN 1 85972 339 X

Library of Congress Catalog Card Number: 96-83221

Printed in Great Britain by
Antony Rowe Ltd, Chippenham, Wiltshire

Contents

Figures and tables   viii
Acknowledgements   xiv

1 Executive summary   1
   Introduction   1
   Impact of the economic system's transformation
   on the Polish economy and the economy of Warsaw   3
   Changes in the spatial structure of the Warsaw metropolitan economy   5
   Demographic profile of Warsaw metropolitan region   7

2 The economic condition of Warsaw in the context
  of the national economy   20
   Introduction: the impact of the transformation of the economic
   system on the economy of Poland and the economy of Warsaw   20
   The structure of the Polish economy   26
   Poland in the international system — the structure of foreign trade   34
   Warsaw's role in the national economy   43
   Chapter 2 Appendix   53

3 Changes in the spatial structure of the Warsaw metropolitan economy   58
   Spatial distribution of economic activity   58
   Spatial patterns of business activity   67
   Spatial distribution of fixed assets and their productivity   72
   Distribution of investment expenditures, their structure and dynamics   77

4 Demographic profile of Warsaw   90
   Introduction   90
   Overall population trends   90
   Components of Warsaw's population change   92

Warsaw's household characteristics 93
Labor force characteristics 94
Spatial distribution of population 95
Household income and expenditures 98
Conclusions 98

5 Warsaw property market assessment 100
Introduction 100
Land use and land ownership 100
Housing conditions and trends 103
City of Warsaw's emerging office sector 106
Retail trade 109
Wholesale trade 112
Industrial activity 114
Lodging 116
Conclusions about property development 117

6 An assessment of the city of Warsaw's infrastructure system 120
Introduction 120
Water supply and waste-water systems 120
Central heating 131
Municipal transport services 138
Roads 146
Sanitation services 152
Telecommunications 157
Electric power 160
Gas supply 162
Summing up Warsaw's infrastructure needs 163

**7 Forecast of economic activity for Warsaw
and the Warsaw metropolitan area** 167
Introduction 167
Review of economic development forecasts for Poland 167
Anticipated goals of economic growth in Poland 169
Economic development scenarios for Warsaw 171
Economic development forecasts for Warsaw 173

8 Future real estate requirements of the Warsaw region 181
Introduction 181
Housing requirements 181
Office space 181
Retailing 183
Industrial facilities 185
Warehousing and distribution centers 186

vi

Overall summary of future property development activity, 1992-1997   190

9 Conclusions and recommendations   192
   Introduction   192
   Economic performance   192
   Warsaw's future economic prospects   195
   What will it cost to modernize and expand Warsaw's economic base?   196
   Making Warsaw more efficient: the role of urban planning   198

Tables and maps

Table 2.1   The rate of change of national-level macroeconomic indices
             in constant prices (1988 = 100.0)   24
Table 2.2   Employment* in Poland, Warsaw metropolitan area
             and Warsaw ('000)   25
Table 2.3   Trends in GDP in constant prices (previous year = 100)   27
Table 2.4   Employment by sectors and forms of ownership for Poland
             in 1989-1992   28
Table 2.5   Employment in industry in Poland ('000)   30
Table 2.6   Employment by branch for Warsaw metropolitan area,
             Warsaw and suburban ring and Poland, 1988,1992 ('000)   31
Table 2.7   Value of exports and imports for Poland, Warsaw, and Warsaw
             metropolitan area in 1988-1992, in constant 1988 zloty   35
Table 2.8   Exports to groups of countries for Poland in 1988-1992,
             in constant 1988 zloty   36
Table 2.9   Imports from groups of countries for Poland in 1988-1992,
             in constant 1988 zloty   37
Table 2.10   Value of exports by branch for Poland, Warsaw metropolitan
             area, and Warsaw in 1988-1992, in constant zloty   38
Table 2.11   Percent distribution of exports by branch for Poland, Warsaw
             metropolitan area and Warsaw in 1988-1992 (in %)   41
Table 2.12   Capital investment outlays by branch for Poland, Warsaw
             metropolitan area and Warsaw, 1988-1992,
             in constant 1988 zlotys   44
Table 2.13   Gross productivity ratios (GPR)* for Poland, Warsaw
             metropolitan area and Warsaw in 1988-1992 (in %)   48
Table 2.14   Net productivity ratios (NPR)* for Poland, Warsaw
             metropolitan area and Warsaw in 1988-1992 (in %)   50

Table 2.15   Warsaw compared to Poland and Warsaw metropolitan area,
1988, 1992   52

Table 2A.1   Value of exports by branch and products for Poland, Warsaw
metropolitan area and Warsaw in 1988-1992,
in constant 1988 zloty (billions)   53

Table 2A.2   Percent distribution of exports by branch and products for Poland,
Warsaw metropolitan area and Warsaw in 1988-1992 (in %)   56

Table 3.1   Number and percent distribution of establishments
by branch for Warsaw metropolitan area, center
and rings in 1988 and 1992   60

Table 3.2   Spatial distribution of employment* in Warsaw
metropolitan area and rings in 1988 and 1992   64

Table 3.3   Declared employment by sectors for Warsaw
metropolitan area and rings in 1988 and 1992   66

Table 3.4   Total income and cost of production by branch in Warsaw
metropolitan area, center and rings in 1988 and 1992,
in millions zlotys, constant 1988 prices   68

Table 3.5   Net and gross profitability for Warsaw metropolitan area
and rings in 1988 and 1992   72

Table 3.6   Gross value of fixed assets estimated by location,
in 1988, 1992, in millions of zlotys, constant 1988 prices   74

Table 3.7   Gross value of fixed assets, total income of enterprises and
gross productivity of fixed assets by branch for Warsaw
metropolitan area, center and rings in 1988 and 1992,
in millions zlotys, constant 1988 prices   76

Table 3.8   Investment outlays by branch for Warsaw metropolitan area,
Warsaw and rings in 1988-1992, in constant 1988 prices (in
millions zlotys)   80

Table 3.9   Percent change of investment outlays for Warsaw metropolitan
area, center and rings in 1988-1992, using constant PLZ figures
(1988 = 100)   84

Table 3.10   Investment outlays and gross value of fixed assets by branch
for Warsaw metropolitan area and rings in 1988-1992   87

Table 4.1   Population trends in Poland and the Warsaw metropolitan area,
1950-1992   91

Table 4.2   Age distribution of Poland and Warsaw metropolitan area,
1980-1992   91

Table 4.3   Components of population change in Warsaw metropolitan
area, 1980, 1990, 1991, 1992   92

Table 4.4   Households trends in Warsaw metropolitan area, 1988-1992   93

Table 4.5   Total and full time workers in the city of Warsaw ('000)   94

Table 4.6   Full time workers in the city of Warsaw, by level of education   95

Table 4.7	Population changes in Warsaw metropolitan area, 1988-1992	96
Table 4.8	Estimated total household income in Warsaw metropolitan area, 1992	98
Table 4.9	Estimate of Warsaw region aggregate household expenditures by type of consumption, 1992 (PLZ 000,000)	99
Table 5.1	Land utilization and availability, 1992	101
Table 5.2	Land ownership patterns, 1992	102
Table 5.3	Trends in housing stock, Warsaw metropolitan area, 1980-1992	104
Table 5.4	Age of housing stock, Warsaw metropolitan area, 1992	104
Table 5.5	Housing quality indicators, Warsaw metropolitan area, 1980-1992	104
Table 5.6	Trends in housing construction, Warsaw metropolitan area, 1980-1992	105
Table 5.7	Housing stock by form of ownership, Warsaw metropolitan area, 1992	105
Table 5.8	Housing rental and mortgage arrears, Warsaw metropolitan area, 1992	105
Table 5.9	Private and public sector construction activities in the Warsaw metropolitan area, office and service buildings, 1980-1992	108
Table 5.10	Trends in employment and establishments in finance and insurance, Warsaw metropolitan area, 1988-1992	108
Table 5.11	Trends in domestic and foreign private sector establishments, Warsaw metropolitan area, 1980-1992	109
Table 5.12	Finance and insurance and foreign companies located Srodmiescie, City of Warsaw and Warsaw metropolitan area, 1988-1992	110
Table 5.13	Trade employment, Warsaw metropolitan area, 1988-1992	110
Table 5.14	Retail shops in Warsaw metropolitan area, 1980-1992	111
Table 5.15	Distribution of retail employment and retail space, 1992	111
Table 5.16	Wholesale employment in Warsaw metropolitan area, 1988-1992	112
Table 5.17	Distribution of warehouse facilities, 1992	113
Table 5.18	Trends in industrial employment, Warsaw metropolitan area, 1988-1992	114
Table 5.19	Estimates of industrial space, metropolitan Warsaw, 1988-1992	115
Table 5.20	Distribution of industrial employment, Warsaw metropolitan area, 1988-1992	115
Table 5.21	Distribution of occupied and vacant or converted industrial space, 1992	116

Table 5.22   Hotel accommodations by type, Warsaw metropolitan area,
             1988-1992   116
Table 5.23   Hotel accommodations by location, 1988-1992   117

Table 6.1   Water production and its structure according to source in
             Warsaw, between 1988-1993   123
Table 6.2   Distribution of water production and treatment of waste-water
             by type of consumer, in Warsaw, 1988-1992   126
Table 6.3   MPWiK revenues by source, 1988-1992,
             in constant 1988 PLZ (000,000)   131
Table 6.4   Cost of water and waste-water services (MPWiK), 1989-1992,
             in constant 1988 PZL (000,000)   132
Table 6.5   MPWiK estimated revenues and cost per cubic meter
             of output, in 1988 constant PLZ   133
Table 6.6   Warsaw's central heating system, 1988-1993   135
Table 6.7   Indicators and physical condition of Warsaw
             central heating system   137
Table 6.8   Central heating costs, in constant 1988 prices, 1988-1992   139
Table 6.9   District heating profit and loss, 1988-1992,
             in constant 1988 (000,000) zlotys   139
Table 6.10   City communications network of Warsaw in 1988-1993   141
Table 6.11   Fleet inventory and kilometers traveled in Warsaw,
             1988-1993   144
Table 6.12   Exploitation ratios of the city (MZK) transportation fleet,
             1988-1993   146
Table 6.13   Fixed assets and investment in transportation fleet,
             in constant 1988 zlotys   147
Table 6.14   Cost structure of basic Warsaw transit operations, 1988-1992,
             in percent   149
Table 6.15   Cost structure of the Warsaw transit system, 1988-1992,
             in percent   150
Table 6.16   Financial performance of MZK operations for 1989-1992,
             in constant 1988 PLZ (000,000)   151
Table 6.17   Lengths and surface areas of national and voivodship roads
             in Warsaw, by type of surface, 1993   151
Table 6.18   MZO fleet description, 1989-1992   155
Table 6.19   Profit and loss account from sanitation activity, 1988-1992,
             in constant 1988 plz (000,000)   156

Table 7.1   Economic growth in Poland, 1993-1997, in percent   168
Table 7.2   Projections of Poland's economic growth, 1993-1997   169
Table 7.3   Projection of employment in Warsaw and the Warsaw
             metropolitan area, in 1993-1997 (in '000), Scenario I —
             Continuation of trends from years 1988-1992   175

xi

Table 7.4   Projection of employment in Warsaw and the Warsaw
                metropolitan area, in 1993-1997 (in '000), Scenario II —
                Diversified growth   177

Table 7.5   Projection of employment in Warsaw and the Warsaw
                metropolitan area, in 1993-1997 (in '000), Scenario III —
                Accelerated growth   178

Table 7.6   Percent change in employment 1992-1997, Warsaw and
                metropolitan Warsaw, three scenarios (in %)   179

Table 7.7   Structure of Warsaw and metropolitan Warsaw area for 1992
                and three scenarios (in %)   180

Table 8.1   Employment projections for finance and insurance and
                administration, metropolitan Warsaw, 1992-1997   182

Table 8.2   Finance and insurance investment outlays for building
                construction, metropolitan Warsaw, 1988-1992   183

Table 8.3   Projected trade employment, 1992-1997, in the Warsaw
                metropolitan area   184

Table 8.4   Projections of industrial employment in the Warsaw
                metropolitan area   186

Table 8.5   Projections of industrial space in the Warsaw
                metropolitan area   187

Table 8.6   Spatial projections of industrial employment in the Warsaw
                metropolitan area   187

Table 8.7   Spatial projections of industrial space in the Warsaw
                metropolitan area (square meters)   187

Table 8.8   Projected future employment in wholesale trade, in the
                Warsaw metropolitan area   188

Table 8.9   Projected demand for warehousing facilities, 1997, in the
                Warsaw metropolitan area   189

Table 8.10   Distribution of warehousing space, metropolitan Warsaw
                ('000) sq. meters   190

Table 8.11   Summary of property development projections, 1992-1997,
                metropolitan Warsaw   191

Map 3.1 Metropolitan Warsaw, center and three rings   59

Map 4.1 Metropolitan Warsaw population change   97

Map 5.1 Office rent patterns in Warsaw's central business district   107

Map 6.1 Warsaw's water supply system   121
Map 6.2 Warsaw's sewage and waste-water treatment system   125
Map 6.3 Warsaw's central heating system   134
Map 6.4 Warsaw's Road and Street System   148
Map 6.5 Warsaw's Waste Collection System   153
Map 6.6 Warsaw's Telecommunications System   158
Map 6.7 Warsaw's Electric Power System   161
Map 6.8 Warsaw's Gas Supply System   164

Acknowledgments

The report was jointly prepared by David Dowall (University of California at Berkeley), and Marta Sadowy and Alojzy Zalewski (Warsaw School of Economics). All three jointly prepared Chapters 1 and 9. Professor Zalewski prepared chapters 2, 3 and 7. Professor Dowall prepared chapters 4, 5 and 8. Professor Sadowy prepared chapter 6.

This report reflects the work of many people, and the authors would like to acknowledge their help. The initial concept for the project came from Mr. Olgierd Dziekonski, Vice Mayor of the City of Warsaw. Ms. Sonia Hammam of U.S. A.I.D. supported the City's interest in promoting economic development and helped to shape the project into a viable and effective program of technical assistance. Mr. Wojciech Matusik, Director of the City of Warsaw's Land Development Department, Chaired the project's steering committee and served as City liaison to the project. Technical Department Director Witold Galinski and Vice Directors Jerzy Kulig and Malgorzata Sosnowska provided access to Warsaw's infrastructure data. Director Serguisz Madurowicz of the Warsaw Development Authority provided excellent logistical support and advice. Mr. Henryk Jablonski of the Technical Department provided logistical support to the project. Mr. Jan Jakobsche of the Development Promotion Department was a superb source of information about the City's growth and development.

Staff of the Voivodship Statistical Office, especially Mrs. Malgorzata Bulska, were extremely helpful in providing data on the Warsaw economy. Ms. Malgorzata Janczak-Roszkowska of the Foreign Trade Information Center was also very helpful. Vast amounts of data were organized, checked, tabulated and archived by Jaroslaw Jukiel and Slawomir Assendi. Ms. Katarzyna Baczyrinska of the Development Authority also assisted in the preparation of tables. Dr. Barbara Sakowska-Knapp organized surveys of businesses in Warsaw and tabulated results on space utilization patterns. She also provided excellent overall management of the office.

Mr. Chris Banks of AID, Ms. Marta Goldsmith and Ms. Laura Cole of the Urban Land Institute provided management support for the project in Washington. Mr. David Kane, graduate research assistant at UC Berkeley, researched materials and assisted in the preparation of the final report.

David E. Dowall
Project Director and
Professor
University of California at Berkeley

1 Executive summary

Introduction

Macroeconomic trends indicate that 1993 was a turning point in the Polish economy, as the massive economic and social reforms launched in the late 1980s began to take hold. The extent to which Warsaw can capitalize on emerging economic opportunities largely depends on its ability to mobilize and efficiently utilize its scarce resources to modernize its economic base. This will require major improvements to the City's urban infrastructure and land use patterns: modernization of its transportation systems, upgrading its telecommunication systems, increasing the supply of modern warehouse and industrial estates and office buildings, improving the quality of its housing stock and boosting the productivity of its labor force.

These challenges are enormous but not insurmountable. Successfully positioning Warsaw requires a careful and realistic assessment of the City's economic strengths and weaknesses, and its competitive advantages compared to cities in other transition economies. The City must also identify and prioritize the critical capital investment projects needed to enhance its competitive position. The City needs to design and implement new initiatives to modify the current structure and process of urban development planning, project finance and urban management. First and foremost, urban planning and master planning reforms must continue to place even more emphasis on economic development. Planning programs and activities should focus on increasing the economic productivity and attractiveness of the City as a place in which to do business. The City needs to aggressively position itself as a major regional center of economic activity in a new unified Europe, and as a bridge to a vast market centered in the Baltics and the Newly Independent States (NIS).

The City should begin by preparing an overall economic development strategy for attracting international capital, enterprises and businesses, and identify what new public and private investment programs are needed to accomplish this task. The strategy should be backed up by a detailed implementation program covering: municipal finance; intergovernmental roles, responsibilities and relationships for the City and the gminas related to public-private real estate development and the planning and development control of new projects.

A major obstacle to preparing such a strategy is the lack of accurate and timely information regarding the City's economic and physical condition. To overcome this problem, the City of Warsaw and the U.S. Agency for International Development launched a year-long program of technical cooperation focused on assessing Warsaw's economic and physical condition. The report was prepared by the newly formed Economic Analysis Unit of the City of Warsaw. The Unit was jointly established by the City of Warsaw and the U. S. Agency for International Development. It is one facet of ongoing technical cooperation between the City and USAID to help modernize and transform Warsaw's urban economy.

Over the past year, the Economic Analysis Unit has designed and constructed a Warsaw economic database consisting of demographic, economic and foreign trade statistics. Data were collected from the Voivodship Statistical Office, the Central Statistical Office, the Foreign Trade Information Center, various Ministries, City Departments, and field surveys. Data on employment, sales revenues, costs of production, profits and investment are tabulated by branch (type of industry), form of ownership and location and size of establishment.

The data cover the period from 1988 to 1992. In most, but not all cases, data are available for the 53 gminas and small towns comprising the Warsaw Voivodship. In some cases, financial data are not available for gminas and small towns located outside of the City of Warsaw. Instead, data are available for the seven City of Warsaw gminas and an aggregation of the 46 gminas outside ring areas. This report will refer to the Warsaw Voivodship as Metropolitan Warsaw or the Warsaw metropolitan region. In addition, the report will refer to the central city area as the City of Warsaw, or the City. The remaining metropolitan area, not including the central city, will be referred to as the Ring.

This report describes the results of the Economic Analysis Unit's work. The group has analyzed the changing economic and spatial structure of the Warsaw economy. Projections of the Warsaw economy have been prepared for the period from 1992 to 1997, providing estimates of employment by branch and location.

Estimates have been made of the current and future stock of office space, housing, industrial facilities, retail shops, and warehouses in the Warsaw metropolitan area. These estimates and projections are based on field surveys of current space utilization per employee, and employment estimates and projections across relevant economic sectors.

A major part of the report examines current infrastructure conditions in the City of Warsaw. Systems covered include: water and waste-water treatment, district heating, transport, roads, sanitation, telecommunications, electricity and gas. Capacity constraints and poor conditions are pinpointed. Estimates of the cost of infrastructure expansion (to 1997), modernization and upgrading are made.

This report attempts to put Warsaw's economic future into concrete terms by providing in one source, baseline assessments and forecasts of economic, real estate and infrastructure trends. The authors hope that the report will assist public and private sector decision makers. The remaining sections of this first chapter provide a short summary of the findings and conclusions of the full report.

Impact of the economic system's transformation on the Polish economy and the economy of Warsaw

When Poland's program of economic reform was launched in 1989, the nation was in the midst of deep economic instability, when economic linkages were dysfunctional. A widespread shortage of goods and services, and hyper-inflation, plagued the economy. In order to assure the success of reform, it was essential to introduce a stabilization program to: choke-off inflation, balance the budget, reduce shortages in the economy, and strengthen the national currency — all simultaneously. The implementation of the stabilization program and economic reform initiated changes in the economy's structure; changes which resulted from the reactions of individual economic sectors to the new economic climate.

The introduction of sharp financial restrictions, together with market instruments and mechanisms, caused a significant drop in basic macroeconomic activity during the first year of reform. The following year, 1990, gross domestic product (GDP) and consumption contracted by almost 12 percent, and capital investment by as much as 25 percent. The fall in GDP and consumer and investment demand was greater than anticipated.

The third year of reform (1991) brought a further decline in GDP (7.6 percent), with a 14.2 percent decline in capital accumulation. Consumption, on the other hand, increased 3.3 percent as households and businesses purchased imported goods. During 1991, the first signs of an economic revival appeared — a 6.7 percent increase in non-residential construction.

The signs of economic revival became increasingly clear in 1992. That year, growth occurred in a majority of sectors in the national economy. Nonetheless, only a few of them managed to achieve growth during the period 1988-1992, including trade (13.5 percent), other branches of material production — mainly publishing and computer firms (4.5 percent), housing (17.2 percent) and education (14 percent). The largest declines in output were noted in: forestry (40 percent), industry (35 percent), and transportation (30 percent). As a result, the contribution of these sectors to GDP decreased, while that of trade and the non-material production sectors rose.

The decline in GDP was accompanied by a fall in employment in the national economy. It was significantly smaller, however than the GDP decrease, especially in 1990, when GDP fell by nearly 12 percent while employment shrank by only 3.6 percent. This was typical of the "wait and see" reaction, in which state enterprises, counting on a softening of the financial rigors of reform, made regular practice of sending employees on unpaid vacations, and making older employees retire early. Only when it became evident that the rigors of reform were not to be softened did these enterprises stave off bankruptcy by laying off employees on a

3

large scale. A modest economic upturn in 1992 slowed the decline of employment. Between 1988 and 1992, employment fell by 9.5 percent, while GDP dropped 17 percent. Thus, labor productivity declined in the state sector.

During the first three years of reform, employment in the Warsaw metropolitan region, fell by 11 percent. Employment decline in the City of Warsaw was markedly lower than in the suburban areas. The very rapid decline in employment in the electric-machinery industry, science and education, and technological development sectors, which are the generators economic growth, has been a particularly unsettling trend. If this trend is not reversed, Poland will be faced with the threat of technological regression and total technological and economic dependence on highly developed countries. Such a situation may not only delay, but actually prevent Poland's genuine integration into the European Union.

The economic situation of the City of Warsaw is better than that of the country as a whole and of the rest of the Warsaw metropolitan region. It appears that the City's economy has demonstrated greater adaptive capabilities to changing market conditions than the national economy. The greater decline in employment in industry and the greater growth in expanding service sectors (finance and insurance, trade, communications and communal services), is an example of the City's adaptive capability.

Poland's foreign trade during the period under discussion underwent significant changes; most notably, it's trade switched orientation from the East to the West. The share of exports to countries of the former USSR declined nearly four-fold, and imports from these countries fell 2.5 times. Germany, on the other hand became Poland's largest trading partner. Exports to Germany grew 2.5 times and their share of national exports increased to 24 from 13 percent.

Shifting trade patterns and demand significantly altered the product structure of exports. The share of electric-machine industry products in total exports declined to 24.3 from 39.1 percent between 1988 and 1992. The share of products undergoing a low degree of processing increased, including metallurgical, wood, paper and food products.

A significant increase in the share of fuels in the structure of Poland's imports occurred, led by the rapid increase in passenger car ownership during the period. The import share of products from the chemical, wood, paper and material industries increased, while the share of imported products from the electric machine, metallurgical and light industries declined.

A characteristic expression of the changes in the structure of Poland's foreign trade is the large decrease in the share of industrial exports, declining from 75 to 35 percent of total volume of exports. Construction industry exports similarly fell from 7.7 to 1 percent of Poland's total exports.

The forces behind these changes in the structure of Poland's foreign trade are varied. To a significant degree, they resulted from the collapse of the Eastern market. The most important cause, however, is the poor competitiveness of many of Poland's products. Errors in Poland's initial approaches to economic reform also contributed to the unfavorable situation in foreign trade. Among the most

4

critical errors were: excessive opening of the domestic market, which went beyond the need of creating competition for domestic producers (in the light manufacturing and food industries), faulty exchange-rate policy, and privatization programs not geared toward modernizing the structure of industry.

The structure of City of Warsaw's and the surrounding Ring area's foreign trade, underwent similar though significantly deeper changes than in the country as a whole. The entire region experienced a greater decline in the share of industrial exports than the nation, and a dramatic collapse in construction industry exports. Despite these declines, Metropolitan Warsaw's share of total national exports remains significant, accounting for 12 percent in 1992. The Warsaw metropolitan region does, however, import more than it exports.

Despite the recession in the economy across Poland, investment expenditures are being made. The growth rate of investment has been linked to the level of profitability of particular sectors of the national economy. In both Metropolitan Warsaw and the nation, the most rapidly growing sectors of the economy are communications and retail and wholesale trade. The growth rate in investments, as measured by the ratio of investment expenditures to the value of fixed assets, was higher in Metropolitan Warsaw, with the exception of 1988, than in the country as a whole. Metropolitan Warsaw's share in total investment expenditures in the national economy increased from 7 percent in 1990 to approximately 10 percent in 1992. It is worth mentioning that these percentages were greater in the suburban ring of Warsaw than in the City, suggesting that investment growth has been greater in the suburbs.

Metropolitan Warsaw's economy is in a better position than that of the nation. In addition to its greater investment possibilities, Metropolitan Warsaw has over 2.5 times the per capita income and local governmental fiscal capacity of the rest of the nation.

Changes in the spatial structure of the Warsaw metropolitan economy

The economic changes under way are characterized by significant spatial differentiation both in terms of the scale of the country as a whole and of the metropolitan area. This is a natural consequence of the effects of market processes, which have fostered the initiation and expansion of economic activity where it generates the greatest profits. From this point of view, of great significance is not only the type of activity, but also its location.

The granting of freedom to undertake economic activity and create new enterprises liberated a great deal of economic energy among the populace. The number of companies in Metropolitan Warsaw increased nearly 15 times between 1988 and 1992 (from 5,600 to 83,800). The greatest increase (20 times) occurred in the City of Warsaw gminas outside of the central gmina. The downtown area had the lowest growth rate (8.5 times).

In industry and transportation, the greatest growth in the number of firms took place in gminas adjacent to the City of Warsaw and in gminas located beyond. On the other hand, in the construction sector, the number of firms grew fastest in gminas around the downtown and around the those gminas adjacent to the City. This trend testifies to the appearance of fairly clear signs of decentralization in some sectors of the economy. On the other hand, communications and finance and insurance are concentrating in the City center.

The greatest amount of economic activity took place in trade, where the number of firms increased over 72 times. This is the result, on one hand, of the relatively high profitability and quick turnover of capital in this sector up until 1990, and on the other hand, of the ease of entry into the market and low start-up costs. Owing to these economic conditions, small firms dominated the trade sector. However, in the near future, a trend toward the concentration of trade activity in larger firms is anticipated.

Important changes also occurred in the spatial distribution of trade firms. The share of firms located downtown fell by about 20 percent, while the share of firms located outside the downtown, but in the City increased by 23 percent. In the gminas just beyond the City limits, the share of trade firms increased by 2 percent. Beyond these gminas, the relative share of trade firms declined (although in absolute terms they increased by 500 percent). Significant growth in the number of firms outside the downtown but in the City testifies to the progressive de-concentration of economic activity in the Warsaw region.

The total value of income (in constant prices) obtained by economic entities in the Warsaw metropolitan area in 1992 slightly exceeded 1988 levels. This occurred thanks to firms located downtown, whose income rose 20.4 percent. The income of economic entities located in other areas was lower in 1992, from as much as 46 percent in the most distant gminas, to 16 percent in those gminas adjacent to the downtown. At the same time, however, the costs of production significantly increased, by over 45 percent for the region as a whole, and by 97 percent for firms operating in the downtown. Nonetheless, income exceeded costs in all gminas.

The relationships between income and cost trends are significantly differentia-ted in the particular sectors of the economy. The fall in industrial production and transportation activity is significantly greater than the decline in employment. In construction, however, the opposite occurred — income reached 1988 levels, while employment fell 21 percent. In other words, as opposed to industry and transportation, labor productivity increased.

The most profitable economic sectors in the metropolitan area in 1988 were trade and communications — thanks to this, they developed quickly between 1988 and 1992. On the other hand, in 1992, the highest profitability rates were in communications and communal services, highly monopolized sectors of the economy. Communal services, it should be noted, achieved these relatively good results because of reduced costs. Income, in constant prices, grew by 13 percent, while real costs declined by 13 percent.

The profitability of the City's and the region's economy, though somewhat higher than the national average, is low. In most cases, investors can make a greater return by placing their money in banks. Such a situation does not foster the development of economic activity, especially of a productive character — quite to the contrary, it is a threat to development.

The distribution of fixed assets and of investment expenditures according to location essentially confirms the aforementioned trends toward decentralization and de-concentration in several economic sectors in the metropolitan region. These trends could be the harbinger of a process of fundamental transformation in the functional structure of the Warsaw metropolitan region.

Demographic profile of Warsaw metropolitan region

Population growth in the Warsaw metropolitan area has steadily decreased since 1980. Over the 1980-5 period, the population of the region increased at a compound annual average rate of 0.8 percent. Between 1985 and 1990, the rate of increase slowed to 0.1 percent per year. Since 1990, the metropolitan area's population has been declining. During 1992, population in the region declined by 11,000 persons. There are several reasons for Warsaw's declining rate of population growth. First, the rate of natural increase is slowing as deaths outpace births. Second, migration to the region is declining and in 1992 turned negative. Third, urban development is spreading outside of Warsaw to surrounding regions.

Despite population declines, the number of households in Warsaw is increasing. During the late 1980s and early 1990s housing production in Warsaw collapsed and production of units fell to an average of 6,000 dwelling units per year. Given such constraints, household formation has slowed, expanding at the same rate as the housing stock. Warsaw's households are considerably smaller than for the nation as a whole, averaging 2.49 persons.

Between 1988 and 1992 labor supply has adjusted to changing labor demand generated by Poland's fundamental economic restructuring. Warsaw's total full-time and part-time supply of labor declined by 19.4 percent between 1988 and 1992. More of the total labor supply is concentrated in part-time employment. In 1980 for example, about 6 percent of the total labor supply, 60,000 persons, offered their services on a part-time basis. By 1992, 11.5 percent of the total labor supply, 84,300 persons, worked part-time.

Employment of male workers, more likely to be employed in industrial sectors, has declined by 20 percent. During the 1980s and into the 1990s, Warsaw's labor quality has markedly improved, reflecting the growing recognition that high skills and advanced education are the key to secure jobs. Structural reforms in the Polish and local economy are profoundly reshaping the labor market. Fast growing sectors such as trade, finance and insurance and services are generating strong demands for highly skilled workers trained in business administration and accounting, marketing, management, finance and logistics. This requires a labor force with vastly different skills.

Voivodship Statistical Office surveys of household income and expenditure estimate that 1992 average household income stood at Plz. 3,700,000. The typical household spends about 91 percent of its income, saving 8.7 percent. In 1992, about 10 percent of household income is devoted to housing, including rent, maintenance and furnishings. The largest budget category is food, accounting for 38.1 percent of total household income. Utility costs run about 8.4 percent of income, covering cooking fuel, electric and heat. Clothing accounts for 8.3 percent of total income.

Property market assessment of the Warsaw metropolitan region

The Warsaw metropolitan region comprises nearly 380,000 hectares. Of the total area, only 11.3 percent is urbanized. Although the City of Warsaw is more intensely urbanized, only 30 percent of the City's total land area is developed. At both the city and regional level, patterns of urban land utilization are well below levels of other comparably sized West European cities. Until 1990, land use planning and development control in Metropolitan Warsaw was highly restrictive. The centerpiece of development control was the master plan, which provided the precise specification of uses and areas. The former master plan, adopted in 1982, restricted development to five main corridors. Besides severely limiting development to these five areas, the plan froze the development of over 2000 parcels of land scattered throughout the city by stipulating precise uses which were either economically infeasible or unwanted.

Despite the vast areas of open space, only a limited amount of land is designated for development — approximately 5,000 hectares. To help promote economic development and attract more investment, the supply of land available for urban development should be expanded, especially in the central areas.

Fortunately, Metropolitan Warsaw's new master plan is more market oriented. It relies on a much more flexible set of development controls. The new master plan designates six general areas for urban development: 1) central area; 2) housing and services; 3) technical and industrial; 4) services and warehousing; 5) green areas; and 6) corridor areas targeted for environmentally friendly activities.

While these new initiatives are a step in the right direction, additional actions are needed to promote redevelopment activity in older and largely derelict industrial areas surrounding the City. Also the City should consider adopting new policies which will promote infill development of serviced but under-utilized parcels.

Another land development constraint facing the City of Warsaw concerns land ownership. In the central area of Warsaw, generally corresponding to the urbanized area of the pre-World War II, land was nationalized, and most of the land in this area is in public ownership. Virtually all of the land in Srodmiescie and over 80 percent of the land in Wola and Zoliborz is in public ownership. In the outlying areas, most urbanized and vacant land approved for development is in private ownership.

Because of the limited supply of developable and privately owned land, many developers and investors are bypassing the City of Warsaw and seeking out sites for development in suburban areas. This tendency is likely to cause an abnormal amount of decentralization of development and limit the ability of the Warsaw economy to generate agglomeration economies. To counter this trend, the City must try to attract a greater share of projects by providing more sites with clear titles and development designation.

Like other Central European capitals, Warsaw's housing market is tight and vacant or newly constructed units are in short supply. New construction is limited by the lack of housing finance credit. The region's stock of occupied housing increased from 734,718 in 1980 to 826,918 in 1992, an annual average increase of 1 percent. Since 1988, the stock has been increasing by about 8,000 units per year. The current stock of housing equals only about 80 percent of the households in Warsaw, and as a result, many households are forced to double up. In 1992, there were about 1.17 households per occupied dwelling. Fortunately, since the average size of households is falling, the number of persons per dwelling unit is gradually declining, falling from 2.96 in 1988 to 2.85 in 1992.

Warsaw's housing stock is relatively young — the median age is about 27 years. This reflects the fact that over 80 percent of the metropolitan area's housing stock was constructed after the Second World War. Despite the relatively slow rate of housing production (averaging about 1 percent of the occupied stock), housing conditions are improving. The size and quality of new units is rising, and housing cooperatives and local governmental units are refurbishing flats. The average size of dwelling units is increasing, rising from 46.6 square meters in 1980 to 51 square meters in 1992.

Most housing production is carried out by housing cooperatives — accounting for some 67 percent of construction in 1992. Private sector construction makes up about 20 to 35 percent of the market, and it can be expected to increase in the future when housing finance is available. In terms of ownership, housing cooperatives are the largest form of ownership, accounting for 41 percent of the stock in 1992. Communal ownership is the second largest, comprising 30 percent.

With the advent of reforms, demand has skyrocketed Given the limited initial response of the market, office rents, especially those in "Class A" facilities have surged and now match or exceed rents found in Western Europe and North America. In 1989, City of Warsaw's total supply of office space stood at 2,480,000 square meters. Of this amount, 2,320,000 square meters was constructed before 1989 for government and state enterprise units. Most of this space is not suitable for multi-tenant occupation and it lacks modern facilities. The remaining stock, 160,000 square meters is "Class A" and is suitable for foreign and domestic private enterprises. Between 1989 and 1992, approximately 120,000 square meters of new Class A office space was added to the City of Warsaw's stock. Since the pace of construction activities has been so low, especially private sector activity, the office market has been very tight, with overall vacancy rates in the City estimated to average around 2 percent.

The City's Development Promotion Department estimates that office space completions will average 30,000 square meters during 1993 and 1994. In 1995, a second wave of office completions will hit the market, providing around 150,000 square meters of new space. While this addition will relieve market pressure, demand for space will continue to dramatically rise.

At the start of Poland's economic reforms in 1989, the annual demand for modern office space averaged 10,000 square meters. By 1993-1994 it had increased to 70-80,000 square meters. Given the rapid growth and the enormous structural changes transforming the Polish economy, the demand for office space will continue to accelerate over the next five years.

Trade (both retail and wholesale) has been one of the fastest growing branches of the economy. Between 1988 and 1992, the region's trade employment increased from 116,200 to 136,700. In 1992, retail trade activities occupied approximately 1,750,000 square meters of space. Nearly 50 percent of retail trade is located in the central gmina of Srodmiescie, and 85 percent of the metropolitan region's total retail employment is concentrated within the City of Warsaw.

No sector of the Warsaw economy is going through as fundamental a change as wholesale trade. Prior to the economic market reforms of 1989, most wholesale distribution was handled through large state production or trading companies. Because of the inefficiencies of the distribution system and the almost complete lack of third party private wholesalers, most retailers were forced to either provide a limited selection of goods or take on the burden of stocking and warehousing inventory.

Metropolitan Warsaw's total stock of warehousing/wholesaling facilities was estimated to occupy approximately 1,900,000 square meters in 1992. Total wholesale trade employment accounted for less than 1 percent of all metropolitan regional employment in 1988 and nearly 1.5 percent in 1992. Over time, as Poland's private sector warehousing and distribution system develops, employment will increase. As one indication of how the sector might grow, consider the fact that in North American cities, wholesale trade employment accounts for between 20 and 30 percent of trade (wholesale and retail) employment and between 4 and 8 percent of total employment in metropolitan areas of similar size to the Warsaw region.

Historically, the backbone of the Warsaw economy was manufacturing. Employment in the industrial sector averaged around 30 percent of total employment. Since the launching of economic reforms and the radical shifts in trade patterns, Warsaw's industrial base has been in decline. In 1988 total industrial employment stood at 352,000. By 1992, employment had fallen to 234,500 a decline of 34 percent. Estimates of future employment trends indicate that even under the most optimistic scenario, manufacturing employment in Warsaw will remain constant over the next five years. It is more probable, however, that manufacturing employment will continue to decline.

At its peak in the mid 1980's, Warsaw's stock of industrial space stood at approximately 24,000,000 square meters. Since 1988, it is estimated that the stock of utilized industrial space fell from 21,200,000 square meters to 14,000,000 square meters in 1992, a decline of over 7,000,000 square meters. At present, approximately 42 percent of the Warsaw region's industrial buildings are either vacant or have been converted to other uses, such as warehouses and offices. Over the next five years, vacancies will continue to grow as the industrial sector restructures.

The most significant issue related to urban land development is the vast under-utilization of land in the City of Warsaw. In comparison to other Western European cities, land use patterns are grossly inefficient. Over the next decade, as the Warsaw economy transforms itself from a manufacturing-oriented to a services- and trade-oriented economy, its requirements for urban facilities, buildings and infrastructure will change as well. In making this transformation, the City faces two basic options. The City can attempt to make the transition by re-utilizing vacant and under-utilized land in already developed and equipped areas, or new development can simply move to the outer edges, mainly outside the current boundaries of the City. The former approach will lead to a more compact city, and probably require less money to upgrade and equip the area with modern infrastructure. The second approach will lead to a sprawling city and require far more money for infrastructure development.

An assessment of Warsaw's infrastructure system

The physical and financial conditions of Warsaw's major infrastructure systems: Water supply and waste-water collection and treatment, central heating, municipal transportation, roads and bridges, sanitation, telecommunications, electric power and gas is assessed in this report. In nearly all cases, technical conditions range from poor to very poor, reflecting years of deferred maintenance. In some cases, service capacity has not kept pace with increased levels of demand.

While gross water supplies are adequate to meet overall demands, water quality is poor, especially those supplies coming from the central waterworks. Treatment technologies need to be modernized at older facilities, and water distribution systems require refurbishment and expansion (especially in the Northern Waterworks service area).

Waste-water treatment is deficient in many respects. First and foremost, only 43 percent of waste-water is treated, and substantial volumes of untreated sewerage flow into the Vistula. The principal cause of the low treatment level is the overloading of existing sewerage treatment plants, as demand has outpaced capacity.

In the case of central heating, the current system is extremely inefficient and cannot produce the levels of energy required. The current deficit amounts to about 8 percent of average demand. During peak periods, the supply-demand gap exceeds 20 percent. Heat and hot water production systems are a major source of air pollution. The system does not adequately treat water used to provide heat and hot water, and the system is plagued with extensive failures from pipe corrosion.

Few buildings have meters to register usage and as a result, there are few opportunities to manage demand. A final problem is that most buildings are poorly insulated, causing an enormous waste of energy.

Warsaw's extensive transportation system operates reasonably well, providing buses, tram and trolley-bus service. In comparison to other Western European cities, Warsaw's transit operation receives a very high percentage of its revenues from the farebox. Subsidies account for about 30 percent of direct operating costs. Major problems center on the lack of financing for fleet replacement.

The condition of Warsaw's roads, bridges and viaducts, is an entirely different story. Here conditions are extremely bad, reflecting decades of deferred maintenance. Over 60 percent of the City's road surface needs total restoration (new construction of roadbeds) and another 10 percent requires surface repairs. Conditions of bridges, viaducts, pedestrian passages, breakwaters and other facilities are in a similar poor state.

Sanitation and solid waste removal is facing a number of challenges. First and foremost, solid waste generation is increasing rapidly, at about 3 percent per year. The City's principal landfill is nearing capacity. Disposal of liquid waste collected from septic tanks, typically dumped in overloaded treatment plants is inadequate. The lack of proper tariffs, has led to the under-financing of sanitation services. This is mostly reflected in the lack of an adequate fleet of vehicles. On the positive side, the private sector has shown interest in providing sanitation services.

Telecommunication service levels are very poor, but improving. Warsaw's level of telephone service is about one-fourth to one-fifth of the levels found in other Western European cities. Fortunately, the sector has been restructured and rates are rising to finance system improvements. Private capital is expected to support telecommunication upgrading.

Electric power service is adequate to good. Deficiencies exist primarily in distribution to districts. Assessments of the sector suggest that about nine regional power supply points are needed to provide adequate service. Downtown power demand is likely to grow if office development increases, and this will require additional capital investments to upgrade and expand the distribution system.

Gas for cooking and heating is supplied from the national grid system. The region is quickly approaching a major supply constraint since the regional distribution network is currently operating at capacity. Increasing capacity will require building a second main pressure line around the metropolitan area, a major project. As more new development seeks to provide independent heating and hot water, the demand for gas is likely to increase.

As will be discussed below, a preliminary order of magnitude estimate suggests that $2 billion dollars will be needed to recondition the City of Warsaw's infrastructure systems. Up to an additional $2.5 billion dollars of investment will be needed to meet the new demand for infrastructure generated by projected economic growth and restructuring. Despite the poor technical condition and high costs of refurbishment and expansion of the City's infrastructure systems, there is reason for much optimism. Economic and financial reforms have sparked considerable liberalization in infrastructure rate setting, leading to relatively strong financial performance in the sector, allowing service providers the option to finance long term improvements from tariffs.

Projections of the Warsaw economy

The economy of Metropolitan Warsaw, as an element of the national economic system, remains under the influence of changes occurring in this system. In addition, local economic conditions also have an important impact on the region's economy. In connection with this, growth forecasts for Metropolitan Warsaw's economy must take into account both macroeconomic and local conditions.

Poland's economic situation is very difficult and complex: unemployment has reached 16 percent of the work force, public and foreign debt is rising, and there is a high deficit in foreign trade. External conditions are also disadvantageous; the weak world-wide economic situation is limiting the access of Polish goods to world markets. Despite the reduction in Poland's credit obligations (first by the Paris Club and recently by the London Club), debt servicing will absorb increasingly large sums, which by 2008 will reach $8 billion.

The internal and external conditions of Poland's economy partly define its long-term development goals. Limiting unemployment will require the creation of an appropriate number of jobs — in other words, guaranteeing a high rate of growth in investments. On the other hand, servicing the foreign debt will require a high rate of growth in exports, with exports exceeding imports.

Basically all economic growth forecasts for Poland take these needs into account. They emphasize continuing economic reform and policy inducements to stimulate growth (investment relief, credit guarantees, etc.), which should set internal growth mechanisms into motion. It is these mechanisms which could become the most important factor in Poland's economic development. Forecasts of annual GDP growth up to 1997 range from 3.7 percent (Economist Intelligence Unit) to 5.1 percent [Central Planning Office (CUP's) latest forecast]. Economic growth forecasts made in this report are based on an analysis and evaluation of recent trends and of local and external conditions of growth in particular branches of the regional economy. Three scenarios have been prepared:

I   continuation of recent trends (during 1988-1992)

II   differentiated growth in particular sectors of Metropolitan Warsaw's economy

III accelerated growth, at a rate nearly twice as fast as that assumed under scenario II.

Scenario I projects that total employment in the metropolitan area decreases from 970,100 in 1992 to 950,900 in 1997. The net decline, masks very significant changes in employment across the various sectors of the economy. The continua-

13

tion of recent trends would lead to an excessive fall in employment in some economic sectors, especially industry, transportation, science, education and technological development; and to excessive employment growth in other sectors, such as finance and insurance (where employment would grow from 30,400 in 1992 to 68,500 in 1997). This disproportionate growth would result in a significant waste of resources, especially labor.

It is unlikely, however, that these trends will continue, because retail trade has already hit the demand barrier, and any further expansion of this sector will depend on increases in consumption. It also seems improbable that the rate of growth in the finance and insurance sector will continue at its recent tempo. Acceleration in the process of bank consolidation should be anticipated, because the majority of small and weak banks will not be able to withstand growing competition from large and powerful competitors. Communications will also fail to maintain its recent growth rate, even if it attains absolute increases on par with those achieved during the 1988-1992 period. This is due to the same dynamic mechanism in development processes, where a saturation point is reached. Unused production capacity in industry, transportation and construction allow for significant expansion of production with little or no employment growth.

Scenarios II and III, which are believed to be more plausible, estimate that total regional employment will increase to between 1,002,300 (II) and 1,045,300 (III). Under both scenarios, the Warsaw region's economy will continue to restructure, but there will be far less retrenchment in industry, science and education and communal services. In the most probable outcome (scenario II) the structure of the economy will shift from primary, to secondary and tertiary activities. As the next sections describes, these changes in the composition of the economy will influence the demand for real estate development and infrastructure investments.

Future real estate requirements of the Warsaw region

Unless there is a radical change in housing finance, we do not expect a dramatic up-turn in housing construction. The metropolitan region's population growth and rate of household formation are projected to be low over the next five years. Most housing construction will be market rate and targeted at upper-income households.

Post-1989 patterns of housing construction will probably continue up until 1997, suggesting that completions will average 6,000 to 8,000 units per year. The metropolitan area will thus absorb an additional 30,000 to 40,000 dwelling units between 1992 and 1997. The majority of these units will be constructed in suburban areas in and around the City of Warsaw.

Demand for office space in the Warsaw region can be expected to grow strongly over the next five years. Projections of employment growth in economic sectors which heavily use office space will increase dramatically. Net new employment in finance and insurance, and administration is projected to increase by between 8,000 and 48,000 workers by 1997. Given the growth in new business start-ups and foreign investment, unmet annual demand for office space will range

14

between 50,000 and 75,000 square meters of space per year. Much of this demand will come from new firms, but a major component of demand will be driven by a move to higher quality accommodations offering advanced telecommunications, modern office layouts and adequate parking. If supply conditions improve and office rents start to decline, demand will ratchet upward as more existing firms move up to modern class "A" structures.

Despite declines in retail trade margins, the sector has a bright future. Household incomes in the metropolitan area are increasing and retail sales volumes are rising. National level projections estimate that real consumption should increase at an annual rate of 3 percent per year. In Metropolitan Warsaw, with higher levels of employment and a more dynamic economy, retail spending is likely to increase at an annual rate of 4 to 5 percent.

As of 1992, total trade employment (covering both retailing and wholesaling) stood at approximately 136,700. Projections to 1997 indicate that total trade employment will grow slowly, increasing to a low of 141,800 or to a high of 167,500. Given the structure of the trade sector, particularly the over-supply of small vendors and the under-representation of wholesale activities, it is expected that most employment growth will be on the wholesale side of the sector. Total retail employment will probably remain about the same under scenarios, II and III. Under the conditions of scenario I, where total trade employment increases to 167,500, retail employment is likely to increase by 12,300 between 1992 and 1997. Much of the increase in employment will be absorbed into existing retail facilities, many of which are under-utilized.

In terms of retail construction activities, net additional retail space is likely to increase by 50,000 to 100,000 square meters by 1997. The high end of the projection, assumes that employment increases by roughly 10,000 and that kiosks and poorly sited and equipped shops upgrade to new facilities. If residential construction picks up in suburban areas, the decentralization of retail establishments to the suburbs will accelerate. By 1997, over one-third of the region's retail construction activity could be located out side the present City of Warsaw boundaries.

Projections of industrial employment reflect continued re-trenchment. Many state-owned factories will be privatized or cease operations. In most cases, privatized firms will be radically reorganized and systematic efforts made to improve labor productivity. This undoubtedly means cutting employment and modernizing facilities. Space utilization requirements (per unit of output) will decline and many older inefficient factories will be closed. Most multi-story facilities will be rejected by foreign investors and if investments are made in new facilities they will largely take place in suburban areas, because of easier access to land, lower prices and less stringent planning controls. Manufacturing, particularly, is expected to decentralize to suburban areas.

Despite the vast over-supply of industrial space, a modest amount of industrial space is expected to be constructed between 1992 and 1997. In fact, between 1990 and 1992, an average of 65,000 square meters of industrial space was constructed annually. This reflects pressure on the sector to modernize and upgrade facilities.

15

Much of the new construction will be stimulated through privatization and foreign investment.

The future demand for warehousing and distribution facilities will grow dramatically over the next three years. Over the course of the next ten years, wholesaling employment in Metropolitan Warsaw will move toward Western European and North American levels. If wholesaling activities in Metropolitan Warsaw were to move half the distance toward levels found in North America by 1997, wholesale activities would account for about 4 percent of total employment. This suggests that by 1997, net new demand for warehousing and distribution facilities in the metropolitan area will range from approximately 3.4 to 4.0 million square meters. On an annual basis this translates to 680,000 to 800,000 square meters of net new demand.

Given the abundant supply of vacant or under-utilized industrial space in the Warsaw metropolitan region, most of the current effective demand for space is directed toward well-located industrial facilities suitable for goods storage and transfer. Based on field surveys, approximately 25 percent of the vacant industrial building space is estimated to be adaptable for warehousing and distribution activities. Therefore, the actual estimated net demand for new warehousing construction ranges from 1,625,000 to 2,225,000 square meters over the 1992-1997 period.

What will it cost to modernize and expand Warsaw's economic base?

The most likely projection, scenario II, estimates that total regional employment will increase from 970,100 to 1,002,300 between 1992 and 1997. This increase in employment and the continuing restructuring of the Warsaw economy will generate a significant increase in the demand for new facilities and supporting infrastructure.

As noted above, projections of population and economic activity suggest that 30,000 to 40,000 housing units will be constructed between 1992 and 1997. Office construction activity will range from 250,000 to 375,000 square meters of new buildings. The construction of new retail space will range from 50,000 to 100,000 square meters. The net demand for industrial facilities will decline in aggregate terms, but some limited new construction of modern facilities will occur over the 1992-1997 period. A significant number of warehousing and distribution buildings will be constructed over the five year period. In total, somewhere between 5,200,000 and 7,350,000 square meters of new housing, offices, shops and warehouses will be constructed over the 1992-1997 period (assuming an average housing size of 75 square meters).

Economic and population growth in the City will require the expansion of infrastructure systems. Available funding may limit this expansion to lengthening networks and connecting new users where reserves of productive capacity of central equipment, and reserves of capacity in main transmission networks exist. In areas where such reserves are lacking, growth will require additional investments in new infrastructure facilities. Given the fact that much of the City of Warsaw's existing systems of infrastructure are deficient and operating beyond capacity, it is very likely that even the modest increments in growth will require major capital expenditures in infrastructure.

To simplify the analysis, Warsaw's future infrastructure requirements can be divided into two types: 1) investments and repairs to remove the backlog of deferred maintenance and to upgrade the system to acceptable standards; and 2) investments to support additional growth in population and economic activity.

Very preliminary estimates of the cost of upgrading the current level of infrastructure services range from $1.8 to $2.2 billion U.S. dollars. About half the amount is needed for central heating, water and waste-water treatment, and solid waste disposal systems. The other half is needed for roads, transportation, tele-communications, electricity and gas.

The actual impact of new construction on the demand for infrastructure investments will greatly depend on the location of new development. For example, if all new growth is channeled into areas with existing infrastructure capacity (using vacant infill sites, or redeveloping derelict industrial areas) the estimated cost of providing infrastructure service to these areas ranges between to $670 and $940 million (in 1993 prices). On the other hand, if all new development was located in "green-field" areas requiring the expansion of trunk infrastructure systems, the total cost would range between $1.8 and $2.5 billion, about 170 percent more.

Warsaw's total infrastructure investment requirements, for both upgrading and repairing existing systems, and providing new service to growth areas, ranges from $2.5 and $4.7 billion dollars. If all of these improvements are financed through long term debt (over 30 years at 8 percent interest), the annual aggregate debt service payment would range from $222 and $420 million. This works out to $230 to $430 per household, and accounts for between 11 to 21 percent of 1992 average household income. Given these high costs, how can the region pay for its infrastructure needs? Are there ways to reduce the necessary costs of infrastructure, without stifling economic growth and development?

Local government budgets will not be capable of financing improvements. The total income from budgets of all the districts of Metropolitan Warsaw up to 1997 would not suffice to finance infrastructure investments needed to meet new demands and make up for the investment backlog. Looking just at the City of Warsaw's needs, it will be difficult to finance future new infrastructure costs, since it is currently impossible to earmark more than Plz. 109,000,000 to Plz. 129,000,000 a year from the local budgets for infrastructure. Assuming infrastructure finance was available at 8 percent for 30 years, these set aside funds would only support Plz. 1.2 to Plz.1.4 billion in debt. Thus the financing of infrastructure, whether it is for upgrading and maintenance or the provision of service to new customers, constitutes a serious problem with which local government will have to confront if the City of Warsaw is to become, in the not too distant future, a modern European city.

There are however, a number of possible solutions to the infrastructure financing problem. Several of the infrastructure sectors can and will successfully attract private capital to finance improvements and expansion. Telecommunications, electric and gas system improvements can all be financed privately through user charges. More "public" services, such as water supply, waste-water treatment and solid waste disposal can also rely on user charges to help finance investments. Charges for road use should be levied through gasoline taxes and vehicle licenses.

There are measures on the production side which can be used as well to address the problem of infrastructure financing. Capital and operating costs can be reduced through systematic efforts to:

1   rationalize the consumption of services through measuring consumption and limiting waste;

2   reduce the costs of services through the introduction of competition (privatization and bidding) and efficiency-enhancing tariff systems; and

3   rationalize budget expenditures by distributing them according to results obtained and not costs incurred, and also distributing them to the truly needy.

With the introduction of instruments and mechanisms to increase efficiency, significant savings in investment outlays and costs are possible; savings which can be used to finance the expansion and modernization of the City's infrastructure. There exists a need to create a system for financing municipal investments which would include not only traditional sources such as fees, budgetary funds and loans, but also modern sources of funds like savings in expenditures (from improvements in efficiency), and the procurement of funds through joint ventures with the private sector and foundations.

Making Warsaw more efficient: the role of urban planning

Another enormous opportunity to reduce the cost of infrastructure expansion is to rethink the spatial pattern of urban development in the Warsaw region. If Metropolitan Warsaw can develop in a more compact pattern, making better use of vacant and under-utilized parcels, it can save an between $1.0 and $1.6 billion in new infrastructure development costs over the 1992-1997 period.

Beyond these cost savings, there are several other benefits likely to result from compact development. First, with more compact form of development, Metropolitan Warsaw will have a better chance of maintaining a high level of transit usage. Secondly, if financial, producer and consumer services are centralized, it will be easier to generate agglomeration economies. If such economies can be created, businesses will be more productive and profitable. Can Metropolitan Warsaw shift its pattern of urban development? The answer depends on whether the City and surrounding towns can alter their basic urban laws, policies and programs.

For Warsaw to fully exploit the cost and productivity benefits of compact development it must address four key issues:

1 public land ownership;

2 promoting high-intensity development;

3 redevelopment of industrial and under-utilized areas; and

4 developing new methods for infrastructure finance.

Virtually all of the land in the central business district of Warsaw is in public ownership, in the remainder of the City private land ownership ranges from 10 to 46 percent. In contrast, suburban areas are mostly in private ownership. At present, it is extremely difficult, time-consuming and risky to try to purchase or obtain the use rights to publicly held land. Titles are uncertain and administrative procedures for disposing of land are complex. As a consequence, private developers and companies seeking land for projects are increasingly attracted to suburban areas where they can easily purchase parcels from private owners. If the City wants to attract development to its central areas it must quickly act to modify land ownership and property rights to facilitate private development.

Planning standards and design criteria should be modified to permit more intensive urban development. The recently revised master plan is a step in the right direction, but additional actions are needed to encourage intensive commercial and residential development. As Poland's market economy expands, the demand for urban land for development is growing rapidly. To facilitate these changes, the City's planning system needs modifications to permit market driven development.

Given the significant decline of industrial districts in the City, many areas are grossly under-utilized. Some are derelict. These and other grossly under-utilized areas are in need of redevelopment. In some areas, multiple land parcels need to be assembled into large tracts to permit modern development. Other areas, for example, garden plots near the airport, should be redeveloped to serve more intensive activities, Relocation of current users will be necessary. Success of these changes will require new legislation and new urban development policies and programs.

Finally, the City needs to develop new methods for financing infrastructure. New mechanisms are needed to get land owners and developers to pay for infrastructure investments which benefit their properties.

Warsaw's greatest challenge is to promote urban land development to support and facilitate economic transformation and growth. If successful, the City is likely to emerge as the leading center of economic activity in Central Europe.

19

2 The economic condition of Warsaw in the context of the national economy

Introduction: the impact of the transformation of the economic system on the economy of Poland and the economy of Warsaw

The principles and goals of the National Economic Program adopted by the Council of Ministers on the 9th of October, 1989 initiated the present process of transformation of Poland's economic system. The purpose of the Program was to stabilize the economy and transform the centrally planned economic system into a market one. Stabilization of the economy was a necessary prerequisite to the transformation of the economic system; at the same time it served as one of the instruments of transition over to a market economy. Such transition could not have been attempted without controlling the hyper-inflation which prevailed in the country at the time.

The goals of the stabilization program were to suppress inflation, balance the state budget, eliminate existing shortages on the supply side of the economy, and strengthen the national currency — the Polish zloty. The program consisted of five principal components:

1 adjustments of the fiscal system;

2 the liberalization of prices;

3 a restrictive monetary policy;

4 the control of wage increases; and

5 the introduction of internal convertibility of the national currency — the Polish zloty.

20

The purpose of fiscal adjustments was to balance the budget by means of: substantial reductions of state budget subsidies, the removal of numerous existing tax breaks and privileges, and more aggressive collection of state taxes, fees and charges. Any temporary deficits were to be financed by limited commercial bank loans and the issue of government bonds. The rigorous fiscal policy led to a surplus in the 1990 state budget amounting to slightly over 2,400 billion Polish zlotys.

The goal of the liberalization of prices was to bring about, as soon as possible, a supply and demand balance in the market. Prices were expected to reach the point of equilibrium and further rise would be contained by the lack of effective demand. The deregulation of prices would not have been possible without the concurrent limitation of money supply by means of restrictive fiscal, monetary and income policies.

Rigorous monetary policy included strict control of the money supply and the regulation of its growth rate by means of positive interest rates. Its purpose was to reduce the demand for credit by enterprises, diminish their demand for capital, and to encourage households to make savings.

The above conditions, i.e. strict budgetary limitations accomplished with the help of restrictive fiscal and monetary policy, prevented the liberalization of price formation from provoking the further resurgence of hyper-inflation.

Wage increases were also subjected to strict regulation. Modification of the principles of wage indexation and the introduction of a special tax penalizing employers for unreasonably high wage rises, were necessary. Its purpose was to discipline enterprises to cooperate, by keeping wages under control despite powerful inflationary pressures. The adopted wage indexation system was based on the principle that the growth of company wage funds was expected not to exceed a predetermined maximum level in relation to the growth of retail prices, represented by an appropriate index. Companies which would allow themselves to raise wages over the above limits would be penalized by a highly progressive tax levied on the excessive wage payments. If a company exceeded the limit by up to 3 percent, the tax on the "excess" was 200 percent, and above 3 percent, it was 500 percent. In 1990 only firms with foreign capital were exempt from that form of taxation.

In 1991 that tax, popularly nick-named as the "beer-tip-tax" ("popiwek"), was modified. Firms with over 50 percent private capital, cooperatives, and firms with mixed foreign-domestic capital structure having a majority of foreign shareholders were exempt from the "beer-tip-tax". Reduced rates of the above tax were also introduced for civil law partnerships and companies incorporated on the basis of commercial law with over 50 percent of the shares held by the state. In addition, companies which accomplished a sound ratio of profit to wages were offered the possibility of additional wage payments (exempt from the above restrictions). The tax under discussion was therefore applied not only as an instrument of a restrictive income policy, but also as an instrument for stimulating ownership transformations (privatization) and as an incentive for attracting more foreign capital into the country.

The introduction of the internal convertibility of the domestic currency — the Polish zloty — was intended to restore its monetary functions, which had been taken over at the beginning of 1989 by convertible foreign currencies. A fundamental role in this respect was played by the discount rate, which was then brought to a realistic level securing the profitability of deposits in zloty. At the same time the exchange rate of the US dollar was fixed at the level of 9,500 Plz. (Polish zloty) to 1 USD. The regulations in the still existing foreign currency shops were changed. First, a 20 percent turnover tax was levied on the goods they offered. Second, as of July, 1989, payment with domestic currency (a dual price system) was introduced. Finally, from the 1st of January 1991, foreign currency prices and payments in retail trade were abolished altogether. Imports were now highly fiscally burdened with 20 percent customs duties and a turnover tax levied on the value of the imported goods which increased by the value of the 20 percent customs duty. In consequence one US dollar in imports was now about 44 percent more expensive than one US dollar obtained by a company from exports. Companies obtaining foreign currencies in payment for their exports were now obliged by law to resell those currencies to the bank at the determined bank exchange rate. The banks, in turn, were now compelled to sell foreign currencies to importers. The stabilization loan of one billion US dollars obtained from the member countries of the OECD was intended to secure financial liquidity. The measures adopted were intended to reduce the demand for foreign currency, to contribute to the stabilization of the foreign exchange rate, and subsequently to enable inflation to be contained and stabilized at a low (acceptable) level.

The measures counteracting inflation and leading to the stabilization of the national economy were accompanied by steps towards the transformation of the still existing centralized economic system (centrally planned and managed). The implementation of such a transformation required the introduction of market economy institutions long established and tested in the highly developed Western countries. This goal was to be obtained by the following means:

1   ownership transformations making the property structure of the national economy similar to the patterns existing in highly developed countries;

2   the full introduction of market mechanisms, especially the liberation of price formation, and the elimination of regulation and compulsory agency services;

3   the establishment of a framework for the emergence of competition on the domestic market through the provision of full liberty of company formation and anti-monopoly policy;

4   the opening of the economy to the external world by the introduction of convertibility for the domestic currency, the Polish zloty, providing for an increase in competition in the domestic market and for the possibility of rational specialization;

5   the reconstruction of the public financial system, including comprehensive reform of the taxation system;

6   the continuation of reforms in the banking system and of the principles of monetary and credit policies;

7   the establishment and initiation of a stock market; and

8   the creation of a labor market.

Generally speaking, the main goal of the transformation process is to improve production efficiency and resource allocation in the national economy. A more detailed analysis and evaluation of these important problems would run beyond the scope of the present paper. Their consideration is therefore limited here to those aspects of economic efficiency which may be affecting further economic growth of the City of Warsaw.

The following is an analysis of the consaequences of the implementation of the National Economic Program for the development of the national economy, the economy of Metropolitan Warsaw, and of the City of Warsaw. The response of the national economy to the measures introduced by the National Economic Program is illustrated in Table 2.1.

The first year of implementation of the Economic Program, 1989, witnessed a substantial decline in principal macroeconomic indices. Most affected was the level of capital investment, which decreased by almost one fourth; the consequence of a decline in demand for capital investment, which had resulted from the reduction of domestic demand and restrictive monetary policy. In the same year, however, exports grew impressively. They had been stimulated by a favorable exchange rate for the Polish zloty, and by numerous companies attempting to counteract their own deteriorating financial condition. At the same time, newly introduced import restrictions brought about a 10 percent decline in imports. It should be stressed, however, that decline of the gross domestic product and other macroeconomic indices was much deeper and more lasting than initially assumed by the government. In the following year a further decrease in most of these factors was observed, with the exception of consumption (which grew slightly) and imports which increased by almost one third due to the elimination of import restrictions and a general opening up of the domestic market. It was only in 1992 that the level of capital investment started to grow. A substantial surplus of imports over exports fed the growth of a foreign trade deficit, which given Poland's massive foreign debt, is likely to be detrimental to the national economic condition in the years to follow.

As Table 2.2 illustrates, the above described changes were accompanied by the decline of employment in the national economy, in Metropolitan Warsaw and in the City of Warsaw. The decline in national employment was notably less than the decrease in the gross domestic product, indicating a reduction in average labor

23

Table 2.1
The rate of change of national-level macroeconomic indices in
constant prices (1988 = 100.0)

	1989	1990	1991	1992	1988 =100.0	1988 -1992
GDP	100.2	88.4	92.4	101.5	—	83.1
Consumption	98.7	88.3	103.3	105.0	94.5	—
Investment	103.1	75.2	85.8	97.5	64.8	—
Imports of Goods & Services	104.3	89.8	131.6	109.2	134.6	—
Exports of Goods & Services	102.6	115.1	98.3	101.4	117.7	—
GDP per capita	99.9	88.1	92.1	101.2	82.0	—

Source: Economic Analysis Unit

efficiency. This decrease resulted from the postponement of adjustments to employment levels in the face of decreasing output levels. This phenomenon was most apparent during the first year of the reform program, when GDP declined by almost 12 percent, and employment decreased by only 3.6 percent. This is a symptom of the "wait and see" reaction: state owned companies expected the financial rigors of the reform to be relaxed, and it was widespread practice to grant many employees unpaid leave or earlier pensions. Only when it became evident that the relaxation would not take place did firms begin to seek refuge from the threat of bankruptcy, instituting mass lay-offs. A greater decrease in the level of employment in 1991 than in 1990, stands as evidence of this trend. Additionally, this decrease can be attributed to the privatization of some state owned companies; resulting in 10-15 percent reductions of personnel in the firms concerned. The decline of employment was still smaller in 1991 than the decrease of the GDP in the same year. Social pressures which discouraged the management of many companies from group lay-offs (especially those located in smaller towns where they provided the main source of jobs), contributed to this continued loss of labor productivity. A slowing in the rate of national employment losses indicated the first signs of economic recovery in 1992.

The economy of the Warsaw metropolitan area is modestly stronger than the economy of the nation. Between 1988 and 1991, City of Warsaw employment losses amounted to 4.7 percent as compared to 8.9 percent for the whole country. The situation of the Ring around central Warsaw, if the City itself is excluded, is however worse than the national average, suffering a decline of employment reaching 20 percent. The relatively good standing of the region as compared to the rest

Table 2.2

**Employment* in Poland, Warsaw metropolitan area
and Warsaw ('000)**

	1988	1990	1991	1992
Poland	17,128.8	16,511.4	15,601.4	15,494.5
Warsaw Metro. Area	1,066.4	1,028.2	972.7	969.9
Warsaw (*)	791.4	781.2	754.2	725.0
Suburban Gminas	275.0	247.0	218.5	244.9
	Poland = 100.0			
Warsaw Metro. Area	6.22	6.22	6.23	6.26
Warsaw	4.62	4.73	4.83	4.68
Suburban Gminas	1.63	1.45	1.40	1.58
Warsaw/Warsaw				
Metro. Area %	74.2%	75.6%	77.5%	74.7%
	previous year = 100.0			
Poland	—	96.4	94.5	99.3
Warsaw Metro. Area	—	96.5	94.6	99.7
Warsaw	—	98.7	96.5	96.1
Suburban Gminas	—	89.8	88.5	112.1
	1988 = 100.0			
Poland	100.0	96.4	91.1	90.5
Warsaw Metro. Area	100.0	96.4	91.2	91.0
Warsaw	100.0	98.7	95.3	91.6
Suburban Gminas	100.0	89.8	79.4	89.1

Source: Economic Analysis Unit

* Actual Employed Persons

of the country is thus led by the City of Warsaw. Data published in the statistical yearbooks of the Central and Regional Statistical Offices are not detailed enough to allow a more profound assessment of the economic situation within different areas of the metropolitan region. Regional statistical data should separate regional capitals from the remainder of the region, since they are usually better off. The assessment of the economy against the background of general economic trends would be incomplete unless transformations of its structure were also taken into account. Structural changes in the economy will be analyzed in the next section.

The structure of the Polish economy

Changes in the national economy's structure are influenced by a variety of factors affecting the growth of particular economic branches and sectors. In analyzing these changes, various economic parameters are utilized, such as gross domestic product (GDP), employment, value of production, etc.. Undoubtedly, gross domestic product is the measure that provides the best synthesis. For this reason, analysis of the Polish economic structure begins with a closer look at the changes in the structure of gross domestic product formation. Table 2.3 presents the pertinent information.

During the first year of reform, the largest decline in GDP occurred in industry (22 percent). Of the remaining sectors of the national economy, only retail and wholesale trade, education, health care, and social services showed an increase of any kind. The second year of reform (1990) was the third year of significant decline in industrial output — 13 percent. In 1991 a further drop in output occurred in forestry, transportation, and communication. Nevertheless, a very early sign of economic rebound became evident in that same year, as a 6.7 percent increase in non-residential construction was noted. Residential construction continued however to regress that year. In the third year of reform (1991), the signs of an economic recovery became increasingly clear. They include an overall widespread rise in GDP across most economic branches. Despite these more recent gains, only a few branches of the economy managed to achieve overall positive growth during the analyzed period (1988-1992). These include trade (13.5 points), the remaining branches of material production, that is, mainly publishing and computer firms (4.5 points), housing services (17.2 points), and education (14 points). On the other hand, output in most other economic sectors had fallen during the period of analysis; declines ranged from a few percent to 30 percent in transportation and 35 percent in industry.

Given the variation in output across branches, the structure of the economy changed. A significant decline in the share of national output originating in industry and transport occurred, while trade and the non-material branches grew and provided a larger percentage of GDP. This transformation in the structure of the national economy was accompanied by changes in the structure of ownership and employment. Table 2.4 provides relevant data.

At the end of the first three years of reform, 2 million fewer persons were working in the national economy. There were 2.7 million fewer persons employed in the public sector, but private sector employment increased by over 500,000. As aresult, a substantial change in the structure of employment occurred, with the private sector increasing its share of national employment by 10.2 percentage points.

Reform also caused a greater increase in unemployment than expected: at the end of 1992, 2.5 million people were unemployed, that is, 13.6 percent of the work force in 1989. The situation in Metropolitan Warsaw and the City of Warsaw in 1992 was significantly better, with unemployment levels at 7 percent and 5 percent, respectively.

Table 2.3

Trends in GDP in constant prices (previous year = 100)

	1989	1990	1991	1992	1992 / 1988 %
Total	100.2	88.4	92.4	101.5	83.1
Industry	97.9	78.0	82.9	102.6	65.0
Construction	99.7	85.5	106.7	103.8	94.4
Agriculture	101.0	99.7	106.8	87.7	94.3
Forestry	94.8	78.1	68.2	118.5	60.1
Transport	101.1	85.2	80.1	100.9	69.6
Communication	105.3	98.1	78.6	114.9	93.0
Whol./Retail Trade	104.7	100.7	107.9	99.8	113.5
Other Branches of Material Production	111.6	88.4	103.3	102.5	104.5
Communal Services	100.8	89.6	124.9	83.8	94.5
Housing	87.7	94.3	95.2	148.8	117.2
Education	100.5	109.4	100.4	103.3	114.0
Health Care	97.6	102.6	96.2	103.4	99.6
Remaining Branches of National Economy	110.2	97.0	79.9	79.8	68.2

Source: Economic Analysis Unit

The drop in the industrial sector's share of national employment is about two times less than the fall in its share of GDP formation. This testifies to the declining productivity of labor in this sector: 21 percent fewer people employed in industry in 1992 produced 35 percent less output than in 1988. Similar phenomena were noted in other sectors of the economy, especially in transportation. The opposite pattern took place in the construction industry: employment during the analyzed period decreased by about 20 percent, while the industry's share in GDP fell by 5.6 percent. Thus, an increase in productivity occurred in the construction industry — a result of the substantial degree of privatization of this sector of the economy and the relatively rapid establishment of market relations based on genuine competition.

The significant fall in production and employment in industry should cause concern, especially since the steepest decline occurred in the electro-machine industry (employment fell 31.5 points). The above industry is considered the vehicle of technological progress in the economy. If the negative trend in this industry is not reversed, Poland will face the prospect of declining living standards. Official government explanations for so great a decline in production in this industry were too one-sided and over-simplified, pointing mainly to the collapse of the Eastern

Table 2.4
Employment by sectors and forms
of ownership for Poland in 1989-1992

	1989	1990	1991	1992
Employment in thousands				
Total	17,558.0	16,474.0	15,861.2	15,494.4
Public sector				
Total Public Sector	9,277.8	8,243.4	7,052.1	6,606.4
State	9,277.8	8,243.4	6,429.5	5,899.8
Communal	0.0	0.0	622.6	663.0
Mixed	0.0	0.0	0.0	43.5
Private sector				
Total Private Sector	8,280.2	8,230.6	8,809.1	8,888.0
Domestic	—	8,063.2	8,386.0	8,583.6
Foreign	—	167.4	89.0	119.8
Mixed	—	0.0	334.1	184.5

Source: Statistical Yearbooks

Percent distribution of employment by sectors
and forms of ownership for Poland in 1989-1992 (in %)

	1989	1990	1991	1992
Total	100.00	100.00	100.00	100.00
Public sector				
Total Public Sector	52.84	50.04	44.46	42.64
State	52.84	50.04	40.54	38.08
Communal	0.00	0.00	3.93	4.28
Mixed	0.00	0.00	0.00	0.28
Private sector				
Total Private Sector	47.16	49.96	55.54	57.36
Domestic	—	48.95	52.87	55.40
Foreign	—	1.02	0.56	0.77
Mixed	—	0.00	2.11	1.19

Source: Economic Analysis Unit

market. An exhaustive analysis of all the different factors that contributed to the decline will not be made here, but the most important factors are discussed below.Such a deep decline in industrial production was not only caused by the collapse of the Eastern market, but also by mistakes in economic policy. The main errors of this policy were: allowing an uncontrolled influx of electronic, light-industry, and food products; a lack of industrial policy laying out the perspectives for individual branches of industry (this had been considered the best industrial policy); overzealous privatization, which began with the best enterprises, capable of competing in international markets; and the failure to set up privatization preferences for branches of industry that would contribute most to the modernization of the economy. These and other mistakes appear to be the result of an exaggerated faith in both the curative powers of the market and the adaptability of economic entities to market conditions.

An analysis of structural change in the economy of the City of Warsaw and the entire Warsaw metropolitan region is conducted in the context of the entire country, based on employment level data. This method was chosen largely because of a lack of other forms of data. National employment levels by economic sector, for 1988 through 1992 are reported in Table 2.5. The size of the work force in Metropolitan Warsaw relative to overall national employment, broken down by economic sector, is presented in Table 2.6.

The following is a discussion of 1988 and 1992 employment levels by economic sector and the performance of the Warsaw metropolitan region to the nation. The decline in the City of Warsaw's work force (8.4 percent) and the metropolitan region's (9.0 percent) was less than that of the country as a whole (9.5 percent). However in the territory of the region outside the City of Warsaw it was higher (10.9 percent). The employment decline in industry, housing, science, scholarship, technological development, culture, and art were greater in Metropolitan Warsaw than in the country as a whole. The losses in the construction, transportation, and sports sectors were less than those for the nation. Significantly higher employment growth occurred in finance and insurance, trade, and communications in Metropolitan Warsaw, than in the nation. The Ring outside of the City of Warsaw recorded better employment gains than the City in the transportation and communication sectors. The Ring also had a gain in state administration employment, where the nation had a loss. In the other economic sectors, the employment changes in the Ring were worse than the City of Warsaw and the nation as a whole.

As a result of the differing growth rates of individual sectors between 1988 and 1992, the structure of employment in the national, regional and City economies were altered. Changes in the structure of national employment were significantly smaller than in those of the City of Warsaw and the Warsaw metropolitan region. The share of industrial employment in the national economy shrank by 3 percentage points, while losing 6 points in the City of Warsaw and 8 points in the surrounding Ring. On the other hand, the increase in the share of trade as well as finance and insurance in the City of Warsaw and the surrounding region was higher than in the country as a whole.

29

Table 2.5
Employment in industry in Poland ('000)

	1988	1990	1991	1992	1992/ 1988
Industry	4,894.2	4,619.9	4,249.9	3,882.1	79.3%
Mining	555.4	511.2	458.1	459.3	82.7%
Fuel & Power	656.4	607.5	560.0	544.0	82.9%
Metallurgical	212.2	194.3	199.0	183.0	86.2%
Electro-Engineering	1,360.6	1,178.3	1,076.0	932.0	68.5%
Chemical	279.5	251.9	257.0	239.0	85.5%
Mineral	219.6	195.5	197.0	188.0	85.6%
Wood & Paper	218.5	181.1	218.0	210.0	96.1%
Light	659.9	557.5	533.0	465.0	70.5%
Food	419.7	400.4	453.0	466.0	111.0%
Other	148.6	110.8	82.0	76.0	51.1%

Source: Statistical Yearbooks

Percent distribution of employment in industry in Poland, 1988-1992 (in %)

	1988	1990	1991	1992
Industry	100.0	100.0	100.0	100.0
Mining	11.3	11.1	10.8	11.8
Fuel & Power	13.4	13.1	13.2	14.0
Metallurgical	4.3	4.2	4.7	4.7
Electro-Engineering	27.8	25.5	25.3	24.0
Chemical	5.7	5.5	6.0	6.2
Mineral	4.5	4.2	4.6	4.8
Wood & Paper	4.5	3.9	5.1	5.4
Light	13.5	12.1	12.5	12.0
Food	8.6	8.7	10.7	12.0
Other	3.0	2.4	1.9	2.0

Source: Economic Analysis Unit

Table 2.6 (page 1 of 3)
Employment by branch for Warsaw metropolitan area,
Warsaw and suburban ring and Poland, 1988,1992 ('000)

	Warsaw metro-politan area		Warsaw		Ring		Poland	
	1988	1992	1988	1992	1988	1992	1988	1992
Total	1,066.4	969.9	791.4	725.0	275.0	244.9	17,128.8	15,494.5
Industry	331.4	234.5	235.7	170.0	95.7	64.5	4,894.2	3,898.4
Construction	116.4	94.1	89.0	76.0	27.4	18.1	1,349.9	1,078.7
Agriculture	14.0	73.2	4.3	21.0	9.7	52.2	4,731.3	4,475.1
Forestry	1.7	0.9	0.4	0.3	1.3	0.6	154.1	88.4
Transport	49.0	39.7	35.6	27.5	13.4	12.2	864.3	593.7
Communication	14.6	16.4	12.2	13.4	2.4	3.0	169.3	179.4
Whol./Retail Trade	117.5	136.7	88.0	105.0	29.5	31.7	1,477.4	1,617.3
Communal Services	34.7	41.6	26.5	35.3	8.2	6.3	437.2	388.7
Housing	31.7	19.7	24.9	17.1	6.8	2.6	223.7	175.8
Science	59.2	27.0	45.6	25.8	13.6	1.2	111.4	70.3
Education	86.2	78.5	60.9	62.3	25.3	16.2	927.3	1,112.0
Culture and Arts	24.1	17.0	18.9	15.3	5.2	1.7	91.4	94.0
Health Care	67.0	64.0	45.7	48.2	21.3	15.8	788.3	849.8
Sports and Recreation	15.5	9.7	13.4	9.2	2.1	0.5	110.9	62.4
State Administration	28.2	34.5	22.5	28.1	5.7	6.4	267.4	254.3
Finance and Insurance	16.3	30.4	13.2	26.5	3.1	3.9	165.3	209.2
Others	59.0	72.2	53.7	44.1	5.3	28.1	365.4	346.9

Table 2.6 (page 2 of 3)
Structure of employment (in %)

	Warsaw metro-politan area		Warsaw		Ring		Poland	
	1988	1992	1988	1992	1988	1992	1988	1992
Total	100.00	100.00	100.00	100.00	100.00	100.00	100.00	100.00
Industry	31.08	24.18	29.78	23.45	34.80	26.34	28.57	25.16
Construction	10.92	9.70	11.25	10.48	9.96	7.39	7.88	6.96
Agriculture	1.31	7.55	0.54	2.90	3.53	21.31	27.62	28.88
Forestry	0.16	0.09	0.05	0.04	0.47	0.24	0.90	0.57
Transport	4.59	4.09	4.50	3.79	4.87	4.98	5.05	3.83
Communication	1.37	1.69	1.54	1.85	0.87	1.22	0.99	1.16
Whol./Retail Trade	11.02	14.09	11.12	14.48	10.73	12.94	8.63	10.44
Communal Services	3.25	4.29	3.35	4.87	2.98	2.57	2.55	2.51
Housing	2.97	2.03	3.15	2.36	2.47	1.06	1.31	1.13
Science	5.55	2.78	5.76	3.56	4.95	0.49	0.65	0.45
Education	8.08	8.09	7.70	8.59	9.20	6.61	5.41	7.18
Culture and Arts	2.26	1.75	2.39	2.11	1.89	0.69	0.53	0.61
Health Care	6.28	6.60	5.77	6.65	7.75	6.45	4.60	5.48
Sports and Recreation	1.45	1.00	1.69	1.27	0.76	0.20	0.65	0.40
State Administration	2.64	3.56	2.84	3.88	2.07	2.61	1.56	1.64
Finance and Insurance	1.53	3.13	1.67	3.66	1.13	1.59	0.97	1.35
Others	5.53	7.44	6.79	6.08	1.91	11.46	2.13	2.24

Table 2.6 (page 3 of 3)
Changes in employment 1992/1988

	Warsaw metro-politan area	Warsaw	Ring	Poland
	0.910	0.916	0.891	0.905
Industry	0.708	0.721	0.674	0.797
Construction	0.808	0.854	0.661	0.799
Agriculture	5.229	4.884	5.381	0.946
Forestry	0.529	0.750	0.462	0.574
Transport	0.810	0.772	0.910	0.687
Communication	1.123	1.098	1.250	1.060
Whol./Retail Trade	1.163	1.193	1.075	1.095
Communal Services	1.199	1.332	0.768	0.889
Housing	0.621	0.687	0.382	0.786
Science	0.456	0.566	0.088	0.631
Education	0.911	1.023	0.640	1.199
Culture and Arts	0.705	0.810	0.327	1.028
Health Care	0.955	1.055	0.742	1.078
Sports and Recreation	0.626	0.687	0.238	0.563
State Administration	1.223	1.249	1.123	0.951
Finance and Insurance	1.865	2.008	1.258	1.266
Others	1.224	0.821	5.334	0.949

Source: Economic Analysis Unit

The ratios indicating changes in employment levels by sector (which compare 1992 employment levels to 1988 levels) suggest that the Warsaw metropolitan area has faired better than the nation as a whole. Among economic sectors involved in material production, only forestry experienced a deeper decline in employment than the nation. Outside of the material production sectors, the situation looks fundamentally different. Only state administration and the financial and insurance industries attained growth in employment which exceeded the national average. Sports and recreation fell less than the national average. In the remaining non-material production sectors, the work force shrank faster than the national average. As a result, these sectors of the metropolitan region's economy, which achieved more favorable ratios, were able to increase their share of overall national employment.

The City of Warsaw's share of the metropolitan region's economy is somewhere between 75 and 80 percent. To analyze the economy of the metropolitan region is thus largely to analyze the City. Such analysis indicates both positive and negative economic processes at work. Metropolitan Warsaw's increase in the national share economic activity in trade, communications, and finance and insurance has certainly been a positive process. Substantial growth in these sectors' share in the national economy testifies to the fact that Metropolitan Warsaw is strengthening its position as a commercial-financial center. At the same time, there are detrimental changes occurring, particularly the decline in the importance of science, scholarship, technology, education, health care, culture, and sports and recreation in the region's economy. The important role that these sectors play in social-economic development is understood. This trend must be reversed, which requires appropriate changes in national economic policy. Such changes will be very difficult to carry out over the next few years given the difficult financial situation of the state and the strong pressure of a multitude of social needs. The sectors mentioned above will require particular support from the Warsaw city government, which must lead efforts to improve the situation of these sectors. The achievement of ambitious and difficult goals for the development of Metropolitan Warsaw depend upon the success of the city government's efforts.

Poland in the international system — the structure of foreign trade

Foreign trade is a prime factor in Poland's economic growth. Not only does it assure the economy of various raw materials and products necessary for production and enriching the market with consumer goods and services, but it also provides the means for servicing Poland's enormous foreign debt.

Table 2.7 indicates a trade surplus occurred through 1990, when the value of exports exceeded imports by 66 percent. But since 1991, imports have substantially exceeded exports, causing an increase in Poland's foreign trade deficit, which has now become a serious threat to the country's development. There are many different reasons for the growth in the foreign trade deficit, the most important of which are: excessive liberalization of import regulations (which caused a largely uncontrolled influx of goods — especially consumer goods), and the erosion of the profitability of exports.

Since 1990, fundamental changes in the structure of Poland's foreign trade have occurred, both geographically and in the types of goods traded. These changes are illustrated in Tables 2.8 and 2.9.

During the period under discussion, Poland's foreign trade patterns shifted orientation from the East to the West. The share of trade with countries from the former USSR has decreased 4-fold in exports and 2.5-fold in imports. Similar changes occurred in trade with the remaining member countries of the defunct COMECON. On the other hand, Germany has become Poland's largest trading partner; its share in Polish exports has increased over 2.5-fold, and in imports by

34

Table 2.7

Table 2.7
Value of exports and imports for Poland, Warsaw,
and Warsaw metropolitan area in 1988-1992, in constant 1988 zloty

	Export 1988		1990		1991		1992	
			In billions zlotys					
Poland	6,011.74	100.00	6,505.27	100.00	6,598.13	100.00	5,969.66	100.00
Warsaw Metro. Area	900.54	14.98	786.95	12.10	2,799.55	42.43	1,905.71	31.92
Warsaw	792.68	13.19	710.08	10.92	2,751.36	41.70	1,835.23	30.74

	Import 1988		1990		1991		1992	
			In billions zlotys					
Poland	5,272.31	100.00	3,799.99	100.00	6,198.45	100.00	7,118.12	100.00
Warsaw Metro. Area	1,475.87	27.99	873.04	22.97	3,079.62	49.68	3,347.62	47.03
Warsaw	1,409.40	26.73	822.49	21.64	2,960.71	47.77	3,164.47	44.46
Export / Import % *	114.3		171.2		106.4		83.9	

Source: Economic Analysis Unit

* For Poland

11 percentage points (from 13 to 24). Germany has essentially taken the former USSR's place in Poland's foreign trade. Italy, Holland, and France have also significantly increased their shares in Poland's foreign trade, while Austria's increased marginally, expanding up until 1991, then contracting by 1.8 percent in imports and 1.4 percent in exports in 1992. Imports from Great Britain and the USA increased, though exports to those nations fell. If tariffs between Poland and the European Union are liberalized, Poland can expect to increase trade with Western Europe.

Important changes have also occurred in the structure of goods in Poland's foreign trade. Table 2.10 reports the value of exports and imports by economic branch for Poland, the Warsaw metropolitan region and the City of Warsaw, in constant prices. Poland's total value of exports remained steady between 1988 and 1992. The Warsaw region experienced a large increase in total export value in 1991 (3-fold greater than 1988). In 1992, export value was lower than 1991, but still over two times greater than the 1988 level. The City of Warsaw increased its share of the region's total value of exports during the 1988-1992 period, from 88 percent in 1988 to over 96 percent in 1992.

In Poland, between 1988 and 1992, heavy losses in export value were recorded in industry (54 percent), construction (86 percent), agriculture (49 percent), forestry (30 percent), communications (75 percent), and non-material production (21 percent). The Warsaw region and the City of Warsaw experienced similar declines in

Table 2.8
Exports to groups of countries for Poland in 1988-1992,
in constant 1988 zloty

	1988	1990	1991	1992
	Exports in billions zlotys			
Total	6,011.745	6,505.274	6,682.881	5,969.668
EEC+Western Europe	2,434.300	3,930.798	4,637.881	4,078.239
Post Communist				
Countries	570.500	278.004	482.076	276.379
Former USSR	1,474.580	993.352	733.559	401.694
Asia	443.037	467.931	292.076	323.355
North and South America	268.802	284.417	267.712	247.475
Australia	9.389	9.960	6.780	10.664
Africa	157.739	142.010	105.890	132.824

Source: Statistical Yearbooks

Percent distribution of exports to groups of countries
for Poland in 1988-1992 (in %)

	1988	1990	1991	1992
Total	100.00	100.00	100.00	100.00
EEC+Western Europe	40.49	60.42	69.40	68.32
Post Communist				
Countries	9.49	4.27	7.21	4.63
Former USSR	24.53	15.27	10.98	6.73
Asia	7.37	7.19	4.37	5.42
North and South America	4.47	4.37	4.01	4.15
Australia	0.16	0.15	0.10	0.18
Africa	2.62	2.18	1.58	2.22

Source: Economic Analysis Unit

Table 2.9
Imports from groups of countries for Poland in 1988-1992, in constant 1988 zloty

	1988	1990	1991	1992
	Imports in billions zlotys			
Total	5,272.313	3,799.993	6,198.453	7,118.123
EEC+Western Europe	2,255.058	2,253.528	3,990.981	4,705.146
Post Communist				
Former USSR	1,228.447	753.407	875.208	678.252
Asia	400.893	341.321	553.962	661.003
North and South America	250.251	99.152	177.925	325.955
Australia	75.707	14.699	9.736	8.123
Africa	22.788	16.464	8.226	26.893

Source: Statistical Yearbooks

Percent distribution of
imports from groups of countries for Poland in 1988-1992 (in %)

	1988	1990	1991	1992
Total	100.00	100.00	100.00	100.00
EEC+Western Europe	42.77	59.30	64.39	66.10
Post Communist				
Former USSR	23.30	19.83	14.12	9.53
Asia	7.60	8.98	8.94	9.29
North and South America	4.75	2.61	2.87	4.58
Australia	1.44	0.39	0.16	0.11
Africa	0.43	0.43	0.13	0.38

Source: Economic Analysis Unit

Table 2.10 (part 1a of 2)
Value of exports by branch for Poland, Warsaw metropolitan area, and Warsaw in 1988-1992, in constant zloty

	1988 Poland	1988 Warsaw metro. area	1988 Warsaw	1990 Poland	1990 Warsaw metro. area	1990 Warsaw
			in billions zlotys			
Total	6,012	901	793	6,837	787	710
Industry	4,512	498	410	4,864	387	327
Construction	461	197	197	520	168	167
Agriculture	157	12	8	206	9	6
Finance & Insurance	0	0	0	0	0	0
Forestry	41	0	0	39	0	0
Transport	14	2	2	8	4	4
Wholesale and Retail Trade	749	149	136	756	155	146
Communication	4	1	1	2	1	1
Other Branches of Material Production	22	7	7	62	36	33
Non-Material Production	52	34	33	48	28	27

Source: Economic Analysis Unit

Table 2.10 (part 1b of 2)
Value of imports by branch for Poland, Warsaw metropolitan area, and Warsaw in 1988-1992, in constant zloty

	1988 Poland	1988 Warsaw metro. area	1988 Warsaw	1990 Poland	1990 Warsaw metro. area	1990 Warsaw
			in billions zlotys			
Total	5,272	1,476	1,409	4,437	873	822
Industry	2,549	421	369	2,374	248	208
Construction	80	24	24	27	6	6
Agriculture	34	6	5	34	5	4
Finance & Insurance	2	2	2	7	6	6
Forestry	3	0	0	2	0	0
Transport	148	72	71	67	32	32
Wholesale and Retail Trade	2,354	687	678	1,152	399	393
Communication	4	3	3	21	15	15
Other Branches of Material Production	18	14	14	78	39	38
Non-Material Production	281	246	244	156	121	119

Source: Economic Analysis Unit

Table 2.10 (part 2a of 2)
Value of exports by branch for Poland, Warsaw metropolitan area, and Warsaw in 1988-1992, in constant zloty

	1991 Poland	1991 Warsaw metro. area	1991 Warsaw	1992 Poland	1992 Warsaw metro. area	1992 Warsaw
			in billions zlotys			
Total	6,683	2,800	2,751	5,970	1,906	1,835
Industry	1,415	118	94	2,076	179	133
Construction	34	10	10	62	16	15
Agriculture	35	6	5	65	24	23
Finance & Insurance	1	1	1	1	1	1
Forestry	18	0	0	12	0	0
Transport	73	10	10	56	23	22
Wholesale and Retail Trade	4,148	2,528	2,506	3,420	1,646	1,627
Communication	0	0	0	1	1	1
Other Branches of Material Production	47	1	1	46	2	2
Non-Material Production	139	125	124	41	13	12

Source: Economic Analysis Unit

Table 2.10 (part 1b of 2)
Value of imports by branch for Poland, Warsaw metropolitan area, and Warsaw in 1988-1992, in constant zloty

	1991 Poland	1991 Warsaw metro. area	1991 Warsaw	1992 Poland	1992 Warsaw metro. area	1992 Warsaw
			in billions zlotys			
Total	6,198	3,080	2,961	7,118	3,348	3,164
Industry	860	189	151	1,999	556	461
Construction	88	23	20	141	35	30
Agriculture	20	3	3	40	5	2
Finance & Insurance	11	5	5	36	28	28
Forestry	2	0	0	1	0	0
Transport	71	35	34	92	43	40
Wholesale and Retail Trade	4,790	2,684	2,612	4,173	2,482	2,411
Communication	7	7	6	25	21	21
Other Branches of Material Production	229	32	31	148	51	50
Non-Material Production	139	103	100	233	127	123

Source: Economic Analysis Unit

these branches of the economy, during the period. For the nation, only finance and insurance, transport services, wholesale and retail trade, and other branches of material production, experienced increases in export value. Again, the Warsaw metropolitan region and the City, followed similar patterns in these sectors. The largest increase in export value, from 1988 to 1992, occurred in the City of Warsaw, in wholesale and retail trade.

The total value of imports, to Poland, decreased between 1988 and 1990, but grew steadily in 1991 and 1992, reaching a value in 1992, 35 percent greater than 1988. The Warsaw metropolitan region and the City of Warsaw followed a similar pattern, though the value of imports in 1992 for both areas was over 100 percent greater than in 1988. By sector, in Poland, industry, forestry, transport services, and non-material production, all had reduced import trade values in 1992, as compared to 1988. The largest and most significant increase in import value occurred in retail and wholesale trade (77 percent for Poland), reflecting increasing demand for such goods. The Warsaw metropolitan region and the City experienced a similar pattern of import value growth in retail and wholesale trade; both areas underwent over a 3.5-fold increase. The value of imported retail and wholesale trade goods was higher in 1991 than 1992, suggesting that the sector may have become saturated, as demand reached a natural limit. The finance and insurance sector experienced a dramatic increase in import value during the period, reflecting demand for these services.

The changes in the structure of goods in Poland's foreign trade pose the danger of becoming permanent, which would further weaken Poland's position in international markets. Reversing this trend will be quite difficult so long as the non-material production sectors which have grown during this period of discussion, remain more profitable than most manufacturing sectors.

Changes in the structure of exports and imports by branch are presented in Table 2.11. Branches experiencing relative increases in exports between 1988 and 1992 include: transport services, retail and wholesale trade, and other branches of material production. Industry's share of polish exports fell from 75 percent in 1988 to 34.8 percent in 1992. Even deeper declines were noted in the region and the City. In all areas, retail and wholesale trade has largely filled the predominant role in foreign trade that industry once played. Branches experiencing relative increases in imports between 1988 and 1992 include: construction, finance and insurance, retail and wholesale trade, communications, and other branches of material production. Tables 2A-1 and 2A-2 in the appendix of this chapter, provide additional data on export and import values, and structure, for further disaggregated sectors of industry.

There are many reasons for the changes in the structure of Poland's foreign trade. To a large extent they were caused by the collapse of the Eastern market — which the accelerated switch-over to dollar-based account settling and the implementation of other short-sighted policies failed to counteract. As a result, Poland lost its trade surplus which it had held until 1990, and has had a deepening trade deficit with the countries of the former USSR, especially Russia (largely due to the importing of energy). Despite certain differences in the structural changes of foreign

40

Table 2.11 (part 1a of 2)
Percent distribution of exports by branch for Poland, Warsaw metropolitan area and Warsaw in 1988-1992 (in %)

| | 1988 | | | 1990 | | |
	Poland	Warsaw metro. area	Warsaw	Poland	Warsaw metro. area	Warsaw
Total	100.0	99.9	100.0	100.0	100.0	100.0
Industry	75.0	55.3	51.7	71.1	49.1	46.0
Construction	7.7	21.9	24.8	7.6	21.3	23.5
Agriculture	2.6	1.4	1.0	3.0	1.1	0.9
Finance & Insurance	0.0	0.0	0.0	0.0	0.0	0.0
Forestry	0.7	0.0	0.0	0.6	0.0	0.0
Transport	0.2	0.2	0.2	0.1	0.5	0.5
Wholesale and Retail Trade	12.5	16.5	17.1	11.1	19.7	20.5
Communication	0.1	0.1	0.1	0.0	0.1	0.1
Other Branches of Material Production	0.4	0.8	0.9	0.9	4.6	4.6
Non-Material Production	0.9	3.8	4.1	0.7	3.6	3.8

Source: Economic Analysis Unit

Table 2.11 (part 1b of 2)
Percent distribution of imports by branch for Poland, Warsaw metropolitan area and Warsaw in 1988-1992 (in %)

| | 1988 | | | 1990 | | |
	Poland	Warsaw metro. area	Warsaw	Poland	Warsaw metro. area	Warsaw
Total	100.0	100.0	100.0	100.0	100.0	100.0
Industry	48.3	28.5	26.2	53.5	28.4	25.3
Construction	1.5	1.6	1.7	0.6	0.7	0.7
Agriculture	0.6	0.4	0.3	0.8	0.6	0.5
Finance & Insurance	0.0	0.1	0.2	0.2	0.7	0.8
Forestry	0.1	0.0	0.0	0.1	0.0	0.0
Transport	2.8	4.9	5.0	1.5	3.7	3.9
Wholesale / Retail Trade	44.7	46.5	48.1	26.0	45.7	47.8
Communication	0.1	0.2	0.2	0.5	1.8	1.9
Other Branches of Material Production	0.4	0.9	1.0	1.8	4.5	4.7
Non-Material Production	5.3	16.7	17.3	3.5	13.9	14.5

Source: Economic Analysis Unit

41

Table 2.11 (part 2a of 2)
Percent distribution of imports by branch for Poland, Warsaw metropolitan area and Warsaw in 1988-1992 (in %)

	1991 Poland	1991 Warsaw metro. area	1991 Warsaw	1992 Poland	1992 Warsaw metro. area	1992 Warsaw
Total	100.0	100.0	100.0	100.0	100.0	100.0
Industry	21.2	4.2	3.4	34.8	9.4	7.2
Construction	0.5	0.4	0.4	1.0	0.9	0.8
Agriculture	0.5	0.2	0.2	1.1	1.3	1.2
Finance & Insurance	0.0	0.1	0.1	0.0	0.0	0.0
Forestry	0.3	0.0	0.0	0.2	0.0	0.0
Transport	1.1	0.3	0.4	0.9	1.2	1.2
Wholesale and Retail Trade	62.1	90.3	91.1	57.3	86.4	88.7
Communication	0.0	0.0	0.0	0.0	0.0	0.0
Other Branches of Material Production	0.7	0.0	0.0	0.8	0.1	0.1
Non-Material Production	2.1	4.5	4.5	0.7	0.7	0.6

Source: Economic Analysis Unit

Table 2.11 (part 2b of 2)
Percent distribution of imports by branch for Poland, Warsaw metropolitan area and Warsaw in 1988-1992 (in %)

	1991 Poland	1991 Warsaw metro. area	1991 Warsaw	1992 Poland	1992 Warsaw metro. area	1992 Warsaw
Total	100.0	100.0	100.0	100.0	100.0	100.0
Industry	13.9	6.1	5.1	28.1	16.6	14.6
Construction	1.4	0.7	0.7	2.0	1.0	0.9
Agriculture	0.3	0.1	0.1	0.6	0.1	0.1
Finance & Insurance	0.2	0.2	0.2	0.5	0.8	0.9
Forestry	0.0	0.0	0.0	0.0	0.0	0.0
Transport	1.1	1.1	1.1	1.3	1.3	1.2
Wholesale / Retail Trade	77.3	87.1	88.2	58.6	74.1	76.2
Communication	0.1	0.2	0.2	0.4	0.6	0.7
Other Branches of Material Production	3.7	1.0	1.0	2.1	1.5	1.6
Non-Material Production	2.2	3.4	3.4	3.3	3.8	3.9

Source: Economic Analysis Unit

trade between Metropolitan Warsaw, and the country as a whole, both reflect general tendencies occurring in the Polish economy in the beginning of the 1990s.

Warsaw's role in the national economy

Metropolitan Warsaw's share in gross domestic product (GDP) formation can be used to determine a city's role in the national economy. This ratio, after all, depends not only on the amount of resources engaged in the process of GDP formation, but also on the efficacy with which they are utilized. In this way, the City and region's role in the national economy can be evaluated in an objective manner. Unfortunately, the statistics available are insufficient to make reliable estimates of GDP at less than the national level. For this reason, an estimate of Metropolitan Warsaw's role in the national economy must be made with the help of a collection of substitute indicators.

In terms of the overall income from the sale of goods and services, the Warsaw region's share of the national economy increased from 20.6 percent on 1988 to 27 percent in 1992. Because these figures are based on reporting of branch activity by location of establishment headquarters, they likely overstate the actual level of national economic activity taking place in Metropolitan Warsaw. Nevertheless, the relative increase in the share offers some ground to assert that Metropolitan Warsaw's economy performed better than the national economy, during the period.

An alternative method of estimating the relative size of the Metropolitan Warsaw economy is to assess capital expenditure data. These data are tabulated according to the location of the investments, and therefore sidestep the problem of headquarters reporting. In 1988, investment outlays in Metropolitan Warsaw accounted for 22.45 percent of national investments. By 1992, Metropolitan Warsaw accounted for only 12.44 percent.

In order to present a more comprehensive picture of the development processes taking place in the economy of the City of Warsaw, the surrounding metropolitan area, and the country, an analysis of the relationship between investment expenditures and gross value of fixed assets is necessary. Table 2.12 provides this data.

Only in 1990 was the ratio of capital outlays to gross value of fixed assets lower in the City of Warsaw and the metropolitan region, than in the country as a whole. In other years it was significantly higher. The most rapidly developing sectors of the national economy are communications and trade. It is also in these sectors where the City and the metropolitan region are farthest ahead of the rest of the nation, indicated by their higher ratios. The construction and industrial sectors experienced a decrease in the ratio under discussion until 1990, and then a gradual rise. The low level of investment in transportation is connected, on the one hand, with a decline in shipments caused by cut-backs in industrial production and construction, and on the other hand, with the rationalization of shipping.In the near future, greater investment intensity would be desirable, especially in those sectors

Table 2.12 (1 of 2)
Capital investment outlays by branch for Poland,
Warsaw metropolitan area and Warsaw, 1988-1992, in constant 1988 zlotys

| | **1988** | | | | | |
| | **Poland** | | **Warsaw metro-politan area** | | **Warsaw** | |
	Investment outlays	Investment outlays / gross value of fixed assets	Investment outlays	Investment outlays / gross value of fixed assets	Investment outlays	Investment outlays / gross value of fixed assets
Total	2,094.9	2.23	470.3	5.41	371.2	4.54
Industry	615.6	2.52	140.5	9.08	102.8	7.90
Construction	52.4	—	20.2	9.19	17.4	9.14
Agriculture	314.6	—	11.2	10.49	1.6	6.03
Forestry	11.9	—	0.7	10.06	0.1	0.13
Transport	157.5	—	66.5	1.52	52.5	1.20
Communi-cation	21.7	—	9.9	11.36	8.9	9.75
Whol./Retail Trade	63.7	—	16.8	4.63	13.9	4.04
Communal Services	162.5	—	26.3	7.10	25.1	6.83

| | **1990** | | | | | |
| | **Poland** | | **Warsaw metro-politan area** | | **Warsaw** | |
	Investment outlays	Investment outlays / gross value of fixed assets	Investment outlays	Investment outlays / gross value of fixed assets	Investment outlays	Investment outlays / gross value of fixed assets
Total	5,790.5	3.42	482.8	3.09	406.6	2.79
Industry	2,025.8	4.12	121.2	4.09	88.8	3.63
Construction	86.9	2.45	6.2	1.73	5.5	1.77
Agriculture	657.3	1.69	3.3	2.01	1.4	8.45
Forestry	21.7	2.61	0.9	23.84	0.0	34.53
Transport	318.9	1.50	94.5	1.15	88.7	1.08
Communi-cation	91.8	8.09	18.4	12.43	17.0	11.47
Whol./Retail Trade	207.0	5.67	24.0	7.52	20.0	7.10
Communal Services	322.7	3.96	26.3	3.48	25.6	3.43

Table 2.12 (2 of 2)
Capital investment outlays by branch for Poland,
Warsaw metropolitan area and Warsaw, 1988-1992, in constant 1988 zlotys

	Poland		Warsaw metro-politan area		Warsaw	
1991						
	Investment outlays	Investment outlays / gross value of fixed assets	Investment outlays	Investment outlays / gross value of fixed assets	Investment outlays	Investment outlays / gross value of fixed assets
Total	6,008.4	4.99	625.9	5.68	542.8	5.26
Industry	2,029.3	5.80	100.2	4.75	69.5	3.92
Construction	116.8	4.62	15.8	6.39	13.5	6.40
Agriculture	381.0	1.37	2.3	2.21	0.7	7.19
Forestry	20.5	3.48	0.4	17.11	0.0	43.98
Transport	304.9	2.02	87.7	1.51	81.4	1.41
Communi cation	110.1	13.63	37.2	30.88	34.9	29.01
Whol./Retail Trade	239.5	9.21	53.1	19.06	49.8	19.91
Communal Services	437.1	7.53	36.3	8.16	36.2	8.18

	Poland		Warsaw metro-politan area		Warsaw	
1992						
	Investment outlays	Investment outlays / gross value of fixed assets	Investment outlays	Investment outlays / gross value of fixed assets	Investment outlays	Investment outlays / gross value of fixed assets
Total	5,964.4	5.68	742.1	7.59	585.1	6.41
Industry	2,015.3	6.61	146.7	8.05	83.7	5.62
Construction	189.7	11.07	30.2	13.98	23.5	12.80
Agriculture	352.1	1.62	33.3	27.03	31.8	72.35
Forestry	13.1	2.72	0.4	16.42	0.0	0.04
Transport	265.9	3.95	75.5	1.54	68.4	1.39
Communi-cation	236.0	29.23	47.8	27.87	44.3	25.80
Whol./Retail Trade	335.6	14.16	73.8	19.99	49.9	14.91
Communal Services	460.6	15.37	36.1	9.53	34.3	9.05

Source: Economic Analysis Unit

of the economy in which the effect of the investment multiplier is particularly strong. However, the level and pace of investments will depend mainly on the financial situation of various sectors of the national economy.

The profitability of Metropolitan Warsaw's economy is generally higher than that of the national economy, as indicated by the gross productivity ratios presented in Table 2.13. Net productivity ratios are found on Table 2.14. Productivity ratios reached their highest levels in 1990. Before reform was initiated, the economy had been sinking deeper into a crisis characterized by ever-increasing shortages, which rendered it incapable of functioning normally and of exploiting its productive capabilities. The early stages of the reform program included, among other things, drastic limitations on subsidies and the freeing up of prices. As a result, the economy was able to achieve a relatively advantageous level of profitability despite a substantial fall in production. This improvement was also facilitated by a significant growth in exports that year, which were favored by an advantageous exchange rate and other factors. In the years that followed, a substantial decline of profitability took place. Income from economic activity only marginally exceeded costs, while net profitability fell into the red. As a result, more and more economic entities were unable to pay their taxes, which further limited government expenditures. The performance of Metropolitan Warsaw's economy during 1991 and 1992 did manage to exceed that of the national economy. The metropolitan region had a lower deficit percentage in 1991 than the nation; and in 1992 when the national economy still experienced a deficit of 1.72 percent, the region managed a marginal net profit.

The financial situation of individual sectors and branches of the national economy is highly differentiated. In 1988, only communal services showed a deficit at the national level. That same year, while trade attained a level of profitability of 35-38 percent across the different levels of geographic aggregation, communications managed a similar level and foreign trade an even higher level, in Metropolitan Warsaw. In 1990, profitability decidedly improved in nearly all sectors and branches of the national economy. A deficit was noted only in transportation and communications in Metropolitan Warsaw's economy. Foreign trade in Metropolitan Warsaw, however, brought net profits exceeding costs incurred. Domestic trade and food processing also attained a relatively high level of profitability. The high level of profitability of these sectors of the economy explains their rapid development. Since 1991, the most profitable sector of the economy has been communications. This profitability, however, has been artificially created by a monopolist, Telekomunikacja Polska SA, which sets rates for its services by itself.

Despite the performance of communications, the majority of examined sectors and branches of the economy noted negative net profitability ratios in 1991. Even the net profitability of trade fell to 1.26 percent in the City of Warsaw and 0.31 percent in the country as a whole. This sector of the economy has reached its saturation point; further growth will depend upon increases in effective demand, which is tied to growth in real income. Substantial growth in net profitability occurred in the financial and insurance sector in 1991, a result primarily of high bank margins

46

connected not only to high inflation, but also to so-called bad debts caused by the failure of many loan takers to fulfill their obligations to banks.

The finances of Polish banks are a matter of serious concern. Improprieties in the extension of credit have resulted in many bad loans. Yet the banks use their relatively high profits to maintain very high salaries, related expenses (salary-increase penalties and taxes) and luxurious interiors, while investing what remains of the profits not in the economy, but in speculative transactions in treasury coupons, paid for by the income of the state budget. In this manner, they increase the budget deficit, which further worsens the financial situation of enterprises that need to borrow money.

In 1992, the financial situation of the country worsened further. Relatively high profitability was maintained in only the communications sector. Even trade suffered losses, largely due to the saturation of this sector.

The performance of Metropolitan Warsaw's economy has been better in many sectors than the nation, during the period of discussion, 1988-1992. Particular sectors of note are: communications, construction, trade, finance, insurance, and the chemical industry.

The more favorable position of the Metropolitan Warsaw economy, over the nation, is confirmed by the indices in Table 2.15. The indices testify to:

1   Metropolitan Warsaw's superior investment possibilities;

2   the far greater consumption capacity of the Metropolitan Warsaw market (retail sales per capita in the region are 180 percent greater than the national average);

3   the superior financial possibilities of Metropolitan Warsaw's local government authorities; and

4   the nearly 2-fold higher per capita income of Metropolitan Warsaw (the local government's 5 percent share of income tax proceeds from physical persons, on a per capita basis, is 101.8 percent higher in Warsaw than the national average).

Warsaw's role in the national economy is undoubtedly significant, and there is much to indicate that this role can increase in the future. This will depend upon the degree to which the economic potential concentrated in Metropolitan Warsaw is developed. The next chapter assesses spatial patterns of economic activity in the Warsaw metropolitan area.

Table 2.13 (1 of 2)
Gross productivity ratios (GPR)* for Poland, Warsaw metropolitan area and Warsaw in 1988-1992 (in %)

	1988	Warsaw metro. area	Warsaw	1990	Warsaw metro. area	Warsaw
	Poland			Poland		
Total	19.88	27.47	25.91	29.94	36.53	37.72
Industry	19.06	22.05	19.17	30.97	36.13	38.54
Mining	—	10.40	10.40	—	22.48	22.48
Manufacturing	—	23.12	20.09	—	37.77	40.85
Fuel and Power	—	7.77	7.51	—	62.94	62.94
Metallurgical	—	13.56	13.56	—	22.88	22.88
Electro-Machine	—	26.18	22.17	—	22.45	22.39
Chemical	—	39.80	37.57	—	47.87	50.41
Mineral	—	16.00	15.41	—	15.74	20.94
Wood and Paper	—	21.94	9.11	—	27.88	57.10
Light	—	28.97	28.71	—	16.24	16.63
Food	—	21.11	20.92	—	58.35	72.89
Other	—	24.79	23.59	—	37.86	36.79
Construction	26.57	28.50	25.50	31.17	32.46	28.90
Transport	11.60	13.48	13.31	17.68	5.43	5.42
Communication	11.35	65.14	65.33	24.76	38.83	38.83
Trade	51.39	89.35	89.76	45.18	118.45	122.52
Domestic	—	67.54	68.00	—	56.69	59.79
Foreign	—	122.16	119.81	—	196.99	196.99
Finance & Insurance	—	11.49	11.49	—	4.86	4.86
Communal Services	-11.05	9.81	9.18	0.00	18.83	18.97
Agriculture	19.20	13.36	9.56	34.37	15.20	15.87
Forestry	9.45	10.23	10.23	17.48	23.18	23.18
Other	—	19.62	18.26	—	21.73	21.98

Source: Economic Analysis Unit

*GPR = Gross Profits (before taxes) / Cost of Production

Table 2.13 (2 of 2)
Gross productivity ratios (GPR)* for Poland, Warsaw metropolitan area and Warsaw in 1988-1992 (in %)

	1991 Poland	1991 Warsaw metro. area	1991 Warsaw	1992 Poland	1992 Warsaw metro. area	1992 Warsaw
Total	4.19	4.59	4.79	1.64	3.63	3.69
Industry	4.59	0.27	0.56	1.17	-1.29	-0.52
Mining	—	-8.14	-8.14	—	-16.06	-16.06
Manufacturing	—	1.18	1.61	—	1.08	2.32
Fuel and Power	—	1.28	1.28	3.88	-0.06	-0.06
Metallurgical	—	-30.06	-30.06	0.66	-29.08	0.48
Electro-Machine	—	-13.36	-12.87	-4.75	-5.61	-4.74
Chemical	—	22.99	29.19	7.33	8.40	12.48
Mineral	—	5.20	13.26	2.98	0.76	3.24
Wood and Paper	—	3.48	1.78	-0.17	-9.21	-15.31
Light	—	-2.86	-4.83	-7.88	-0.94	-1.37
Food	—	9.99	10.72	2.83	0.42	0.32
Other	—	23.90	24.92	—	5.92	7.19
Construction	12.31%	16.46	16.69	5.32	8.50	8.13
Transport	-1.59	-7.35	-7.40	0.68	-0.73	-0.77
Communication	51.94	49.27	53.41	35.96	40.55	40.55
Trade	2.19	4.18	3.94	1.84	2.50	1.99
Domestic	—	3.31	3.77	0.00	1.26	1.21
Foreign	—	5.08	4.56	0.00	4.17	3.01
Finance & Insurance	—	27.09	23.07	—	10.92	10.92
Communal Services	19.27	20.43	19.93	11.54	15.42	15.55
Agriculture	-9.17	-10.07	-12.36	-9.41	-3.75	-4.83
Forestry	9.72	31.49	31.49	5.63	11.59	11.59
Other	—	11.40	11.69	—	8.09	8.42

Source: Economic Analysis Unit

*GPR = Gross Profits (before taxes) / Cost of Production

49

Table 2.14 (1 of 2)
Net productivity ratios (NPR)* for Poland, Warsaw metropolitan area and Warsaw in 1988-1992 (in %)

	1988			1990		
	Poland	Warsaw metro. area	Warsaw	Poland	Warsaw metro. area	Warsaw
Total	20.30	13.21	13.09	14.53	15.56	15.91
Industry	18.20	11.42	10.86	14.52	17.52	18.64
Mining	—	8.18	8.18	—	2.18	2.18
Manufacturing	—	11.72	11.14	—	19.37	21.02
Fuel and Power	—	5.93	5.93	—	28.00	28.00
Metallurgical	—	6.04	6.04	—	11.30	11.30
Electro-Machine	—	12.48	11.89	—	11.41	11.40
Chemical	—	19.14	17.19	—	21.50	21.11
Mineral	—	8.99	11.35	—	-0.16	1.29
Wood and Paper	—	13.25	22.34	—	11.44	31.14
Light	—	14.72	15.10	—	9.12	9.04
Food	—	11.84	11.60	—	29.50	36.56
Other	—	17.19	17.24	—	22.62	22.31
Construction	26.00	10.18	10.24	14.64	14.17	15.61
Transport	17.40	8.04	8.04	3.50	-6.75	-6.79
Communication	11.40	35.28	35.28	5.67	-36.48	-36.48
Trade	38.10	34.65	35.73	23.82	62.16	64.30
Domestic	—	28.42	29.73	—	28.69	30.24
Foreign	—	44.02	44.02	—	104.73	104.73
Finance & Insurance	—	5.69	5.69	—	2.60	2.60
Communal Services	8.50	3.47	3.47	7.54	7.25	7.25
Agriculture	25.90	11.45	12.51	27.80	7.76	12.74
Forestry	8.10	6.05	6.05	7.50	11.86	11.86
Other	—	13.30	13.28	—	14.51	14.47

Source: Economic Analysis Unit

*NPR = Net Profit (after taxes) / Costs of Production

Table 2.14 (2 of 2)

Net productivity ratios (NPR)* for Poland, Warsaw metropolitan area and Warsaw in 1988-1992 (in %)

| | 1991 | | | 1992 | | |
	Poland	Warsaw metro. area	Warsaw	Poland	Warsaw metro. area	Warsaw
Total	-1.70	-1.47	-1.32	-1.72	0.70	0.92
Industry	-2.97	-4.90	-4.51	-3.58	-4.09	-3.71
Mining	—	-8.43	-8.43	—	-16.09	-16.09
Manufacturing	—	-4.52	-4.04	—	-2.17	-1.45
Fuel and Power	—	-1.07	-1.07	-1.52	-2.14	-2.14
Metallurgical	—	-35.66	-35.66	-6.17	-33.36	-33.36
Electro-Machine	—	-19.95	-19.31	-9.36	-9.53	-8.26
Chemical	—	7.59	10.99	0.59	2.12	5.00
Mineral	—	-7.14	-1.08	-4.65	-5.57	-2.38
Wood and Paper	—	0.87	0.76	-3.76	-10.94	-15.97
Light	—	-4.81	-6.92	-10.80	-2.32	-3.25
Food	—	4.38	4.79	-0.10	-1.25	-1.14
Other	—	8.40	8.57	—	1.47	1.84
Construction	4.10	6.80	7.04	1.76	4.27	4.37
Transport	-13.74	-25.06	-25.21	-2.34	-2.29	-2.35
Communication	18.88	31.96	31.16	19.97	24.42	24.22
Trade	0.31	1.25	1.26	0.44	0.64	0.65
Domestic	—	0.50	0.52	0.00	-0.20	-0.22
Foreign	—	2.03	2.02	0.00	1.77	1.80
Finance & Insurance	—	16.02	15.76	—	6.08	6.08
Communal Services	5.57	3.74	3.66	6.85	8.72	8.80
Agriculture	-12.39	-11.33	-12.58	-11.25	-5.08	-5.00
Forestry	2.83	14.85	14.85	5.42	7.36	7.36
Other	—	6.36	6.50	—	4.97	5.08

Source: Economic Analysis Unit

*NPR = Net Profit (after taxes) / Costs of Production

Table 2.15
Warsaw compared to Poland and Warsaw metropolitan area, 1988, 1992

	1988			1992		
	Poland	Warsaw	Warsaw	Poland	Warsaw	Warsaw
Investment outlays per capita in thousand zlotys	55.3	210.2	220.1	5,249.8	10,412.3	12,025.9
Poland = 100.0	100.0	381.8	398.0	100.0	197.0	229.0
Sales of goods and services per inhabitant in thousand zlotys	357.4	498.6	551.9	17,517.5	45,364.3	49,850.0
Poland = 100.0	100.0	139.5	154.4	100.0	258.9	280.5
Income of local government budgets per inhabitant in thousand zlotys	—	—	—	1,677.1	2,850.0	3,187.6
Poland = 100.0	—	—	—	100.0	170.0	190.1
Investment outlays from local budgets per inhabitants in thousand zlotys	—	—	—	392.3	917.8	1,054.0
Poland = 100.0	—	—	—	100.0	234.2	268.8
Value of local government 's share in personal income tax per inhabitant in thousand zlotys	—	—	—	328.5	645.1	663.1
Poland = 100.0	—	—	—	100.0	196.3	201.8

Source: Economic Analysis Unit

Chapter 2 Appendix

Table 2A.1 (part 1a of 2)
Value of exports by branch and products for Poland, Warsaw metropolitan
area and Warsaw in 1988-1992, in constant 1988 zloty (billions)

	1988 Warsaw metro.			1990 Warsaw metro.		
	Poland	area	Warsaw	Poland	area	Warsaw
Fuels and Power	611.6	34.4	34.4	691.4	38.8	38.8
Products of Metallurgical Industry	2,350.5	450.4	391.5	2,005.5	371.5	333.9
Products of Electro-Engineering Ind.	604.8	35.6	35.2	996.1	56.8	56.5
Products of Chemical Industry	655.9	6.5	4.4	821.1	50.5	37.1
Products of Mineral Industry	63.3	3.9	0.5	117.5	6.4	2.4
Products of Wood & Paper Industry	104.2	34.6	33.2	277.2	15.9	14.9
Products of Light Industry	330.5	31.0	28.6	437.7	10.1	8.1
Products of Food Industry	468.3	41.2	29.8	684.9	50.7	39.7
Other branches	84.9	12.7	10.1	43.6	10.2	8.5
Products of Industry	4,662.5	615.9	533.3	5,383.5	572.2	501.2
Products of Construction	239.8	144.9	144.8	327.2	109.1	108.6
Agricultural Products	210.9	25.2	18.9	368.7	45.8	41.1
Forestry Products	4.2	1.0	1.0	26.9	1.9	1.9
Other	282.7	21.0	20.9	37.8	19.2	18.5
Total	6,011.7	900.5	792.7	6,836.9	787.0	710.1

Source: Economic Analysis Unit

53

Table 2A.1 (part 1b of 2)
Value of imports by branch and products for Poland, Warsaw metropolitan area and Warsaw in 1988-1992, in constant 1988 zloty (billions)

	1988 Poland	1988 Warsaw metro. area	1988 Warsaw	1990 Poland	1990 Warsaw metro. area	1990 Warsaw
Fuels and Power	781.20	214.7	214.6	928.5	133.0	132.5
Products of Metallurgical Industry	1,882.30	698.3	668.2	1,782.1	416.6	389.6
Products of Electro-Engineering Ind.	431.70	40.7	38.3	297.8	30.3	27.5
Products of Chemical Industry	837.20	213.2	198.3	509.3	111.3	102.7
Products of Mineral Industry	635.00	13.0	9.5	53.2	9.4	7.6
Products of Wood & Paper Industry	104.20	30.9	26.4	70.1	14.5	13.6
Products of Light Industry	330.50	58.5	53.1	270.6	34.9	33.2
Products of Food Industry	468.20	102.1	98.6	337.2	76.2	71.5
Other branches		37.2	36.3	94.6	27.5	26.3
Products of Industry		1,408.5	1,343.3	4,343.5	853.8	804.4
Products of Construction		0.5	0.5	1.8	0.5	0.5
Agricultural Products	266.30	63.3	62.1	83.9	16.5	15.3
Forestry Products		0.3	0.3	1.3	0.2	0.2
Other		3.2	3.2	6.5	2.0	2.0
Total	5,272.30	1,475.9	1,409.4	4,436.9	873.0	822.5

Source: Economic Analysis Unit

Table 2A.1 (part 2a of 2)
Value of exports by branch and products for Poland, Warsaw metropolitan area and Warsaw in 1988-1992, in constant 1988 zloty (billions)

	1991 Poland	Warsaw metro. area	Warsaw	1992 Poland	Warsaw metro. area	Warsaw
Fuels and Power	712.0	124.4	124.4	630.9	81.6	81.5
Products of Metallurgical Industry	1,497.4	700.8	695.1	1,450.5	470.8	442.3
Products of Electro-Engineering Ind.	1,064.8	435.3	422.2	1,002.4	212.9	203.5
Products of Chemical Industry	774.3	583.7	581.2	724.3	376.5	372.0
Products of Mineral Industry	228.1	76.5	69.6	188.8	58.0	55.6
Products of Wood & Paper Industry	437.1	160.2	158.0	455.3	149.9	147.0
Products of Light Industry	408.4	39.9	37.3	507.0	57.7	52.4
Products of Food Industry	667.9	375.0	366.9	585.2	299.1	287.7
Other branches	28.4	19.3	18.7	39.5	13.9	13.2
Products of Industry	5,106.5	2,390.7	2,348.9	4,953.0	1,638.7	1,573.5
Products of Construction						
Agricultural Products	439.1	264.1	257.7	321.2	162.0	157.3
Forestry Products	31.7	19.7	19.7	35.9	16.2	16.0
Other	18.9	0.7	0.7	28.7	3.9	3.9
Total	6,683.3	2,799.6	2,751.4	5,969.7	1,902.5	1,832.3

Source: Economic Analysis Unit

Table 2A.1 (part 2b of 2)
Value of imports by branch and products for Poland, Warsaw metropolitan area and Warsaw in 1988-1992, in constant 1988 zloty (billions)

	1991 Poland	Warsaw metro. area	Warsaw	1992 Poland	Warsaw metro. area	Warsaw
Fuels and Power	1,166.9	809.6	808.9	1,196.7	1,033.3	1,031.6
Products of Metallurgical Industry	2,332.1	1,113.4	1,064.3	2,530.8	990.7	914.2
Products of Electro-Engineering Ind.	248.6	63.0	62.0	321.5	75.6	71.7
Products of Chemical Industry	778.3	430.8	412.9	1,241.4	525.2	483.0
Products of Mineral Industry	107.2	48.1	43.0	161.6	61.2	51.8
Products of Wood & Paper Industry	152.8	74.6	71.5	253.6	100.6	94.6
Products of Light Industry	380.6	115.7	106.2	318.6	92.4	80.7
Products of Food Industry	642.1	265.7	248.3	606.4	242.5	228.7
Other branches	193.6	87.0	82.4	219.0	105.6	100.5
Products of Industry	6,002.2	3,007.9	2,899.4	6,849.7	3,227.2	3,056.7
Products of Construction						
Agricultural Products	189.4	69.8	59.5	254.8	115.5	103.5
Forestry Products	1.1	0.6	0.5	2.3	0.7	0.5
Other	3.6	1.3	1.3	11.3	1.9	1.8
Total	6,198.5	3,079.6	2,960.7	7,118.1	3,345.3	3,162.5

Source: Economic Analysis Unit

Table 2A.2 (part 1a of 2)
Percent distribution of exports by branch and products for Poland, Warsaw metropolitan area and Warsaw in 1988-1992 (in %)

	1988 Poland	1988 Warsaw metro. area	1988 Warsaw	1990 Poland	1990 Warsaw metro. area	1990 Warsaw
Fuels and Power	10.17	3.82	4.34	1.05	4.93	5.47
Products of Metallurgical Industry	39.10	50.01	49.39	29.33	47.21	47.02
Products of Electro-Engineering Ind.	10.06	3.96	4.45	14.57	7.22	7.96
Products of Chemical Industry	10.91	0.72	0.55	12.01	6.42	5.22
Products of Mineral Industry	1.05	0.43	0.07	1.72	0.81	0.34
Products of Wood & Paper Industry	1.73	3.84	4.18	4.05	2.02	2.10
Products of Light Industry	5.50	3.44	3.61	6.40	1.28	1.14
Products of Food Industry	7.79	4.58	3.76	10.02	6.44	5.60
Other branches	1.41	1.41	1.27	0.64	1.29	1.20
Products of Industry	77.56	68.39	67.28	78.74	72.71	70.58
Products of Construction	3.99	16.09	18.27	4.79	13.86	15.29
Agricultural Products	3.51	2.79	2.38	5.39	5.81	5.79
Forestry Products	0.07	0.11	0.12	0.39	0.25	0.27
Other	4.70	2.34	2.64	0.55	2.44	2.61
Total	100.00	100.00	100.00	100.00	100.00	100.00

Source: Economic Analysis Unit

Table 2A.2 (part 1b of 2)
Percent distribution of exports by branch and products for Poland, Warsaw metropolitan area and Warsaw in 1988-1992 (in %)

	1988 Poland	1988 Warsaw metro. area	1988 Warsaw	1990 Poland	1990 Warsaw metro. area	1990 Warsaw
Fuels and Power	14.82	14.55	15.22	20.93	15.24	16.11
Products of Metallurgical Industry	35.70	47.31	47.41	40.17	47.72	47.36
Products of Electro-Engineering Ind.	8.19	2.76	2.72	6.71	3.47	3.34
Products of Chemical Industry	15.88	14.45	14.07	11.48	12.75	12.49
Products of Mineral Industry	12.04	0.88	0.68	1.20	1.08	0.93
Products of Wood & Paper Industry	1.98	2.09	1.87	1.58	1.67	1.65
Products of Light Industry	6.27	3.96	3.76	6.10	4.00	4.03
Products of Food Industry	8.88	6.92	7.00	7.60	8.73	8.69
Other branches		2.52	2.58	2.13	3.15	3.20
Products of Industry		95.44	95.31	97.89	97.80	97.81
Products of Construction		0.03	0.04	0.04	0.06	0.06
Agricultural Products	5.05	4.29	4.41	1.89	1.89	1.86
Forestry Products		0.02	0.02	0.03	0.02	0.03
Other		0.22	0.23	0.15	0.23	0.25
Total	100.00	100.00	100.00	100.00	100.00	100.00

Source: Economic Analysis Unit

Table 2A.2 (part 2a of 2)
Percent distribution of exports by branch and products for Poland, Warsaw metropolitan area and Warsaw in 1988-1992 (in %)

	1991 Poland	Warsaw metro. area	Warsaw	1992 Poland	Warsaw metro. area	Warsaw
Fuels and Power	10.65	4.44	4.52	10.57	4.53	4.45
Products of Metallurgical Industry	22.41	25.03	25.26	24.30	26.12	24.14
Products of Electro-Engineering Ind.	15.93	15.55	15.34	16.79	11.81	11.10
Products of Chemical Industry	11.59	20.85	21.12	12.13	20.89	20.30
Products of Mineral Industry	3.41	2.73	2.53	3.16	3.22	3.03
Products of Wood & Paper Industry	6.54	5.72	5.74	7.63	8.32	8.02
Products of Light Industry	6.11	1.42	1.36	8.49	3.20	2.86
Products of Food Industry	9.99	13.40	13.33	9.80	16.60	15.70
Other branches	0.43	0.69	0.68	0.66	0.77	0.72
Products of Industry	76.41	85.39	85.37	82.97	90.93	85.88
Products of Construction						
Agricultural Products	6.57	9.43	9.37	5.38	8.99	8.58
Forestry Products	0.47	0.70	0.72	0.60	0.90	0.87
Other	0.28	0.03	0.03	0.48	0.22	0.21
Total	100.00	100.00	100.00	100.00	105.56	100.00

Source: Economic Analysis Unit

Table 2A.2 (part 2b of 2)
Percent distribution of exports by branch and products for Poland, Warsaw metropolitan area and Warsaw in 1988-1992 (in %)

	1991 Poland	Warsaw metro. area	Warsaw	1992 Poland	Warsaw metro. area	Warsaw
Fuels and Power	18.83	26.29	27.32	16.81	30.89	32.62
Products of Metallurgical Industry	37.62	36.15	35.95	35.55	29.62	28.91
Products of Electro-Engineering Ind.	4.01	2.05	2.09	4.52	2.26	2.27
Products of Chemical Industry	12.56	13.99	13.95	17.44	15.70	15.27
Products of Mineral Industry	1.73	1.56	1.45	2.27	1.83	1.64
Products of Wood & Paper Industry	2.46	2.42	2.41	3.56	3.01	2.99
Products of Light Industry	6.14	3.76	3.59	4.48	2.76	2.55
Products of Food Industry	10.36	8.63	8.39	8.52	7.25	7.23
Other branches	3.12	2.83	2.78	3.08	3.16	3.18
Products of Industry	96.83	97.67	97.93	96.23	96.47	96.65
Products of Construction						
Agricultural Products	3.06	2.27	2.01	3.58	3.45	3.27
Forestry Products	0.02	0.02	0.02	0.03	0.02	0.02
Other	0.06	0.04	0.04	0.16	0.06	0.06
Total	100.00	100.00	100.00	100.00	100.00	100.00

Source: Economic Analysis Unit

3 Changes in the spatial structure of the Warsaw metropolitan economy

Spatial distribution of economic activity

In 1990 the easing of restrictions on new enterprise creation resulted in a significant increase in economic activity in Poland. This chapter analyses the dynamics of this process and its effect upon the spatial distribution of economic activity in Metropolitan Warsaw. For this purpose, Metropolitan Warsaw is divided into four distinct areas:

- the Center, comprising Srodmiescie gmina and including Warsaw's central business district;

- Ring I, comprising the remaining six gminas of the City of Warsaw (prior to the 1994 municipal reorganization);

- Ring II, covering the townships contiguous to the administrative borders of the City of Warsaw; and

- Ring III, consisting of the remaining townships of the metropolitan region.

Map 3.1 shows the boundaries of the zones. The number of registered economic enterprises and their declared employment, provide the basis for analysis. Relevant data on number and distribution of enterprises within the region is set forth in Table 3.1.

The total number of firms in Metropolitan Warsaw increased nearly 15-fold between 1988 and 1992. The increase in the number of firms in Ring I was the greatest (20-fold), while the Center noted the smallest increase (8.5-fold). As a result, the spatial distribution of firms within Metropolitan Warsaw was altered: the Center's share substantially decreased (from 30.6 to 17.9 percent), while that of

MAP 3.1

Metropolitan Warsaw,
Center and Three Rings

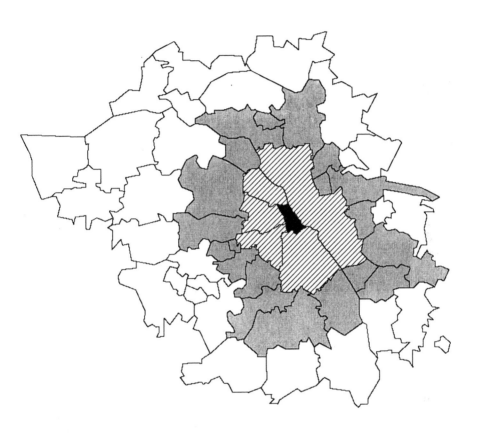

SPATIAL ANALYSIS ZONES

■	CENTER	(1)
▨	ZONE I	(7)
▦	ZONE II	(20)
☐	ZONE III	(26)

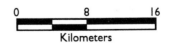

0   8   16
Kilometers

Table 3.1 (part 1 of 3)
Number and percent distribution of establishments by branch for Warsaw metropolitan area, center and rings in 1988 and 1992

	Number of establishments									
	1988					1992				
	Warsaw metro. area	Center	Ring 1	Ring 2	Ring 3	Warsaw metro. area	Center	Ring 1	Ring 2	Ring 3
Total	5,647	1,725	2,480	767	675	83,837	14,999	50,805	11,790	6,243
Industry	773	133	448	100	92	15,484	1,712	8,426	3,681	1,665
Construction	350	112	180	32	20	7,440	987	5,039	816	598
Transport	118	12	76	7	11	2,184	173	1,312	343	356
Communication	11	3	5	0	0	186	35	130	9	12
Wholesale/Retail Trade	513	193	204	59	53	37,276	6,298	23,488	4,933	2,557
Finance & Insurance	114	44	13	22	28	569	241	251	32	45
Communal Services	65	8	28	9	10	1,495	206	1,089	99	101
Agriculture	179	22	21	52	81	757	58	245	187	267
Forestry	15	5	4	4	1	91	30	49	6	6
Other	3,509	1,193	1,491	443	382	18,355	5,259	10,776	1,424	896

Source: Economic Analysis Unit

Table 3.1 (part 2 of 3)

	Percent distribution of establishments (in %)									
	1988					1992				
	Warsaw metro. area	Center	Ring 1	Ring 2	Ring 3	Warsaw metro. area	Center	Ring 1	Ring 2	Ring 3
Total	100	30.5	43.9	13.6	12.0	100	17.9	60.6	14.1	7.4
Industry	100	17.2	58.0	12.9	11.9	100	11.1	54.4	23.8	10.8
Construction	100	32.0	51.4	9.1	5.7	100	13.3	67.7	11.0	8.0
Transport	100	10.2	64.4	5.9	9.3	100	7.9	60.1	15.7	16.3
Communication	100	27.3	45.5	0.0	0.0	100	18.8	69.9	4.8	6.5
Wholesale/Retail	100	37.6	39.8	11.5	10.3	100	16.9	63.0	13.2	6.9
Finance &	100	38.6	11.4	19.3	24.6	100	42.4	44.1	5.6	7.9
Communal Services	100	12.3	43.1	13.8	15.4	100	13.8	72.8	6.6	6.8
Agriculture	100	12.3	11.7	29.1	45.3	100	7.7	32.4	24.7	35.3
Forestry	100	33.3	26.7	26.7	6.7	100	33.0	53.8	6.6	6.6
Other	100	34.0	42.5	12.6	10.9	100	28.7	58.7	7.8	4.9

Source: Economic Analysis Unit

Table 3.1 (part 3 of 3)

	Percent change in distribution, 1988-1992 (in %)				
	Warsaw metro. area	Center	Ring 1	Ring 2	Ring 3
Total	6.74	11.50	4.88	6.51	10.81
Industry	4.99	7.77	5.32	2.72	5.53
Construction	4.70	11.35	3.57	3.92	3.34
Transport	5.40	6.94	5.79	2.04	3.09
Communication	5.91	8.57	3.85	0.00	0.00
Wholesale/Retail	1.38	3.06	0.87	1.20	2.07
Finance &	20.04	18.26	5.18	68.75	62.22
Communal Services	4.35	3.88	2.57	9.09	9.90
Agriculture	23.65	37.93	8.57	27.81	30.34
Forestry	16.48	16.67	8.16	66.67	16.67
Other	19.12	22.68	13.84	31.11	42.63

Source: Economic Analysis Unit

Ring I increased (from 44.0 to 60.6 percent). A negligible increase in Ring II's share occurred, while Ring III's share declined by 4.5 percentage points. The changes under discussion are the result of two conditions: uneven rates of development, which existed during the years preceding reform, and spatial differentiation of demand. In this context, the low firm growth in the Center and its declining share of total metropolitan activity becomes understandable. Even before reform, downtown Warsaw was an area with a diverse concentration of firms, while the other areas were clearly under-invested.

The disproportionate development levels across the Rings have started to even out since 1988. It is no longer necessary to travel to downtown Warsaw — as it was for instance 5 years ago — to obtain even the most basic goods and services. Basic goods and services are currently available throughout most areas of the region.

In industry, a process of decentralization has become evident. Over half of all firms continue to be concentrated in Ring I, but that area's share within the region shrunk from 58.0 to 54.4 percent between 1988 and 1992. As of 1992, Zone II's share has doubled, almost 24 percent of all industrial firms were located there.

The distribution of construction firms within the region has undergone a significantly higher degree of decentralization than that of industrial firms. Particularly deep changes occurred in the Center and in Ring I. The Center lost share, a decrease of 19 percentage points, while Ring I's share increased by 16 percentage points. The share of construction firm activity in Ring II and III also increased in the period.

The greatest growth in the number of transportation firms took place in Rings II and III. They significantly increased their share at the cost of declines in the Center's and Ring I's shares.

61

In communications, firms are concentrated in the Center and in Ring I. This pattern is appropriate, as demand for their services is also concentrated in these areas.

The greatest increase in economic activity took place in retail and wholesale trade, in which the number of firms increased 72-fold. This is the result of two conditions: the relatively high profitability of this sector of the economy until 1990, and the ease of entering the market. Regarding the latter, one need not have a large amount of capital to enter the market and the cycle of capital turnover is relatively short. As a result of these economic conditions, small firms dominate in this sector of Poland's economy. A trend toward the concentration of this activity into larger firms should be anticipated in the near future.

Important changes took place in the spatial distribution of retail and wholesale trading firms as well. The share of such firms located in the Center fell by about 20 percentage points, while that of firms in Ring I substantially increased (by 23 percentage points). A small increase in the share of firms occurred in Ring II, and Ring III experienced a decline in share of over 3 percentage points. As a result of these changes, a fundamental correction occurred in the proximity of retail and wholesale trade firms to the needs of the public. Spatial disproportions in trade services that existed in the period before economic reform have largely been removed.

Finance and insurance firms have shown a clear tendency toward concentrating in the Center and Ring I. This is an expected result, linked to the orientation of the transit system. These firms gain significant economic benefits by locating close to their clients.

The growth in the number of firms providing communal services is tied to the establishment of numerous private firms and to the splitting up of multi-plant and multi-industry state enterprises, and single-industry enterprises. An example of this break-up is MPWiK in Warsaw (the water and waste-water utility for the City) which handed over its branches outside central Warsaw to the townships in which they are located. The distribution of firms should correspond to the spatial distribution of service demand, which depends primarily on the distribution of the populace and economic activity, especially industrial economic activity. The low share of communal services in Rings II and III testifies to spatial disproportions in this sector of Metropolitan Warsaw's economic structure. This situation is due mainly to varying levels of municipal infrastructure development within the metropolitan region.

In the farming and forestry sectors, a significant increase in the number of firms in the Center and Ring I has been fueled by the establishment of various firms which support these branches of the economy.

In the remaining economic sectors, such as education, health care, sports and recreation, tourism, etc., the largest number of new firms were established in Ring I (an over 7-fold increase). As a result, Ring I's share in the region approached 60 percent (a growth of 26 percentage points), while that of the other areas, including the Center, decreased.

The significant increase in the total number of firms in the region has been accompanied by the progressive decentralization of economic activity. Growth in the share of Ring I and Ring II in many branches of the economy provides statistical representation of this decentralization.

To verify this thesis, analysis of the spatial distribution of employment is necessary, and is presented in the next section. A look at the distribution of income and fixed assets according to value, will also add to the analysis.

There is a lack of employment data for the region, and for the townships and city districts of the metropolitan region. The analysis is therefore conducted on the basis of employment declared by firms when they registered in the REGON system (government required business registration). Declared employment significantly varies from the actual number of persons employed, because the original declarations are not continually updated, and thus only reflects employment figures at the moment the firms are registered. Moreover, some of the firms registered do not undertake economic activity, yet still show employment and thus figure on the registers. Furthermore, a portion of the firms are run by people who work on the basis of employment contracts signed with other firms. These people are counted twice, sometimes even more times. Assuming that the share of those supposedly employed and working in a second, third or fourth workplace (besides their place of permanent employment) is the same in all four areas of the metropolitan region, it is possible to obtain a picture of the spatial distribution of economic activity in Metropolitan Warsaw which corresponds closely to reality. Table 3.2 provides information on declared employment patterns within the region.

An analysis of the overall spatial distribution of employment in the four areas of the metropolitan region leads to the conclusion that during the 1988-1992 period, a decentralization of economic activity occurred. The Center's and Ring I's share of economic activity decreased, while that of the two Rings outside the City of Warsaw increased. The intensity of the decentralization varied by each particular economic sector. There are sectors of the economy which are indicating a tendency to concentrate in the City of Warsaw, such as communications, retail and wholesale trade, and finance and insurance. It is thus correct to say that the spatial distribution of employment confirms tendencies noted as a result of the analysis of the location of firms within Metropolitan Warsaw.

The private sector demonstrated a particularly high level of economic activity during the analyzed period. This was the result of the easing of restrictions upon undertaking economic activity since 1988, and the complete removal of restrictions in 1990. In all four areas of the metropolitan region, a 2- to 3-fold increase in the private sector's share of economic activity occurred. In 1988, the farther away from the Center, the greater the share of the private sector. This trend is fully understandable, because the farther away from the center, the greater the share of agriculture which was for the most part private that year. This tendency is continuing. The private sector's share in economic activity substantially increases the further one moves from the Center; in Rings I and II it attains, respectively, 58 percent and 55 percent. The fact that the private sector's lowest share in economic activity is in downtown Warsaw, stems from the concentration of the majority of state insti-

Table 3.2 (part 1 of 2)
Spatial distribution of employment* in Warsaw metropolitan area and rings in 1988 and 1992

	Total	Industry	Construc-tion	Transport	Communi-cation	Whol./ Retail Trade
Warsaw Metropolitan Area (1988)	1,340,61	280,54	66,65	342,71	167,06	119,28
Warsaw Metropolitan Area (1992)	1,942,99	418,74	133,91	364,76	186,39	343,48
Change (1992-1988)	602,37	138,19	67,26	22,04	19,32	224,20
1992 to 1988 Ratio	144.93%	149.26%	200.92%	106.43%	111.57%	287.95%
Center (1988)	823,25	79,86	23,93	317,13	165,82	88,46
Center (1992)	990,86	97,46	28,43	318,78	175,19	183,05
Change (1992-1988)	167,60	17,59	4,50	1,65	9,36	94,58
1992 to 1988 Ratio	120.36%	122.03%	118.81%	100.52%	105.65%	206.92%
Center to Warsaw Metro. Area (1988)	61.41%	28.47%	35.91%	92.53%	99.26%	74.16%
Center to Warsaw Metro. Area (1992)	51.00%	23.27%	21.24%	87.39%	93.99%	53.29%
Ring 1 (1988)	422,88	172,49	35,66	23,64	1,23	23,09
Ring 1 (1992)	755,18	248,61	85,68	41,02	9,40	128,63
Change (1992-1988)	332,30	76,11	50,01	17,37	8,16	105,53
1992 to 1988 Ratio	178.58%	144.12%	240.23%	173.48%	760.68%	556.91%
Ring 1 to Warsaw Metro. Area (1988)	31.54%	61.49%	53.52%	6.90%	0.74%	19.36%
Ring 1 to Warsaw Metro. Area (1992)	38.87%	59.37%	63.99%	11.25%	5.04%	37.45%
Ring 2 (1988)	53,41	14,93	3,84	1,07		4,16
Ring 2 (1992)	118,60	43,49	11,11	2,16	1,76	21,24
Change (1992-1988)	65,18	28,55	7,26	1,08	1,76	17,08
1992 to 1988 Ratio	222.05%	291.20%	289.15%	201.30%		510.13%
Ring 2 to Warsaw Metro. Area (1988)	3.98%	5.32%	5.77%	0.31%	0.00%	3.49%
Ring 2 to Warsaw Metro. Area (1992)	6.10%	10.39%	8.30%	0.59%	0.95%	6.19%
Ring 3 (1988)	41,05	13,13	3,20	86		3,55
Ring 3 (1992)	78,33	29,17	8,67	2,79	3	10,55
Change (1992-1988)	37,27	16,04	5,47	1,93	3	6,99
1992 to 1988 Ratio	190.80%	222.16%	270.85%	324.27%		296.63%
Ring 3 to Warsaw Metro. Area (1988)	3.06%	4.68%	4.81%	0.25%	0.00%	2.98%
Ring 3 to Warsaw Metro. Area (1992)	4.03%	6.97%	6.48%	0.77%	0.02%	3.07%

Source: Economic Analysis Unit

* Employment data are based on the registration of firm system.

Table 3.2 (part 2 of 2)
Spatial distribution of employment* in Warsaw metropolitan area and rings in 1988 and 1992

	Finance & Insurance	Communal Services	Agriculture	Forestry	Other
Warsaw Metropolitan Area (1988)	33,35	30,91	13,09	3,94	283,04
Warsaw Metropolitan Area (1992)	39,21	34,12	17,35	2,35	402,63
Change (1992-1988)	5,86	3,21	4,26	-1,58	119,58
1992 to 1988 Ratio	117.58%	110.40%	132.57%	59.77%	142.25%
Center (1988)	28,52	15,29	1,14	2,09	100,98
Center (1992)	27,69	15,65	1,53	37	142,67
Change (1992-1988)	-82	35	39	-1,71	41,69
1992 to 1988 Ratio	97.09%	102.31%	135.00%	18.02%	141.29%
Center to Warsaw Metro. Area (1988)	85.52%	49.49%	8.71%	53.03%	35.68%
Center to Warsaw Metro. Area (1992)	70.62%	45.86%	8.87%	15.99%	35.44%
Ring 1 (1988)	4,07	13,87	2,73	1,17	144,87
Ring 1 (1992)	9,50	15,49	3,72	1,24	211,86
Change (1992-1988)	5,42	1,61	98	7	66,99
1992 to 1988 Ratio	233.04%	111.66%	135.92%	106.39%	146.24%
Ring 1 to Warsaw Metro. Area (1988)	12.22%	44.88%	20.90%	29.76%	51.18%
Ring 1 to Warsaw Metro. Area (1992)	24.23%	45.39%	21.43%	52.97%	52.62%
Ring 2 (1988)	34	97	3,71	58	23,77
Ring 2 (1992)	1,02	1,60	5,10	72	30,36
Change (1992-1988)	67	62	1,39	14	6,58
1992 to 1988 Ratio	293.95%	163.43%	137.60%	124.57%	127.70%
Ring 2 to Warsaw Metro. Area (1988)	1.04%	3.17%	28.34%	14.75%	8.40%
Ring 2 to Warsaw Metro. Area (1992)	2.60%	4.69%	29.41%	30.75%	7.54%
Ring 3 (1988)	40	76	5,50	9	13,41
Ring 3 (1992)	1,00	1,38	6,99		17,72
Change (1992-1988)	59	62	1,48	-9	4,31
1992 to 1988 Ratio	246.55%	182.00%	127.01%	7.22%	132.17%
Ring 3 to Warsaw Metro. Area (1988)	1.22%	2.46%	42.05%	2.46%	4.74%
Ring 3 to Warsaw Metro. Area (1992)	2.55%	4.06%	40.29%	0.30%	4.40%

Source: Economic Analysis Unit

* Employment data are based on the registration of firm system.

Table 3.3
Declared employment by sectors for Warsaw
metropolitan area and rings in 1988 and 1992

	Total	Public Sector	Private Sector
Warsaw Metropolitan Area (1988)	1,340,612	1,192,116	148,496
Warsaw Metropolitan Area 1988=100	100.00%	88.92%	11.08%
Warsaw Metropolitan Area (1992)	1,942,990	1,350,303	592,687
Warsaw Metropolitan Area 1992=100	100.00%	69.50%	30.50%
Change (1992-1988)	602,378	158,187	444,191
1992 to 1988 Ratio	144.93%	113.27%	399.13%
Center (1988)	823,258	759,973	63,285
Center (1988)=100	100.00%	92.31%	7.69%
Center (1992)	990,867	829,081	161,786
Center (1992)=100	100.00%	83.67%	16.33%
Change (1992-1988)	167,609	69,108	98,501
1992 to 1988 Ratio	120.36%	109.09%	255.65%
Center to Warsaw Metro. Area (1988)	61.41%	63.75%	42.62%
Center to Warsaw Metro. Area (1992)	51.00%	61.40%	27.30%
Ring 1 (1988)	422,887	362,107	60,780
Ring 1 (1988)=100	100.00%	85.63%	14.37%
Ring 1 (1992)	755,188	436,392	318,796
Ring 1 (1992)=100	100.00%	57.79%	42.21%
Change (1992-1988)	332,301	74,285	258,016
1992 to 1988 Ratio	178.58%	120.51%	524.51%
Ring 1 to Warsaw Metro. Area (1988)	31.54%	30.38%	40.93%
Ring 2 to Warsaw Metro. Area (1992)	38.87%	32.32%	53.79%
Ring 2 (1988)	53,412	40,011	13,401
Ring 2 (1988)=100	100.00%	74.91%	25.09%
Ring 2 (1992)	118,601	49,675	68,926
Ring 2 (1992)=100	100.00%	41.88%	58.12%
Change (1992-1988)	65,189	9,664	55,525
1992 to 1988 Ratio	6.10%	514.02%	124.14%
Ring 2 to Warsaw Metro. Area (1988)	3.98%	3.36%	9.02%
Ring 2 to Warsaw Metro. Area (1992)	6.10%	3.68%	11.63%
Ring 3 (1988)	41,055	30,025	11,030
Ring 3 (1988)=100	100.00%	73.13%	26.87%
Ring 3 (1992)	78,334	35,155	43,179
Ring 3 (1992)=100	100.00%	44.88%	55.12%
Change (1992-1988)	37,279	5,130	32,149
1992 to 1988 Ratio	190.80%	117.09%	391.47%
Ring 3 to Warsaw Metro. Area (1988)	3.06%	2.52%	7.43%
Ring 3 to Warsaw Metro. Area (1992)	4.03%	2.60%	7.29%

Source: Economic Analysis Unit

tutions there. Table 3.3 presents employment broken down by public and private sector activity.

Currently, it is still difficult to ascertain with complete certainty whether these patterns of change in the spatial distribution of economic activity in Metropolitan Warsaw are permanent. One thing, however, is not in doubt: that the structure of Metropolitan Warsaw's economy will gradually become similar to the economic structure of cities of the same size and functions in highly developed Western countries. In connection with this, the further decentralization of manufacturing and transportation functions (transport of goods), and concentration of services, especially highly specialized services, should be anticipated.

Spatial patterns of business activity

This portion of the study is devoted to an analysis of the financial performance attained by enterprises located in the four areas of Metropolitan Warsaw. First, however, is a look at corporate income trends from the sale of goods and services, and costs of production in constant 1988 prices. In order to establish these prices, appropriately converted indices of changes in prices published by GUS [Main Bureau of Statistics] in the Annual Yearbook for 1993 (p. 167), were used. Income and the costs of production in constant 1988 prices are presented in Table 3.4.

The overall value of income earned by the metropolitan region's economic units in 1992 modestly exceeded 1988 levels. This occurred largely due to firms located downtown, whose income grew 20.4 percent. The income of economic units in the other areas, however, were lower in 1992 by as much as 46 percent in Ring III; Ring I experienced a 16 percent lower income level. Between 1988 and 1992, a substantial increase occurred in the costs of production, which on a region-wide scale exceeded 45 percent, and in the downtown area climbed 97 percent. The main reason for the growth in costs was a fall in the degree of utilization of factors of production. In particular, labor and fixed assets have suffered a loss, as a result of the fall in demand and resulting reduction in production. The situation of each sector of the economy, however, is significantly differentiated.

In industry, the largest economic sector of the metropolitan region, income fell by almost half, while costs shrank by only 14 percent. The largest difference in the dynamic of income and costs was noted by downtown firms. Large differences in income and cost of production trends are due to the reactions of enterprises that, as mentioned earlier, are "biding their time". These firms continue to maintain excessive employment and delay adaptation to changes occurring in the market.

In 1992, construction attained the level of income it held in 1988. This was the result of the following three conditions: first, over the course of the last few years before reform, the construction industry (as one of the sectors of the economy which reacts most rapidly to changes in the economic situation) was in a state of crisis, and the level of building production in 1988 was low; second, this sector of the economy was privatized to a significant degree (about 70 percent) during the period under dis-

67

Table 3.4 (part 1 of 2)

Total income and cost of production by branch in Warsaw metropolitan area, center and rings in 1988 and 1992, in millions zlotys, constant 1988 prices

		Warsaw metropolitan area (WMA)			Center			Center / WMA		Ring 1			Ring 1/ WMA	
		1988	1992	1992/ 1988	1988	1992	1992/ 1988	1988	1992	1988	1992	1992/ 1988	1988	1992
Total	Total Income	10,653,18	10,895,17	102.27%	5,614,321	6,760,202	120.41%	52.70%	62.05%	4,371,616	3,654,098	83.59%	41.04%	33.54%
	Cost of Production	7,228,154	10,488,43	145.11%	3,295,311	6,501,318	197.29%	45.59%	61.99%	3,414,876	3,506,587	102.69%	47.24%	33.43%
Industry	Total Income	5,489,350	2,990,768	54.48%	2,111,751	1,500,512	71.06%	38.47%	50.17%	2,852,316	1,181,620	41.43%	51.96%	39.51%
	Cost of Production	3,460,804	2,987,410	86.32%	891,583	1,531,472	171.77%	25.76%	51.26%	2,172,031	1,142,116	52.58%	62.76%	38.23%
Construction	Total Income	715,153	716,369	100.17%	357,248	283,669	79.40%	49.95%	39.60%	313,999	371,110	118.19%	43.91%	51.80%
	Cost of Production	557,596	672,968	120.69%	272,840	263,539	96.59%	48.93%	39.16%	249,942	352,606	141.08%	44.82%	52.40%
Transport	Total Income	1,424,308	1,010,271	70.93%	899,738	868,921	96.57%	63.17%	86.01%	520,156	120,673	23.20%	36.52%	11.94%
	Cost of Production	1,478,793	995,405	67.31%	1,006,415	874,863	86.93%	68.06%	87.89%	468,637	100,219	21.39%	31.69%	10.07%
Communication	Total Income	87,141	590,903	678.10%	81,419	585,208	718.77%	93.43%	99.04%	5,722	5,695	99.52%	6.57%	0.96%
	Cost of Production	56,174	443,618	789.72%	49,277	437,596	888.04%	87.72%	98.64%	6,898	6,022	87.31%	12.28%	1.36%
Trade	Total Income	1,912,752	4,120,694	215.43%	1,583,554	2,645,997	167.09%	82.79%	64.21%	283,833	1,390,295	489.83%	14.84%	33.74%
	Cost of Production	741,312	4,022,079	542.56%	555,601	2,576,414	463.72%	74.95%	64.06%	149,063	1,361,863	913.61%	20.11%	33.86%
Finance & Insurance	Total Income	39,181	68,062	173.71%	6,155	8,506	138.20%	15.71%	12.50%	33,026	59,556	180.33%	84.29%	87.50%
	Cost of Production	34,839	61,039	175.20%	4,754	8,326	175.14%	13.65%	13.64%	30,085	52,713	175.21%	86.35%	86.36%
Communal Services	Total Income	114,476	129,766	113.36%	94,538	97,781	103.43%	82.58%	75.35%	19,038	30,978	162.71%	16.63%	23.87%
	Cost of Production	128,789	112,471	87.33%	109,730	84,973	77.44%	85.20%	75.55%	18,140	26,508	146.12%	14.09%	23.57%
Agriculture	Total Income	24,931	26,282	105.42%	31	1,987	6387.71%	0.12%	7.56%	16,424	14,215	86.55%	65.88%	54.08%
	Cost of Production	21,367	26,335	123.25%	27	1,586	5793.08%	0.13%	6.02%	13,981	14,660	104.86%	65.43%	55.67%
Forestry	Total Income	10,704	5,230	48.86%	7,517	2,457	32.68%	70.23%	46.97%	3,187	2,773	87.03%	29.77%	53.03%
	Cost of Production	9,914	4,720	47.61%	7,351	2,361	32.11%	74.15%	50.02%	2,563	2,359	92.04%	25.85%	49.98%
Other	Total Income	835,194	719,384	86.13%	472,369	334,686	70.85%	56.56%	46.52%	323,915	357,481	110.36%	38.78%	49.69%
	Cost of Production	738,564	655,873	88.80%	397,733	304,382	76.53%	53.85%	46.41%	303,537	324,990	107.07%	41.10%	49.55%

Source: Economic Analysis Unit

Table 3.4 (part 2 of 2)

Total income and cost of production by branch in Warsaw metropolitan area, center and rings in 1988 and 1992, in millions zlotys, constant 1988 prices

		Ring 2			Ring 2/ WMA		Ring 3			Ring 3/ WMA	
		1988	1992	1992/ 1988	1988	1992	1988	1992	1992/ 1988	1988	1992
Total	Total Income	334,303	301,994	90.34%	3.14%	2.77%	332,948	178,884	53.73%	3.13%	1.64%
	Cost of Production	259,259	301,932	116.46%	3.59%	2.88%	258,708	178,595	69.03%	3.58%	1.70%
Industry	Total Income	265,297	208,411	78.56%	4.83%	6.97%	259,986	100,224	38.55%	4.74%	3.35%
	Cost of Production	199,579	211,446	105.95%	5.77%	7.08%	197,612	102,375	51.81%	5.71%	3.43%
Construction	Total Income	12,727	31,129	244.60%	1.78%	4.35%	31,179	30,461	97.70%	4.36%	4.25%
	Cost of Production	10,080	28,567	283.41%	1.81%	4.24%	24,735	28,256	114.24%	4.44%	4.20%
Transport	Total Income	4,413	6,854	155.30%	0.31%	0.68%	0	13,823	—	0.00%	1.37%
	Cost of Production	3,742	6,619	176.91%	0.25%	0.66%	0	13,704	—	0.00%	1.38%
Communication	Total Income	0	0	—	0.00%	0.00%	0	0	—	0.00%	0.00%
	Cost of Production	0	0	—	0.00%	0.00%	0	0	—	0.00%	0.00%
Trade	Total Income	22,720	51,661	227.38%	1.19%	1.25%	22,645	32,742	144.59%	1.18%	0.79%
	Cost of Production	18,003	51,421	285.62%	2.43%	1.28%	18,645	32,381	173.67%	2.52%	0.81%
Finance & Insurance	Total Income	0	0	—	0.00%	0.00%	0	0	—	0.00%	0.00%
	Cost of Production	0	0	—	0.00%	0.00%	0	0	—	0.00%	0.00%
Communal Services	Total Income	518	274	52.86%	0.45%	0.21%	381	734	192.73%	0.33%	0.57%
	Cost of Production	489	268	54.78%	0.38%	0.24%	430	723	168.11%	0.33%	0.64%
Agriculture	Total Income	2,383	5,373	225.45%	9.56%	20.44%	6,092	4,707	77.27%	24.44%	17.91%
	Cost of Production	2,110	5,010	237.49%	9.87%	19.03%	5,249	5,078	96.75%	24.57%	19.28%
Forestry	Total Income	0	0	—	0.00%	0.00%	0	0	—	0.00%	0.00%
	Cost of Production	0	0	—	0.00%	0.00%	0	0	—	0.00%	0.00%
Other	Total Income	26,245	17,524	66.77%	3.14%	2.44%	12,665	9,693	76.53%	1.52%	1.35%
	Cost of Production	25,257	17,189	68.06%	3.42%	2.62%	12,037	9,312	77.36%	1.63%	1.42%

Source: Economic Analysis Unit

cussion and as a result, went through deep restructuring; and third, a substantial increase in building production (beginning in 1991) occurred rapidly.

Important changes took place in transport services; as a result of these changes, the decline in costs was greater than the fall in income. Significant reductions in subsidies caused cut-backs in reduced ticket prices for passenger travel, especially travel by rail. As a result, the number of passengers transported fell, as did income from ticket sales (despite fairly high and frequent price increases). In freight transport, income fell as a result of a steep drop in the amount of freight transported, which was mainly due to the crash in industrial production. Reductions in costs were achieved by liquidation of the worst money-losing railroad and bus lines, together with the restructuring of freight transport by road, accomplished as a consequence of the industry's substantial degree of privatization.

Communications is decidedly the fastest growing sector of the metropolitan region's economy. Financial results include the activities of the post office, telecommunications, radio communications, and of subsidiary units of communications. Income of communications firms, in the course of the four years under discussion, increased by 578 percent, while costs went up 690 percent. This economic sector's rapid growth in the last few years can be attributed mainly to telecommunications, which undoubtedly is the most profitable sector of communications. A contributing factor to the success of telecommunications, as mentioned above, is its monopolistic position in the market. True, telecommunications enterprises lie within the category of natural monopolies (one producer is able to satisfy the needs of a given market at a lower cost than several competing producers), but Polish Telecommunications S.A. is a monopoly of a particular sort, setting its own prices for its services. Thus it is different from natural monopolies in that it is essentially not subject to regulation. Natural monopolies in highly developed countries are regulated by public authorities or by special commissions appointed by public authorities, which set or approve prices proposed by the enterprises after an analysis of the costs of the services. In this situation, Polish Telecommunications S.A. has no incentives to efficiently manage itself. This partially explains the outstripping of income by costs, as well as the frequent and steep price increases needed to boost the lagging income. The price increases have also been crucial to support the costs resulting from network modernization efforts.

Retail and Wholesale trade is the second most dynamically growing sector of the metropolitan region's economy. Income from trade increased over 2-fold between 1988 and 1992, while costs climbed 5.5-fold. This large difference is due to relatively low growth in effective demand and an enormous increase in the number of firms in trade, which contributed to such a high increase in costs, especially the rental of shops and the bidding up of labor costs.

The finance and insurance sector is the third fastest growing sector of the region's economy. Income and costs of production rose similarly during the period under discussion.

Important changes also occurred in communal services. Income increased by 13 percent, while costs fell by the same percentage, resulting in a strong income over costs surplus. The rationalization of tariff policy carried out through cut-backs in subsidies, made this surplus possible. Prices for communal services, with the exception of those for energy, have remained under the reasonably tight control of local authorities, who have also undertaken various actions aimed at restructuring this segment of the City's economy. The effect of this control has been, among other things, the reduction in costs that has occurred. This however does not mean that everything possible was undertaken to improve efficiency, for much remains to be done.

In comparison to 1988, some improvement was noted in the agricultural sector in 1992. Unfortunately, during the years in between, the sector suffered significantly because of unfavorable atmospheric conditions. Forestry experienced over a 50 percent decline in income and costs from 1988 to 1992. Remaining sectors of the economy showed a decline in these economic figures as well.

Rendering the values of income and costs into constant 1988 prices provides an accurate picture of changes in the economy of the Warsaw metropolitan region. These figures show that the metropolitan region's economy, as a whole, attained a level of income in 1992 which was 2.3 percent higher than in 1988. This occurred largely due to income growth in the downtown area of 20.4 percent, between 1988 and 1992. The other three areas experienced declines in income during this time; from a 9.7 percent loss in Ring II to a 46.3 percent loss in Ring III. The figures also show that the fall in production in industry and transport was substantially greater than the fall in employment in these sectors. In construction, the opposite occurred — income attained 1988 levels in 1992 and employment fell by 21 percent, thus the productivity of labor rose.

Trends in income and costs have a direct impact on the level of financial performance achieved in the individual economic sectors of the metropolitan region. The following is an analysis of the financial performance of individual economic sectors, and how it affects the spatial configuration of the metropolitan region. Table 3.5 presents a matrix of financial performance by economic sector.

Gross profits (gross income less costs before taxes), and net profits (profits after taxation) fell between 1988 and 1992: from 27.5 to 3.6 percent, and from 13.2 to 0.7 percent respectively. The economy of the city center achieved the best results, while the economy in Ring II performed the worst. Industry, transport, and farming suffered losses at the metropolitan region level in 1992, though in Rings I and II, transport achieved a relatively high surplus of income over costs. The most profitable sectors of the region's economy in 1988 were trade and communications — this was a crucial factor in their rapid growth from 1989 to 1992. In 1992, highest profitability was recorded by communications and communal services. Both are highly monopolized sectors of the economy, though communal services achieved these good results largely on account of a strong reduction in costs. Finance and insurance, forestry, and construction also obtained relatively good results.

In general, the profitability of the City of Warsaw's and the surrounding region's economy is low, though somewhat higher than the national average. It is possible to obtain profits several times greater by putting money in a bank, for example. Such

71

Table 3.5 (part 1 of 2)
Net and gross profitability for Warsaw metropolitan area and rings in 1988 and 1992

			Total	Industry	Construc-tion	Trans-port	Communi-cation	Whol./Retail Trade
Warsaw Metro. Area	1992	Gross profitability	3.63	-1.29	8.50	-0.73	40.55	2.50
	1992	Net profitability	0.70	-4.09	4.27	-2.29	24.42	0.64
	1988	Gross profitability	27.47	22.05	28.50	13.48	65.14	89.35
	1988	Net profitability	13.21	11.42	10.18	8.04	35.28	34.65
Center	1992	Gross profitability	4.06	-1.77	10.12	-3.08	41.18	2.56
	1992	Net profitability	1.06	-3.38	5.71	-3.53	24.88	0.46
	1988	Gross profitability	29.99	15.59	31.68	9.37	76.50	95.60
	1988	Net profitability	13.46	8.56	10.85	5.65	42.46	36.14
Ring 1	1992	Gross profitability	3.49	0.07	7.29	19.36	-5.16	2.51
	1992	Net profitability	0.67	-4.15	3.36	7.97	-9.18	1.01
	1988	Gross profitability	25.24	23.70	25.42	22.26	547.61	81.61
	1988	Net profitability	12.73	11.80	9.58	13.18	304.46	34.20
Ring 2	1992	Gross profitability	-1.53	-3.67	9.12	3.33	—	-0.09
	1992	Net profitability	-4.60	-7.81	4.96	2.33	—	-0.49
	1988	Gross profitability	23.63	24.12	24.88	17.90	—	31.07
	1988	Net profitability	12.74	12.44	12.72	6.79	—	16.51
Ring 3	1992	Gross profitability	-1.02	-4.23	7.74	0.66	—	0.93
	1992	Net profitability	-2.98	-6.31	1.36	-0.15	—	0.52
	1988	Gross profitability	28.67	30.86	26.15	—	—	21.22
	1988	Net profitability	16.95	19.07	7.83	—	—	11.16

Source: Economic Analysis Unit

a situation does not favor the development of economic activity, especially activity of a profitable nature. In fact, it is a serious threat to growth.

Spatial distribution of fixed assets and their productivity

A precise determination of the spatial distribution of fixed assets within the metro-politan region is very difficult, because of the current method used by the Voivod-ship Bureau of Statistics (WUS). The WUS calculates fixed assets according to the enterprise method, which records all fixed assets of an enterprise as occurring in the township of the registered office of the board of directors (management) of the firm. Mulit-plant enterprises which hold plants and or equipment outside of the township in which the company is registered, will cause obvious inaccuracies in the use of this method. To overcome his problem, WUS also calculates the value of assets by location. This method yields more accurate results, but often under-estimates the genuine figures, since only enterprises are counted. This section will look at the

Table 3.5 (part 2 of 2)

**Net and gross profitability for Warsaw metropolitan area and rings
in 1988 and 1992**

			Finance & Insurance	Communal Services	Agriculture	Forestry	Other
Warsaw	1992	Gross profitability	10.92	15.42	-3.75	11.59	8.09
Metro.	1992	Net profitability	6.08	8.72	-5.08	7.36	4.97
Area	1988	Gross profitability	11.49	9.81	13.36	10.23	19.62
	1988	Net profitability	5.69	3.47	11.45	6.05	13.30
	1992	Gross profitability	2.30	14.80	1.26	5.87	6.78
Center	1992	Net profitability	-2.27	8.32	0.23	5.87	1.50
	1988	Gross profitability	29.57	9.22	13.68	5.62	22.05
	1988	Net profitability	22.38	3.30	13.68	3.37	13.65
	1992	Gross profitability	12.29	17.94	-5.49	17.32	9.76
Ring 1	1992	Net profitability	7.40	10.34	-5.56	8.86	8.43
	1988	Gross profitability	7.45	68.94	12.51	23.45	16.91
	1988	Net profitability	2.64	24.46	12.51	13.74	12.81
	1992	Gross profitability	—	1.75	3.70	—	2.17
Ring 2	1992	Net profitability	—	0.82	-1.20	—	1.64
	1988	Gross profitability	—	21.00	13.13	—	15.74
	1988	Net profitability	—	5.81	10.00	—	13.61
	1992	Gross profitability	—	1.19	-7.66	—	3.91
Ring 3	1992	Net profitability	—	-0.89	-9.17	—	3.66
	1988	Gross profitability	—	4.76	15.73	—	4.00
	1988	Net profitability	—	1.12	9.18	—	4.00

Source: Economic Analysis Unit

changes in the spatial distribution of fixed asset value in the region (using the location data), and the productivity of these assets (utilizing the enterprise data).

Table 3.6 presents data on the spatial distribution of gross value of fixed assets by location in constant prices. In total, the Warsaw metropolitan area experienced real growth in the value of its fixed assets between 1988 and 1992. By economic branch, fixed asset values increased for all sectors except construction and forestry, during the period.

In the period under discussion, industry experienced fixed asset value growth in all four areas of the region. In construction, mild declines in fixed asset value were noted in all but Ring II. Growth occurred in transport services in all but Ring I, where over a 47 percent decline in fixed asset value was reported between 1988 and 1992.

Perhaps the strongest fixed asset value increases during the period occurred in communication and finance and insurance. Fixed asset value in communication increased nearly 2-fold for the Center, and over 2.5-fold for Ring I. There is little or no fixed asset value in communications in the Ring II and Ring III areas, confirm-

73

Table 3.6 (part 1 of 2)
Gross value of fixed assets estimated by location, in 1988, 1992, in millions of zlotys, constant 1988 prices

	Total	Industry	Construc-tion	Transport	Communi-cation	Whol./ Retail Trade
1988						
Warsaw Metro. Area	8,687,386	1,547,745	220,843	4,384,900	87,788	364,658
Center	5,239,257	173,446	64,513	3,912,708	83,002	300,391
Ring 1	2,932,949	1,129,247	126,667	469,696	4,785	45,398
Ring 2	317,601	170,745	8,065	2,496	0	9,024
Ring 3	197,579	74,307	21,598	0	0	9,844
1992						
Warsaw Metro. Area	9,781,923	1,823,104	216,665	4,918,759	171,760	369,458
Center	5,891,552	271,297	57,094	4,662,065	159,580	191,117
Ring 1	3,233,822	1,218,510	126,562	247,844	12,158	143,987
Ring 2	402,075	208,479	13,829	5,208	21	22,062
Ring 3	254,473	124,818	19,180	3,642	1	12,291

Source: Economic Analysis Unit

Table 3.6 (part 2 of 2)
Gross value of fixed assets estimated by location, in 1988, 1992, in millions of zlotys, constant 1988 prices

	Finance & Insurance	Communal Services	Agriculture	Forestry	Other
1988					
Warsaw Metro. Area	19,909	370,862	106,982	7,654	1,576,048
Center	18,049	352,489	2,827	5,936	325,896
Ring 1	784	15,449	24,486	1,717	1,114,720
Ring 2	526	1,161	35,346	0	90,237
Ring 3	549	1,764	44,322	0	45,194
1992					
Warsaw Metro. Area	161,859	379,390	123,352	2,506	1,615,069
Center	139,514	155,009	284	80	219,202
Ring 1	20,616	224,089	43,798	79	1,232,490
Ring 2	672	283	37,416	2,348	111,755
Ring 3	1,057	8	41,854	0	51,622

Source: Economic Analysis Unit

ing the earlier noted trend of this sector's concentration in the city center. During the period under discussion, finance and insurance experienced over an 8-fold increase in real fixed asset value, in the region. The vast majority of this growth occurred in the Center and Ring I areas.

While gross fixed asset value in retail and wholesale trade remained nearly constant between 1988 and 1992 across the region, changes within the four areas of the region were significant. Retail and wholesale trade underwent a one-third decline in fixed asset value in the Center area, while experiencing a significant increase in all three other areas; Ring I and Ring II had 3- and 2-fold increases respectively. Communal services similarly experienced explosive growth in fixed asset value in Ring I (14.5-fold increase), while suffering significant asset losses in the Center (a 56 percent decrease).

The agriculture and forestry sectors both experienced very heavy fixed asset value losses in the Center area between 1988 and 1992, though for the region, agriculture increased its asset value. Forestry lost asset value in the region during the period under discussion. In other sectors of the economy, the gross fixed asset value rose modestly for the region. Within the region, the Center experienced losses in these other sectors, while the outside Rings underwent growth in asset value.

In general, as growth in fixed asset value has occurred during this period across all sectors, a decentralizing tendency has been evident in several sectors; particularly in retail and wholesale trade, communal services, agriculture and other sectors. A centralizing tendency has been noted only in the communication and finance and insurance sectors. These general trends support previous conclusions.

The next section analyses the productivity of fixed assets by looking at the ratio of earnings from the sale of goods and services over the gross value of fixed assets. In this analysis, both numbers are calculated according to the enterprise method in constant 1988 prices. The ratio of productivity of fixed assets is the opposite of the ratio of capital intensiveness of production or services. The ratio is calculated for sectors of the economy. The ratio is thus higher in less capital-intensive sectors of production or services. Table 3.7 reports ratios for all sections of the metropolitan area, by economic sector. Trade has the highest productivity of fixed assets for the region, while agriculture and communal services have the lowest. The productivity of fixed assets varies in particular areas of the metropolitan region. In 1988, Ring II had the highest total productivity, while the Center had the lowest.

Productivity losses were noted in all areas of the region in 1992, particularly in Rings II and III. Between 1988 and 1992, productivity in construction decreased by over 50 percent. In nearly all other branches, including finance and insurance, productivity losses were noted. The fall in productivity of the finance and insurance sector is surprising, considering its exuberant growth during the period under discussion. This most likely suggests that the sector has reached a temporary saturation level. Further development, especially of banks, will be achieved through restructuring as the result of unavoidable consolidation. The only productivity increase during the period was attained by retail and wholesale trade. Within this sector, Ring I had the highest productivity level, two times the level of productivity in the Center

75

area, and over four times the productivity level of Rings II and III. This confirms earlier observations about retail and wholesale trade: its rapid growth was fueled by the high profitability of the sector, and by the relatively low capital requirements necessary for undertaking trade activity. Despite the productivity losses noted in the communication and finance and insurance sectors, demand for these services will continue to increase in the long run as the region continues to develop.

Table 3.7 (part 1 of 2)
Gross value of fixed assets, total income of enterprises and gross productivity of fixed assets by branch for Warsaw metropolitan area, center and rings in 1988 and 1992, in millions zlotys, constant 1988 prices

		Total	Industry	Construc-tion	Transport	Commu-nication	Whol./Retail
Warsaw Metro.Area 1988	Gross Value	9,771,549	2,631,907	220,843	4,384,900	87,788	364,658
	Total Income	10,653,188	5,489,350	715,153	1,424,308	87,141	1,912,752
	Productivity	1.090	2.086	3.238	0.325	0.993	5.245
Center 1988	Gross Value	6,056,631	990,819	64,513	3,912,708	83,002	300,391
	Total Income	5,614,321	2,111,751	357,248	899,738	81,419	1,583,554
	Productivity	0.927	2.131	5.538	0.230	0.981	5.272
Ring 1 1988	Gross Value	3,162,178	1,358,476	126,667	469,696	4,785	45,398
	Total Income	4,371,616	2,852,316	313,999	520,156	5,722	283,833
	Productivity	1.382	2.100	2.479	1.107	1.196	6.252
Ring 2 1988	Gross Value	285,215	169,901	8,065	2,496	0	7,498
	Total Income	334,303	265,297	12,727	4,413	0	22,720
	Productivity	1.172	1.561	1.578	1.768	—	3.030
Ring 3 1988	Gross Value	267,525	112,711	21,598	0	0	11,370
	Total Income	332,948	259,986	31,179	0	0	22,645
	Productivity	1.245	2.307	1.444	—	—	1.992
Warsaw Metro. Area 1992	Gross Value	11,153,180	2,943,837	223,770	4,924,781	807,095	608,317
	Total Income	10,294,498	2,990,768	716,369	1,010,271	468,003	4,120,694
	Productivity	0.923	1.016	3.201	0.205	0.580	6.774
Center 1992	Gross Value	7,101,244	414,358	60,164	4,662,926	800,920	628,247
	Total Income	6,223,517	1,500,512	283,669	868,921	463,493	2,645,997
	Productivity	0.876	3.621	4.715	0.186	0.579	4.212
Ring 1 1992	Gross Value	3,402,846	1,356,234	131,234	253,004	6,153	128,399
	Total Income	3,554,668	1,181,620	371,110	120,673	4,510	1,390,295
	Productivity	1.045	0.871	2.828	0.477	0.733	10.828
Ring 2 1992	Gross Value	504,746	206,053	12,778	5,021	21	19,697
	Total Income	323,044	208,411	31,129	6,854	0	51,661
	Productivity	0.640	1.011	2.436	1.365	0.000	2.623
Ring 3 1992	Gross Value	290,690	113,655	19,594	3,830	1	14,129
	Total Income	193,269	100,224	30,461	13,823	0	32,742
	Productivity	0.665	0.882	1.555	3.609	0.000	2.317

Source: Economic Analysis Unit

Distribution of investment expenditures, their structure and dynamics

The following section provides analysis of the distribution of investment expenditures, their typological structure, and dynamics of change, as well as an evaluation of investment processes in Metropolitan Warsaw. Because of a lack of data available for the separate townships of Ring I, the analysis is conducted for Rings II and

Table 3.7 (part 2 of 2)
Gross value of fixed assets, total income of enterprises and gross productivity of fixed assets by branch for Warsaw metropolitan area, center and rings in 1988 and 1992, in millions zlotys, constant 1988 prices

		Finance & Insurance	Communal Services	Agriculture	Forestry	Other
Warsaw	Gross Value	19,909	370,862	106,982	7,654	1,576,048
Metro.Area	Total Income	39,181	114,476	24,931	10,704	835,194
1988	Productivity	1.968	0.309	0.233	1.399	0.530
Center	Gross Value	18,049	352,489	2,827	5,936	325,896
1988	Total Income	6,155	94,538	31	7,517	472,369
	Productivity	0.341	0.268	0.011	1.266	1.449
Ring 1	Gross Value	784	15,449	24,486	1,717	1,114,720
1988	Total Income	39,181	19,038	16,424	3,187	323,915
	Productivity	49.953	1.232	0.671	1.856	0.291
Ring 2	Gross Value	314	1,161	35,346	0	60,433
1988	Total Income	0	518	2,383	0	26,245
	Productivity	0.000	0.447	0.067	—	0.434
Ring 3	Gross Value	761	1,764	44,322	0	74,999
1988	Total Income	0	381	6,092	0	12,665
	Productivity	0.000	0.216	0.137	—	0.169
Warsaw	Gross Value	165,038	379,390	167,877	4,321	2,510,061
Metro. Area	Total Income	53,906	102,777	26,282	9,086	796,342
1992	Productivity	0.327	0.271	0.157	2.103	0.317
Center	Gross Value	141,320	155,009	83,935	80	336,440
1992	Total Income	6,737	77,444	1,987	4,268	370,489
	Productivity	0.048	0.500	0.024	53.669	1.101
Ring 1	Gross Value	21,989	224,089	10,056	1,893	1,269,796
1992	Total Income	47,169	24,535	14,215	4,818	395,723
	Productivity	2.145	0.109	1.414	2.545	0.312
Ring 2	Gross Value	568	283	33,817	2,348	77,813
1992	Total Income	0	217	5,373	0	19,399
	Productivity	0.000	0.767	0.159	0.000	0.249
Ring 3	Gross Value	1,161	8	40,068	0	98,244
1992	Total Income	0	581	4,707	0	10,730
	Productivity	0.000	68.703	0.117	—	0.109

Source: Economic Analysis Unit

77

III, the City of Warsaw (including the Center and Ring I), and the metropolitan region as a whole.

The following account divisions make up the typological structure of investment expenditures: construction-installation works, machine and equipment purchases, and other expenditures. Tables 3.8 and 3.9 present actual investment outlays by branch, as well as structure and percent change in structure of investment outlays for 1988 to 1992 in constant prices. In total, for the Warsaw metropolitan region, accounting for all economic sectors, construction-installation works have held a greater share of total investment outlay than equipment purchases. Since 1990, Ring II has had the highest share (greater than 64 percent) of construction-installation expenditures of any of the areas (see Table 3.8). Until 1991, growth in total investment expenditures in Metropolitan Warsaw was minimal; in 1991 and 1992, strong increases were experienced. The City of Warsaw and Ring II led this regional trend. However, in Ring III the level of investment expenditures decreased through 1991, rebounding only partly in 1992 (see Table 3.9).

When the typological structure is applied to individual economic branches, differences in investment outlays arise. In industry, for nearly every year, and in every area of the region, equipment purchase expenditures have held a larger share of investment outlays. This suggests that new equipment was being installed in older existing facilities. Growth in total industry expenditures took place only in Ring II, in 1992. In the City and Ring III, 1992 expenditures fell in comparison with 1988 by 18.5 and 34.8 percent respectively. Similar to industry, investment expenditures in construction were largely for the purchase of machinery and equipment during the 1988-1992 period. In construction, a decline in total expenditures occurred until 1991, with the greatest decrease taking place in 1990 (70 percent). In 1992 total investment expenditures in construction exceeded 1988 levels by nearly 50 percent. A similar pattern occurred in the City and Ring II.

In transport services, the share of expenditures for construction-installation works predominated, particularly in Ring III (ranging from 82 to 95 percent during the period). Total investment expenditures increased only in the City of Warsaw between 1988 and 1992, while decreasing dramatically in Rings II and III.

In communication, the region and the City spent significantly more on equipment purchases than construction in all years. However, construction-installation expenditures outpaced equipment purchases in Rings II and III in 1988 and 1990, and were on par with construction expenditures in 1991 and 1992. This trend suggests that network expansion projects are taking place more intensively in the outer areas of the region. Total investment expenditures in communication recorded a high level of growth in all areas during the period.

In retail and wholesale trade, the situation varies depending on the area under consideration. In 1988, about 70 percent of expenditures in the City of Warsaw were made for the purchase of machinery and equipment, because construction work was largely limited to the adaptation of previously existing buildings. On the other hand, in Rings II and III, expenditures on construction installation works predominate. In these areas, there were relatively fewer buildings to be adapted as a result of the lower level of development of trade services in these zones. In the following years, an increase in the share of construction installation projects undertaken in the City of Warsaw occurred; a trend which is connected to the increasing exploitation of existing stores and the subsequent need to build new ones. In the remaining Rings, the predominance of expenditures on construction-installation works continued over the entire period. Total expenditure in retail and wholesale trade grew from 1988 to 1992.

Investment expenditures in finance and insurance in the City of Warsaw were concentrated, until 1991, on machinery and equipment purchases, because the development of this sector of the economy has occurred by means of the relatively simple adaptation of previously existing buildings. In 1992, the situation changed and increasing expenditures were made on construction-installation works. In the other areas, with the exception of Ring III in 1992, a decided majority of expenditures were made on construction-installation works over the entire period. The highest level of growth in total expenditures, of all sectors, took place in finance and insurance, where in 1992 the investment level was 10 times higher in the region than in 1988.

In the structure of investment expenditures for the development of communal services, expenditures on construction-installation works predominate. In 1992, machinery and equipment purchases increased as a result of expenditures on sanitation and public transit equipment. From 1988 to 1992, total investment in communal services increased in the City of Warsaw and Ring III, while decreasing dramatically in Ring II.

In agriculture and forestry, during the 1988-1992 period, the majority of investment expenditures were also made for construction-installation works. In agriculture, a large fall in total investment expenditures occurred until 1991, while in the following year a nearly 3-fold increase over 1988 levels was noted. Forestry, in 1990 only, experienced a 20 percent increase in expenditures, while the following years brought a significant decline.

The dynamic of investment expenditures informs us only about the tempo of changes in the level of these expenditures, while telling us nothing about their scale. Therefore, in order to fill this gap, trends in the relationship of investment expenditures to the value of fixed assets must be explored. Table 3.10 presents the ratio of investment outlay to fixed asset value.

In general, trends in the ratio of investment expenditures to the value of fixed assets reflect trends in the dynamics of the expenditures discussed above. This ratio in most cases significantly shrank through 1990, and then increased in 1991, re-attaining 1988 levels, which it then significantly exceeded in 1992. Departures from this tendency took place mainly in geographic areas and economic sectors of low investment, thus particularly occurring in the outer zones.

The ratio under discussion is higher in the outer zones than in the City of Warsaw in the following sectors of the economy: industry, transportation, retail and wholesale trade, communal services, agriculture, and others. In the remaining sectors, significantly higher ratios were noted in the City.

Table 3.8 (part 1a of 2)
Investment outlays by branch for Warsaw metropolitan area, Warsaw and rings in 1988-1992, in constant 1988 prices (in millions zlotys)

		1988				1990			
		Warsaw metro. area	City of Warsaw	Ring 2	Ring 3	Warsaw metro. area	City of Warsaw	Ring 2	Ring 3
Total	Total	470,390	371,243	45,116	46,377	482,847	406,691	40,871	34,193
Invest-.	Construction wks.	244,537	185,681	27,921	26,714	278,366	232,383	22,130	23,061
ment	Purch. of equipmt.	195,001	161,942	13,629	16,626	164,982	141,046	15,164	8,518
Outlays	Other	30,853	23,620	3,566	3,037	39,499	33,262	3,578	2,614
	Total	140,543	102,867	20,723	15,971	121,238	88,844	20,628	10,674
Industry	Construction wks.	49,153	34,474	9,649	4,604	41,811	29,560	7,913	3,547
	Purch. of equipmt.	82,899	61,872	9,627	10,875	74,909	55,652	12,200	6,803
	Other	8,491	6,521	1,447	493	4,517	3,632	515	324
	Total	20,286	17,477	846	1,963	6,233	5,508	195	530
Construc-	Construction wks.	4,722	4,121	310	291	1,870	1,793	11	66
tion	Purch. of equipmt.	14,209	12,078	472	1,659	3,924	3,292	171	462
	Other	1,355	1,278	64	13	439	423	13	2
	Total	66,587	52,548	871	6,825	94,564	88,754	98	5,713
Transport	Construction wks.	39,228	29,534	128	5,920	72,046	66,561	51	5,435
	Purch. of equipmt.	24,385	20,869	693	715	13,162	12,994	45	124
	Other	2,973	2,145	50	189	9,356	9,199	2	154
	Total	9,970	8,982	388	271	18,415	16,999	1,036	380
Commu-	Construction wks.	4,037	3,410	220	258	5,369	4,274	717	378
nication	Purch. of equipmt.	5,615	5,293	151	0	12,798	12,496	300	1
	Other	318	279	16	13	248	229	18	1
Whole-	Total	16,884	13,973	1,491	1,420	24,003	20,051	2,307	1,645
sale &	Construction wks.	5,889	3,989	954	946	13,982	11,238	1,347	1,398
Retail	Purch. of equipmt.	10,321	9,538	423	360	8,212	7,092	943	177
Trade	Other	674	446	114	114	1,809	1,722	18	70
	Total	5,998	5,846	55	97	18,457	17,551	642	264
Finance	Construction wks.	382	256	42	85	5,585	5,010	369	206
& Insur-	Purch. of equipmt.	5,468	5,458	3	8	11,965	11,900	9	56
ance	Other	148	133	10	5	907	641	263	2
	Total	26,321	25,118	1,178	24	26,326	25,651	646	30
Com-	Construction wks.	20,112	19,056	1,032	24	21,008	20,409	574	24
munal	Purch. of equipmt.	4,919	4,874	45	0	4,051	4,006	43	2
Services	Other	1,290	1,188	102	1	1,268	1,235	29	4
	Total	11,218	1,646	3,428	6,144	3,365	1,462	672	1,231
Agricul-	Construction wks.	7,409	852	2,496	4,061	2,300	1,029	362	909
ture	Purch. of equipmt.	3,264	748	726	1,790	923	356	280	287
	Other	544	45	206	293	142	77	30	35
	Total	770	179	420	172	924	72	293	559
Forestry	Construction wks.	514	11	339	163	380	6	92	283
	Purch. of equipmt.	243	167	71	6	265	50	202	13
	Other	13	1	9	3	279	16	0	263
	Total	171,814	142,609	15,716	13,488	169,322	141,800	14,356	13,166
Other	Construction wks.	113,090	89,978	12,749	10,363	114,014	92,504	10,696	10,814
	Purch. of equipmt.	43,678	41,045	1,420	1,213	34,773	33,207	971	594
	Other	15,045	11,586	1,547	1,913	20,535	16,088	2,688	1,758

Source: Economic Analysis Unit

80

Table 3.8 (part 1b of 2)
Investment outlays by branch for Warsaw metropolitan area, Warsaw and rings in 1988-1992, in constant 1988 prices (in millions zlotys)

		1991				1992			
		Warsaw metro. area	City of Warsaw	Ring 2	Ring 3	Warsaw metro. area	City of Warsaw	Ring 2	Ring 3
Total Invest-. ment Outlays	Total	625,949	542,818	45,477	33,917	742,106	585,107	64,103	39,688
	Construction wks.	347,467	296,700	24,830	22,416	409,807	339,547	27,564	25,682
	Purch. of equipmt.	202,929	182,562	13,566	6,657	293,865	214,238	33,819	11,386
	Other	75,553	63,556	7,081	4,844	38,434	31,322	2,720	2,619
Industry	Total	100,241	69,528	19,240	7,999	146,700	83,786	34,459	10,418
	Construction wks.	41,512	26,767	8,386	2,970	46,342	29,987	6,112	4,482
	Purch. of equipmt.	53,012	39,103	9,409	4,476	95,207	50,464	27,668	5,438
	Other	5,718	3,658	1,445	553	5,151	3,335	679	498
Construc- tion	Total	15,835	13,575	1,162	1,098	30,283	23,516	987	531
	Construction wks.	5,432	5,289	52	91	18,583	16,256	172	154
	Purch. of equipmt.	8,911	7,529	573	809	10,722	6,404	807	369
	Other	1,491	757	537	198	978	855	9	8
Transport	Total	87,714	81,420	79	6,215	75,544	68,401	268	3,984
	Construction wks.	60,078	54,182	13	5,883	55,789	52,101	15	3,282
	Purch. of equipmt.	15,090	14,854	61	174	13,529	10,485	251	338
	Other	12,546	12,384	5	158	6,225	5,816	2	365
Commu- nication	Total	37,230	34,974	1,472	785	47,873	44,305	2,433	1,123
	Construction wks.	13,014	11,613	616	785	17,930	16,305	1,104	519
	Purch. of equipmt.	22,265	21,449	817	-1	27,925	26,163	1,205	546
	Other	1,951	1,912	39	1	2,018	1,837	123	58
Whole- sale & Retail Trade	Total	53,132	49,877	1,339	1,916	73,836	49,977	4,402	7,778
	Construction wks.	25,375	23,539	780	1,055	28,443	18,065	2,526	4,052
	Purch. of equipmt.	24,923	23,918	552	453	42,234	29,906	1,596	3,276
	Other	2,834	2,420	6	407	3,160	2,007	280	450
Finance & Insur- ance	Total	35,967	34,749	963	256	59,194	58,250	777	167
	Construction wks.	9,359	8,373	774	212	30,463	29,911	481	71
	Purch. of equipmt.	23,841	23,681	133	27	25,340	25,009	243	88
	Other	2,768	2,696	55	16	3,391	3,330	53	8
Com- munal Services	Total	36,346	36,207	66	72	36,138	34,297	666	41
	Construction wks.	28,743	28,699	44	0	23,492	22,693	390	21
	Purch. of equipmt.	6,079	6,006	1	71	10,025	9,073	233	18
	Other	1,524	1,503	21	0	2,620	2,531	43	2
Agricul- ture	Total	2,352	721	999	632	33,344	31,895	977	468
	Construction wks.	1,712	659	572	481	28,581	27,783	609	189
	Purch. of equipmt.	598	59	405	135	4,039	3,421	343	271
	Other	42	4	22	16	725	691	25	8
Forestry	Total	471	55	98	318	412	69	287	16
	Construction wks.	397	20	98	280	261	29	220	9
	Purch. of equipmt.	36	34	0	2	140	39	58	7
	Other	38	1	0	37	11	1	9	0
Other	Total	256,660	221,712	20,061	14,626	238,782	190,612	18,845	15,162
	Construction wks.	161,844	137,560	13,495	10,658	159,923	126,418	15,935	12,902
	Purch. of equipmt.	48,175	45,930	1,615	510	64,705	53,275	1,416	1,037
	Other	46,641	38,221	4,951	3,458	14,155	10,919	1,495	1,222

Source: Economic Analysis Unit

81

Table 3.8 (part 2a of 2)
Structure of investment outlays by branch for Warsaw metropolitan area, Warsaw and rings in 1988-1992, in constant 1988 prices (in %)

		1988				1990			
		Warsaw metro. area	City of Warsaw	Ring 2	Ring 3	Warsaw metro. area	City of Warsaw	Ring 2	Ring 3
Total Invest- ment Outlays	Total	100.00	100.00	100.00	100.00	100.00	100.00	100.00	100.00
	Construction wks.	51.99	50.02	61.89	57.60	57.65	57.14	54.15	67.44
	Purch. of equipmt.	41.46	43.62	30.21	35.85	34.17	34.68	37.10	24.91
	Other	6.56	6.36	7.90	6.55	8.18	8.18	8.75	7.65
Industry	Total	100.00	100.00	100.00	100.00	100.00	100.00	100.00	100.00
	Construction wks.	34.97	33.51	46.56	28.83	34.49	33.27	38.36	33.23
	Purch. of equipmt.	58.98	60.15	46.45	68.09	61.79	62.64	59.14	63.73
	Other	6.04	6.34	6.98	3.09	3.73	4.09	2.50	3.04
Construc- tion	Total	100.00	100.00	100.00	100.00	100.00	100.00	100.00	100.00
	Construction wks.	23.28	23.58	36.68	14.82	30.00	32.55	5.57	12.52
	Purch. of equipmt.	70.04	69.11	55.72	84.50	62.96	59.77	87.53	87.05
	Other	6.68	7.31	7.60	0.68	7.04	7.68	6.90	0.43
Transport	Total	100.00	100.00	100.00	100.00	100.00	100.00	100.00	100.00
	Construction wks.	58.91	56.20	14.75	86.74	76.19	74.99	51.87	95.14
	Purch. of equipmt.	36.62	39.71	79.56	10.48	13.92	14.64	45.72	2.16
	Other	4.47	4.08	5.69	2.78	9.89	10.37	2.41	2.70
Commu- nication	Total	100.00	100.00	100.00	100.00	100.00	100.00	100.00	100.00
	Construction wks.	40.49	37.96	56.76	95.04	29.15	25.14	69.24	99.41
	Purch. of equipmt.	56.32	58.93	39.03	0.00	69.50	73.51	29.00	0.30
	Other	3.19	3.10	4.21	4.96	1.35	1.34	1.76	0.29
Whole- sale & Retail Trade	Total	100.00	100.00	100.00	100.00	100.00	100.00	100.00	100.00
	Construction wks.	34.88	28.55	64.00	66.61	58.25	56.04	58.36	85.00
	Purch. of equipmt.	61.13	68.26	28.37	25.35	34.21	35.37	40.87	10.74
	Other	3.99	3.19	7.63	8.04	7.54	8.59	0.76	4.26
Finance & Insur- ance	Total	100.00	100.00	100.00	100.00	100.00	100.00	100.00	100.00
	Construction wks.	6.37	4.37	76.18	87.24	30.26	28.54	57.54	78.08
	Purch. of equipmt.	91.16	93.36	4.94	7.84	64.83	67.80	1.41	21.03
	Other	2.46	2.27	18.88	4.93	4.91	3.65	41.04	0.89
Com- munal Services	Total	100.00	100.00	100.00	100.00	100.00	100.00	100.00	100.00
	Construction wks.	76.41	75.87	87.57	97.29	79.80	79.57	88.80	82.12
	Purch. of equipmt.	18.69	19.40	3.80	0.00	15.39	15.62	6.68	5.23
	Other	4.90	4.73	8.64	2.71	4.82	4.81	4.52	12.65
Agricul- ture	Total	100.00	100.00	100.00	100.00	100.00	100.00	100.00	100.00
	Construction wks.	66.05	51.78	72.82	66.09	68.35	70.40	53.87	73.83
	Purch. of equipmt.	29.10	45.48	21.16	29.14	27.43	24.33	41.70	23.33
	Other	4.85	2.74	6.02	4.77	4.21	5.27	4.43	2.84
Forestry	Total	100.00	100.00	100.00	100.00	100.00	100.00	100.00	100.00
	Construction wks.	66.70	6.12	80.86	95.18	41.16	8.58	31.21	50.55
	Purch. of equipmt.	31.60	93.24	16.92	3.29	28.65	69.39	68.76	2.40
	Other	1.70	0.64	2.22	1.54	30.19	22.04	0.03	47.05
Other	Total	100.00	100.00	100.00	100.00	100.00	100.00	100.00	100.00
	Construction wks.	65.82	63.09	81.12	76.82	67.34	65.24	74.51	82.13
	Purch. of equipmt.	25.42	28.78	9.03	9.00	20.54	23.42	6.77	4.51
	Other	8.76	8.12	9.84	14.18	12.13	11.35	18.73	13.35

Source: Economic Analysis Unit

Table 3.8 (part 2b of 2)
Structure of investment outlays by branch for Warsaw metropolitan area, Warsaw and rings in 1988-1992, in constant 1988 prices (in %)

		1991				1992			
		Warsaw metro. area	City of Warsaw	Ring 2	Ring 3	Warsaw metro. area	City of Warsaw	Ring 2	Ring 3
Total Invest-ment Outlays	Total	100.00	100.00	100.00	100.00	100.00	100.00	100.00	100.00
	Construction wks.	55.51	54.66	54.60	66.09	55.22	58.03	43.00	64.71
	Purch. of equipmt.	32.42	33.63	29.83	19.63	39.60	36.62	52.76	28.69
	Other	12.07	11.71	15.57	14.28	5.18	5.35	4.24	6.60
Industry	Total	100.00	100.00	100.00	100.00	100.00	100.00	100.00	100.00
	Construction wks.	41.41	38.50	43.59	37.12	31.59	35.79	17.74	43.02
	Purch. of equipmt.	52.88	56.24	48.90	55.96	64.90	60.23	80.29	52.20
	Other	5.70	5.26	7.51	6.92	3.51	3.98	1.97	4.78
Construc-tion	Total	100.00	100.00	100.00	100.00	100.00	100.00	100.00	100.00
	Construction wks.	34.31	38.96	4.49	8.29	61.37	69.13	17.39	29.08
	Purch. of equipmt.	56.27	55.46	49.31	73.71	35.41	27.23	81.70	69.40
	Other	9.42	5.58	46.20	18.00	3.23	3.64	0.91	1.53
Transport	Total	100.00	100.00	100.00	100.00	100.00	100.00	100.00	100.00
	Construction wks.	68.49	66.55	16.55	94.66	73.85	76.17	5.57	82.37
	Purch. of equipmt.	17.20	18.24	77.73	2.80	17.91	15.33	93.80	8.47
	Other	14.30	15.21	5.73	2.54	8.24	8.50	0.63	9.15
Commu-nication	Total	100.00	100.00	100.00	100.00	100.00	100.00	100.00	100.00
	Construction wks.	34.96	33.20	41.82	—	37.45	36.80	45.38	46.21
	Purch. of equipmt.	59.80	61.33	55.52	—	58.33	59.05	49.55	48.66
	Other	5.24	5.47	2.66	0.07	4.22	4.15	5.07	5.14
Whole-sale & Retail Trade	Total	100.00	100.00	100.00	100.00	100.00	100.00	100.00	100.00
	Construction wks.	47.76	47.19	58.30	55.09	38.52	36.15	57.38	52.10
	Purch. of equipmt.	46.91	47.95	41.23	23.67	57.20	59.84	36.25	42.11
	Other	5.33	4.85	0.47	21.24	4.28	4.02	6.37	5.79
Finance & Insur-ance	Total	100.00	100.00	100.00	100.00	100.00	100.00	100.00	100.00
	Construction wks.	26.02	24.10	80.41	82.96	51.46	51.35	61.88	42.65
	Purch. of equipmt.	66.28	68.15	13.85	10.61	42.81	42.93	31.25	52.62
	Other	7.69	7.76	5.74	6.43	5.73	5.72	6.87	4.74
Com-munal Services	Total	100.00	100.00	100.00	100.00	100.00	100.00	100.00	100.00
	Construction wks.	79.08	79.26	66.22	0.44	65.01	66.17	58.56	51.79
	Purch. of equipmt.	16.72	16.59	2.20	98.87	27.74	26.45	34.93	42.41
	Other	4.19	4.15	31.58	0.69	7.25	7.38	6.50	5.80
Agricul-ture	Total	100.00	100.00	100.00	100.00	100.00	100.00	100.00	100.00
	Construction wks.	72.79	91.31	57.28	76.16	85.71	87.11	62.31	40.49
	Purch. of equipmt.	25.44	8.18	40.51	21.31	12.11	10.72	35.10	57.84
	Other	1.77	0.51	2.20	2.53	2.17	2.17	2.59	1.67
Forestry	Total	100.00	100.00	100.00	100.00	100.00	100.00	100.00	100.00
	Construction wks.	84.24	35.99	100.00	87.80	63.42	42.53	76.77	56.19
	Purch. of equipmt.	7.71	61.38	0.00	0.74	33.95	55.71	20.04	41.47
	Other	8.06	2.63	0.00	11.47	2.63	1.75	3.18	2.33
Other	Total	100.00	100.00	100.00	100.00	100.00	100.00	100.00	100.00
	Construction wks.	63.06	62.04	67.27	72.87	66.97	66.32	84.56	85.10
	Purch. of equipmt.	18.77	20.72	8.05	3.48	27.10	27.95	7.51	6.84
	Other	18.17	17.24	24.68	23.64	5.93	5.73	7.93	8.06

Source: Economic Analysis Unit

83

Table 3.9 (part 1 of 2)
Percent change of investment outlays for Warsaw metropolitan area, center and rings in 1988-1992, using constant PLZ figures (1988 = 100)

		Warsaw metro. area				Warsaw			
		1988	1990	1991	1992	1988	1990	1991	1992
Total	Total	100.0	102.6	133.1	157.8	100.0	109.5	146.2	157.6
Invest-	Construction wks.	100.0	115.0	137.7	166.1	100.0	126.4	154.8	181.3
ment	Purch. of equipmt.	100.0	85.9	118.4	162.2	100.0	88.4	128.3	142.4
Outlays	Other	100.0	128.0	244.9	124.6	100.0	140.8	269.1	132.6
	Total	100.0	86.3	71.3	104.4	100.0	86.4	67.6	81.5
Industry	Construction wks.	100.0	85.9	81.8	93.5	100.0	86.6	75.2	86.2
	Purch. of equipmt.	100.0	91.7	72.7	123.6	100.0	91.3	71.9	87.8
	Other	100.0	53.2	67.3	60.7	100.0	55.7	56.1	51.1
	Total	100.0	30.7	78.1	149.3	100.0	31.5	77.7	134.6
Construc-	Construction wks.	100.0	40.0	111.5	390.1	100.0	44.0	124.4	391.0
tion	Purch. of equipmt.	100.0	28.0	71.3	81.2	100.0	27.7	70.9	57.1
	Other	100.0	32.4	110.0	72.1	100.0	33.1	59.2	66.9
	Total	100.0	142.0	131.7	113.5	100.0	168.9	154.9	130.2
Transport	Construction wks.	100.0	185.5	148.4	141.0	100.0	227.6	177.8	174.9
	Purch. of equipmt.	100.0	54.8	70.4	59.7	100.0	63.2	81.0	54.1
	Other	100.0	314.7	422.0	209.4	100.0	428.8	577.3	271.1
	Total	100.0	184.7	373.4	480.2	100.0	189.3	389.4	493.3
Commu-	Construction wks.	100.0	134.3	312.4	440.2	100.0	126.6	330.0	474.0
nication	Purch. of equipmt.	100.0	231.4	451.1	535.4	100.0	239.7	461.0	532.1
	Other	100.0	77.9	613.1	634.1	100.0	82.0	686.1	659.2
	Total	100.0	142.2	314.7	437.3	100.0	143.5	357.0	357.7
Wholesal	Construction wks.	100.0	239.8	417.5	478.7	100.0	284.6	571.8	448.9
and	Purch. of equipmt.	100.0	80.8	274.7	440.5	100.0	75.5	285.3	337.5
Trade	Other	100.0	268.6	420.7	469.1	100.0	386.3	543.0	450.3
	Total	100.0	307.7	599.7	986.9	100.0	300.2	594.4	996.4
Finance	Construction wks.	100.0	1,476.4	2,373.1	7,901.6	100.0	1,979.9	3,174.2	11,599.
& Insur-	Purch. of equipmt.	100.0	222.1	496.0	498.8	100.0	221.4	493.6	493.3
ance	Other	100.0	613.5	1,872.6	2,294.7	100.0	483.3	2,032.7	2,510.8
	Total	100.0	100.0	138.1	137.3	100.0	102.1	144.1	136.5
Com-	Construction wks.	100.0	105.5	138.5	115.8	100.0	108.2	145.9	118.0
munal	Purch. of equipmt.	100.0	83.6	140.6	219.4	100.0	83.4	140.2	200.4
Services	Other	100.0	98.3	118.1	203.1	100.0	104.0	126.5	213.1
	Total	100.0	30.0	21.0	297.2	100.0	88.8	43.8	1,937.9
Agricul-	Construction wks.	100.0	31.4	22.4	382.3	100.0	122.0	74.9	3,231.0
ture	Purch. of equipmt.	100.0	28.7	20.9	133.2	100.0	48.2	9.0	491.9
	Other	100.0	26.0	7.6	133.1	100.0	170.9	8.1	1,533.8
	Total	100.0	120.0	61.2	53.5	100.0	40.1	31.0	38.7
Forestry	Construction wks.	100.0	74.8	74.9	50.4	100.0	56.8	176.4	266.3
	Purch. of equipmt.	100.0	110.5	17.0	61.8	100.0	30.3	23.2	24.9
	Other	100.0	2,130.5	290.0	82.7	100.0	1,388.4	128.2	106.6
	Total	100.0	98.5	149.4	139.0	100.0	99.4	155.5	133.7
Other	Construction wks.	100.0	101.8	138.7	140.2	100.0	103.8	148.1	139.3
	Purch. of equipmt.	100.0	80.8	125.5	159.5	100.0	82.1	127.3	139.7
	Other	100.0	136.5	310.0	94.1	100.0	138.9	329.9	94.2

Source:Economic Analysis Unit

Table 3.9 (part 2 of 2)
Percent change of investment outlays for Warsaw metropolitan area, center and rings in 1988-1992, using constant PLZ figures (1988 = 100)

		Ring 2				Ring 3			
		1988	1990	1991	1992	1988	1990	1991	1992
Total	Total	100.0	90.6	100.8	142.1	100.0	73.7	73.1	85.6
Invest-	Construction wks.	100.0	80.1	86.2	97.9	100.0	87.2	81.3	95.3
ment	Purch. of equipmt.	100.0	113.0	113.2	267.1	100.0	52.0	45.6	73.7
Outlays	Other	100.0	100.3	198.6	76.3	100.0	86.1	159.5	86.2
	Total	100.0	99.5	92.8	166.3	100.0	66.8	50.1	65.2
Industry	Construction wks.	100.0	82.8	84.2	62.8	100.0	77.8	62.5	96.5
	Purch. of equipmt.	100.0	128.7	111.2	309.4	100.0	63.5	46.8	53.8
	Other	100.0	35.6	99.8	46.9	100.0	65.8	112.2	101.0
	Total	100.0	23.0	137.3	116.7	100.0	27.0	55.9	27.1
Construc-	Construction wks.	100.0	3.5	16.3	54.8	100.0	23.1	30.3	52.6
tion	Purch. of equipmt.	100.0	36.7	138.2	184.1	100.0	28.3	55.5	23.9
	Other	100.0	20.9	834.1	14.0	100.0	17.3	1,483.6	60.9
	Total	100.0	11.2	9.1	30.8	100.0	83.7	91.1	58.4
Transport	Construction wks.	100.0	39.8	9.9	11.5	100.0	92.7	96.3	54.9
	Purch. of equipmt.	100.0	6.5	10.1	39.0	100.0	17.5	27.7	50.8
	Other	100.0	4.7	9.1	3.4	100.0	81.4	83.4	192.4
	Total	100.0	267.3	379.8	627.8	100.0	140.4	289.6	414.3
Commu-	Construction wks.	100.0	329.3	271.2	497.6	100.0	148.3	295.6	199.7
nication	Purch. of equipmt.	100.0	201.6	614.6	857.9	100.0			
	Other	100.0	111.9	240.3	756.7	100.0	8.2	4.2	429.0
Whole-	Total	100.0	154.7	89.8	295.2	100.0	115.8	134.9	547.7
sale &	Construction wks.	100.0	142.5	79.2	262.3	100.0	149.2	108.1	424.6
Retail	Purch. of equipmt.	100.0	226.4	148.4	406.1	100.0	49.8	143.3	979.4
Trade	Other	100.0	15.5	5.6	246.5	100.0	61.4	356.5	394.3
	Total	100.0	1,166.5	1,750.3	1,413.6	100.0	272.5	263.3	171.9
Finance	Construction wks.	100.0	890.1	1,790.2	1,138.1	100.0	246.3	242.6	83.3
& Insur-	Purch. of equipmt.	100.0	338.0	5,581.3	9,620.9	100.0	742.1	405.6	1,241.9
ance	Other	100.0	2,535.9	531.9	514.6	100.0	49.2	343.9	165.2
	Total	100.0	54.8	5.6	56.6	100.0	121.2	295.5	168.9
Com-	Construction wks.	100.0	56.2	4.1	37.5	100.0	103.4	1.3	89.1
munal	Purch. of equipmt.	100.0	98.0	3.7	560.1	100.0			
Services	Other	100.0	28.7	20.6	42.6	100.0	564.8	75.0	360.9
	Total	100.0	19.6	29.1	28.5	100.0	20.0	10.3	7.6
Agricul-	Construction wks.	100.0	14.6	22.2	24.2	100.0	22.6	11.5	4.6
ture	Purch. of equipmt.	100.0	39.2	63.4	50.9	100.0	16.3	8.6	16.3
	Other	100.0	14.4	10.7	12.3	100.0	11.9	5.5	2.7
	Total	100.0	69.9	23.3	68.4	100.0	325.7	185.5	9.6
Forestry	Construction wks.	100.0	27.2	27.9	64.4	100.0	174.7	165.8	5.6
	Purch. of equipmt.	100.0	288.3	0.0	87.3	100.0	241.2	47.4	130.4
	Other	100.0	1.1	0.0	98.2	100.0	9,960.2	1,382.5	14.6
	Total	100.0	91.3	127.6	119.9	100.0	97.6	108.4	112.4
Other	Construction wks.	100.0	84.7	102.6	123.9	100.0	105.4	99.7	123.4
	Purch. of equipmt.	100.0	69.5	129.4	107.3	100.0	49.7	47.8	92.0
	Other	100.0	173.8	320.1	96.6	100.0	91.9	180.8	63.9

Source: Economic Analysis Unit

The level of investment in the economy of the metropolitan region, with the exception of finance and insurance, communications and retail and wholesale trade, is relatively low. Investment levels are not strong enough to ensure, outside of the sectors mentioned, that the process of de-capitalization will be stopped. Evidence of this is the increase in the degree of wear and tear on the fixed assets of the City, during the study period. The measure of this deterioration increased in the City, from 36.4 percent in 1988 to 41.2 percent in 1989. In the metropolitan region the increase was from 36.5 to 41.2 percent in the same time period. By comparison, in the country as a whole, the wear and tear of fixed assets increased from 36.7 to 44.0 percent during the period.

This chapter has analyzed the effects of new enterprise creation and economic restructuring upon the spatial distribution of economic activity in the Warsaw metropolitan region. The analysis supports the assertion that particular sectors of the Warsaw economy have been decentralizing to the outer Rings; most notably, manufacturing, transport services and retail and wholesale trade. Other sectors have concentrated their services in the City of Warsaw, such as communication and finance and insurance. Profitability and investment levels are low in the region. These conditions continue to be a threat to the future growth and economic development of the region.

Table 3.10 (part 1 of 3)
Investment outlays and gross value of fixed assets by branch for Warsaw metropolitan area and rings in 1988-1992

			Total	Industry	Construction	Transport	Communication
Warsaw Metro. Area	1988	Investment outlays	470,390	140,543	20,286	66,587	9,970
		Gross value of fixed assets	8,687,386	1,547,745	220,843	4,384,900	87,788
		Investment/gross value of F.A.	0.0541	0.0908	0.0919	0.0152	0.1136
	1990	Investment outlays	9,656,935	2,424,752	124,663	1,891,286	368,292
		Gross value of fixed assets	312,711,331	59,274,265	7,226,344	164,838,854	2,963,673
		Investment/gross value of F.A.	0.0309	0.0409	0.0173	0.0115	0.1243
	1991	Investment outlays	17,589,178	2,816,782	444,956	2,464,765	1,046,167
		Gross value of fixed assets	309,845,440	59,242,930	6,963,375	162,792,417	3,388,228
		Investment/gross value of F.A.	0.0568	0.0475	0.0639	0.0151	0.3088
	1992	Investment outlays	25,083,166	4,958,469	1,023,551	2,553,377	1,618,097
		Gross value of fixed assets	330,628,983	61,620,918	7,323,266	166,254,069	5,805,484
		Investment/gross value of F.A.	0.0759	0.0805	0.1398	0.0154	0.2787
Warsaw	1988	Investment outlays	371,243	102,867	17,477	52,548	8,982
		Gross value of fixed assets	8,172,207	1,302,693	191,180	4,382,403	87,788
		Investment/gross value of F.A.	0.0454	0.0790	0.0914	0.0120	0.1023
	1990	Investment outlays	8,133,817	1,776,877	110,159	1,775,084	339,973
		Gross value of fixed assets	291,477,871	48,939,496	6,225,339	164,014,490	2,963,673
		Investment/gross value of F.A.	0.0279	0.0363	0.0177	0.0108	0.1147
	1991	Investment outlays	15,253,190	1,953,739	381,458	2,287,900	982,757
		Gross value of fixed assets	290,238,240	49,807,611	5,957,056	162,500,683	3,388,228
		Investment/gross value of F.A.	0.0526	0.0392	0.0640	0.0141	0.2901
	1992	Investment outlays	19,776,626	2,831,951	794,828	2,311,970	1,497,493
		Gross value of fixed assets	308,437,662	50,355,477	6,207,565	165,954,909	5,804,732
		Investment/gross value of F.A.	0.0641	0.0562	0.1280	0.0139	0.2580

Table 3.10 (part 2 of 3)
Investment outlays and gross value of fixed assets by branch for
Warsaw metropolitan area and rings in 1988-1992

			Total	Industry	Construc-tion	Transport	Commu-nication
Ring		Investment/gross value of F.A.	0.0646	0.0590	0.0159	0.0120	
2		Investment outlays	1,277,907	540,644	32,650	2,218	41,357
	1991	Gross value of fixed assets	11,668,978	5,745,434	376,939	178,269	0
		Investment/gross value of F.A.	0.1095	0.0941	0.0866	0.0124	
		Investment outlays	2,166,666	1,164,720	33,375	9,051	82,232
	1992	Gross value of fixed assets	13,590,146	7,046,605	467,429	176,046	722
		Investment/gross value of F.A.	0.1594	0.1653	0.0714	0.0514	113.8947
		Investment outlays	46,377	15,971	1,963	6,825	271
	1988	Gross value of fixed assets	197,579	74,307	21,598	0	0
		Investment/gross value of F.A.	0.2347	0.2149	0.0909		
		Investment outlays	683,856	213,488	10,608	114,251	7,606
	1990	Gross value of fixed assets	8,573,053	3,343,163	755,623	662,135	0
Ring		Investment/gross value of F.A.	0.0798	0.0639	0.0140	0.1725	
3		Investment outlays	953,065	224,770	30,848	174,647	22,053
	1991	Gross value of fixed assets	7,938,222	3,689,885	629,380	113,465	0
		Investment/gross value of F.A.	0.1201	0.0609	0.0490	1.5392	
		Investment outlays	1,341,442	352,118	17,952	134,657	37,947
	1992	Gross value of fixed assets	8,601,175	4,218,836	648,272	123,114	30
		Investment/gross value of F.A.	0.1560	0.0835	0.0277	1.0938	1264.9000

Source: Economic Analysis Unit

Table 3.10 (part 3 of 3)
Investment outlays and gross value of fixed assets by branch for Warsaw metropolitan area and rings in 1988-1992

			Whol./ Retail	Finance & Insurance	Communal Services	Agriculture	Forestry	Other
Warsaw Metro. Area	1988	Investment outlays	16,884	5,998	26,321	11,218	770	171,814
		Gross value of fixed assets	364,658	19,909	370,862	106,982	7,654	1,576,048
		Investment/gross value of F.A.	0.0463	0.3013	0.0710	0.1049	0.1006	0.1090
	1990	Investment outlays	480,063	369,135	526,529	67,293	18,480	3,386,442
		Gross value of fixed assets	6,386,015	788,800	15,150,650	3,342,610	77,529	52,662,591
		Investment/gross value of F.A.	0.0752	0.4680	0.0348	0.0201	0.2384	0.0643
	1991	Investment outlays	1,493,009	1,010,685	1,021,310	66,103	13,246	7,212,155
		Gross value of fixed assets	7,834,156	2,265,292	12,510,836	2,994,291	77,427	51,776,488
		Investment/gross value of F.A.	0.1906	0.4462	0.0816	0.0221	0.1711	0.1393
	1992	Investment outlays	2,495,671	2,000,764	1,221,449	1,127,039	13,914	8,070,835
		Gross value of fixed assets	12,487,673	5,470,843	12,823,380	4,169,312	84,719	54,589,319
		Investment/gross value of F.A.	0.1999	0.3657	0.0953	0.2703	0.1642	0.1478
Warsaw	1988	Investment outlays	13,973	5,846	25,118	1,646	179	142,609
		Gross value of fixed assets	345,789	18,834	367,937	27,313	7,654	1,440,616
		Investment/gross value of F.A.	0.0404	0.3104	0.0683	0.0603	0.0234	0.0990
	1990	Investment outlays	401,029	351,017	513,011	29,242	1,434	2,835,996
		Gross value of fixed assets	5,649,308	742,734	14,965,244	346,146	4,153	47,627,288
		Investment/gross value of F.A.	0.0710	0.4726	0.0343	0.0845	0.3453	0.0595
	1991	Investment outlays	1,401,539	976,455	1,017,417	20,273	1,556	6,230,096
		Gross value of fixed assets	7,037,654	2,228,008	12,436,778	289,959	3,538	46,596,553
		Investment/gross value of F.A.	0.1991	0.4383	0.0818	0.0699	0.4398	0.1337
	1992	Investment outlays	1,689,226	1,968,851	1,159,252	1,078,041	2,337	6,442,677
		Gross value of fixed assets	11,326,538	5,412,404	12,813,523	1,489,992	5,354	49,067,168
		Investment/gross value of F.A.	0.1491	0.3638	0.0905	0.7235	0.4365	0.1313
Ring 2	1988	Investment outlays	1,491	55	1,178	3,428	420	15,716
		Gross value of fixed assets	9,024	526	1,161	35,346	0	90,237
		Investment/gross value of F.A.	0.1652	0.1045	1.0152	0.0970		0.1742
	1990	Investment outlays	46,144	12,830	12,925	13,435	5,864	287,120
		Gross value of fixed assets	270,599	18,557	10,327	1,112,398	42,946	1,739,329
		Investment/gross value of F.A.	0.1705	0.6914	1.2516	0.0121	0.1365	0.1651
	1991	Investment outlays	37,614	27,049	1,862	28,069	2,742	563,702
		Gross value of fixed assets	449,919	22,639	8,961	1,272,165	73,889	3,540,763
		Investment/gross value of F.A.	0.0836	1.1948	0.2078	0.0221	0.0371	0.1592
	1992	Investment outlays	148,782	26,276	22,526	33,026	9,704	636,974
		Gross value of fixed assets	745,685	22,726	9,571	1,264,663	79,365	3,777,334
		Investment/gross value of F.A.	0.1995	1.1562	2.3536	0.0261	0.1223	0.1686
Ring 3	1988	Investment outlays	1,420	97	24	6,144	172	13,488
		Gross value of fixed assets	9,844	549	1,764	44,322	0	45,194
		Investment/gross value of F.A.	0.1443	0.1768	0.0139	0.1386		0.2985
	1990	Investment outlays	32,890	5,288	593	24,616	11,182	263,326
		Gross value of fixed assets	466,108	27,509	175,079	1,884,066	30,430	3,295,974
		Investment/gross value of F.A.	0.0706	0.1922	0.0034	0.0131	0.3675	0.0799
	1991	Investment outlays	53,838	7,181	2,031	17,761	8,948	410,988
		Gross value of fixed assets	346,583	14,645	65,097	1,432,167	0	1,639,172
		Investment/gross value of F.A.	0.1553	0.4903	0.0312	0.0124		0.2507
	1992	Investment outlays	262,899	5,637	1,396	15,814	557	512,465
		Gross value of fixed assets	415,450	35,713	286	1,414,657	0	1,744,817
		Investment/gross value of F.A.	0.6328	0.1578	4.8811	0.0112		0.2937

Source: Economic Analysis Unit

89

4 Demographic profile of Warsaw

Introduction

This chapter reviews trends in population, migration, households and household income in Poland and the Warsaw metropolitan area. Data used in this chapter are drawn from the statistical office of the Warsaw Voivodship. The survey reveals the relatively slow rate of population growth in Poland and Warsaw, due principally to a very low rate of natural increase and negative migration flows.

Overall population trends

Poland's current population currently stands at 38,400,000, and has increased slowly since the mid-1980s, averaging an annual compound growth rate of 0.4 percent. Over the past decade, population growth has gradually slowed in the Warsaw metropolitan area and is now declining. As a result, the Warsaw Metropolitan area's share of Poland's total population has been decreasing since 1985. Table 4.1 presents population trends since 1950. Demographic patterns in the country mirror those found in other Western and Central European nations — declining birth rates and a rising elderly population. Between 1980 and 1992, the "post-productive" portion of Poland's elderly population (over 59 for women, and over 64 for men) increased from 11.8 to 13.2 percent of the total population. Post-productive population grew at an annual rate of 1.5 percent, about double the overall population growth rate. In the Warsaw metropolitan region, the share of the post-productive population increased from 13.5 to 15.8 percent. Post-productive population grew at an annual rate of 1.7 percent, over five times the overall population growth rate. Table 4.2 reports population by age range for Poland and Metropolitan Warsaw.

90

Table 4.1
Population trends in Poland and the Warsaw metropolitan area, 1950-1992

Year	Poland ('000)	Average percent change from previous date	Warsaw metropolitan area ('000)	Annual percent change from previous date	Warsaw as a percent of Poland
1950	24,824	—	1,265	—	5.1
1960	29,561	1.8	1,726	3.2	5.8
1970	32,536	1.0	1,998	1.5	6.1
1980	35,578	0.9	2,319	1.5	6.5
1985	37,203	0.9	2,412	0.8	6.5
1990	38,119	0.5	2,422	0.1	6.4
1991	38,245	0.3	2,420	-0.1	6.3
1992	38,365	0.3	2,409	-0.5	6.3

Source: Economic Analysis Unit

Table 4.2
Age distribution of Poland and Warsaw metropolitan area, 1980-1992

Poland

	Population ('000)			Annual percent change	Share		
	1980	1990	1992		1980	1990	1992
Pre-productive Age	10,297	11,318	11,175	0.7	28.8	29.6	29.1
Productive Age	21,211	21,262	22,181	0.4	59.4	57.5	57.7
Post-productive Age	4,227	4,903	5,062	1.5	11.8	12.8	13.2
Total	35,735	38,183	38,418	0.6	100.0	100.0	100.0

Source: Economic

Warsaw Metropolitan Area

	Population ('000)			Annual percent change	Share		
	1980	1990	1992		1980	1990	1992
Pre-productive Age	516.6	584.6	569.5	0.8	22.3	24.1	23.6
Productive Age	1,490.2	1,471.5	1,458.8	-0.2	64.3	60.8	60.6
Post-productive Age	312.3	365.5	380.7	1.7	13.5	15.1	15.8
Total	2,319.1	2,421.6	2,409.0	0.3	100.0	100.0	100.0

Source: Economic

Components of Warsaw's population change

Population growth in the Warsaw metropolitan region has steadily decreased since 1980. Over the 1980-85 period, the population of the region increased at a compound annual average rate of 0.8 percent. Between 1985 and 1990, the rate of increase decreased to 0.1 percent per year. Since 1990, the metropolitan region's population has been declining. During 1992, population in the region declined by 11,000 persons. Table 4.3 presents components of population change between 1980 and 1992.

Table 4.3

Components of population change in Warsaw metropolitan area, 1980, 1990, 1991, 1992

Year	Births	Deaths	Net migration	Total population change
1980	35,448	24,325	13,108	24,231
1990	24,561	27,239	5,041	2,363
1991	23,836	28,880	3,087	-1,957
1992	22,746	28,187	-5,559	-11,000

Source: Economic Analysis Unit

There are several reasons for Metropolitan Warsaw's declining rate of population growth. First, the rate of natural increase is slowing as deaths outpace births. Second, migration to the region is declining, and in 1992 turned negative. Third, urban development is spreading outside of Metropolitan Warsaw to surrounding regions. Crude birth rates have been falling. In 1980, females averaged 1.65 births over their reproductive cycle. In 1991, the average declined 6 percent to 1.55 births. As is common in urban areas, fertility rates are low. This rate does not provide enough births to replace the population. As more women enter the labor force and as social factors influence attitudes about marriage and raising families, the region's birth rates will continue to decline. At the same time, mortality rates are increasing. Between 1980 and 1990, annual mortality rates for the Warsaw population increased 12.3 percent rising from 10.6 to 11.9 deaths per year per 1000 of population.

In 1980, the Warsaw metropolitan region's total population increased by 24,231. Of this number, natural increase accounted for 11,123 or 46 percent of the total increase in population. Net migration flows accounted for an increase of 13,108, or 54 percent of the increase. By 1990, total annual population change was one tenth the rate in 1980, or 2,363. Of this amount, natural increase accounted for -2,678 (-113 percent). Migration into the region was by 5,041, or 213 percent of the increase, more than offsetting the loss of population from an excess of deaths over births.

During 1991, Metropolitan Warsaw's natural increase continued to be negative, and deaths exceeded births by 5,044. Net migration into Metropolitan Warsaw continued to fall, reaching 3,087. By 1991, migration was not sufficient to offset the region's negative natural increase and the region's total population started to decline. The same pattern held for 1992 as well, when the natural increase of the region was -5,441. Net migration to Metropolitan Warsaw turned negative, and a total of 5,559 persons left the region. The combined effect of the declining natural increase and the negative net migration caused the region's population to decline by 11,000 during 1992. Preliminary demographic data for 1993, indicate that both natural increase and net migration rates into Warsaw have remained negative, causing the region's overall population to continue to decline in 1993.

Warsaw's household characteristics

Based on trends in occupied housing units, the 1988 Census of Poland and construction trends in Metropolitan Warsaw, estimates have been made of the number and size of households in the Warsaw Metropolitan area. Estimates are provided for 1988 through 1992 in Table 4.4. Despite a declining population, the number of households is increasing. This pattern is commonly found in cities with an aging population. Households decline in size as family members depart to establish new households. During the late 1980s and early 1990s housing production in Metropolitan Warsaw collapsed and production of units averaged around 6,000 dwelling units. Given such constraints, household growth is limited, expanding at the same rate as the housing stock.

Table 4.4
Households trends in Warsaw metropolitan area, 1988-1992

Year	Number of households	Population	Average house-hold size
1988	939,000	2,412,900	2.57
1990	949,300	2,422,000	2.55
1991	958,200	2,420,000	2.53
1992	967,500	2,409,000	2.49

Source: Economic Analysis Unit

Metropolitan Warsaw's households are considerably smaller than the national average. For example, between 1988 and 1992, the national average household size in Poland ranged between 3.51 and 3.55, about 40 percent larger than the

93

region's. The difference reflects the fact that rural households are quite large in Poland, averaging over 4.5 persons in 1988.

Labor force characteristics

Between 1988 and 1992 labor supply adjusted to changing labor demand generated by Poland's fundamental economic restructuring. As illustrated in Table 4.5 the total full-time and part-time supply of labor has declined by 19.4 percent between 1988 and 1992, in the City of Warsaw. Over the longer term, between 1980 and 1992, it declined by 38 percent. More of the total labor supply is concentrated in part-time employment. In 1980 for example, about 6 percent of the total labor supply, 60,000 persons, offered their services on a part-time basis. By 1992, that number had risen to 11.5 percent (84,300 persons).

Table 4.5
Total and full time workers in the city of Warsaw ('000)

Year	Total			Full Time		
	Total	Male	Female	Total	Male	Female
1980	1,011.3	524.3	487.8	951.6	496.1	455.5
1988	908.3	456.9	451.4	791.8	406.4	385.4
1990	720.6	343	377.6	625.8	303.4	321.9
1991	703.1	340.1	363	604.8	295.8	309.0
1992	732.0	359.2	372.8	647.7	322.2	325.5
Percent Change 1988-1992	-19.4	-21.4	-17.4	18.2	-20.7	-15.5

Source: Economic Analysis Unit

Male workers, more likely to be employed in industrial sectors, were also more likely to have withdrawn their services from the labor market than were women. Male labor supply declined by 21.4 percent between 1988 and 1992, while female labor supply fell by 17.4 percent. As a consequence, by 1992, Metropolitan Warsaw's labor force was dominated by women (51 percent). Data on retirements and layoffs indicate that older men working in industrial sectors are more likely to lose their jobs than women working mainly in the growing retail and service sectors.

Despite declines in educational expenditures by government, during the 1980s and into the 1990s, Warsaw's labor quality has markedly improved, reflecting the growing recognition that high skills and advanced education are the key to secure jobs. As Table 4.6 reveals, over 80 percent of the 1992 Warsaw metropolitan area

Table 4.6
Full time workers in the city of Warsaw, by level of education

Type of School	1980	1988	1990	1991	1992
Trade School	171,693	156,248	128,753	125,333	140,225
General High School	75,329	59,849	47,955	47,931	51,506
Technical School	231,499	217,592	183,265	180,187	194,478
Higher Ed. Institution	145,691	135,054	115,398	119,019	129,169
Total	944,500	768,834	621,688	598,007	638,952
	%	%	%	%	%
Trade School	18.2	20.3	20.7	21.0	21.9
High School	8.0	7.8	7.7	8.0	8.1
Technical School	24.5	28.3	29.5	30.1	30.4
Higher Ed. Institution	15.4	17.6	18.6	19.4	20.2
Completed No Program	33.9	26.0	23.5	21.0	19.4
Total	100.0	100.0	100.0	100.0	100.0

Source: Economic Analysis Unit

labor supply had completed some form of technical or academic training, up from 66.1 percent in 1980. Workers who have completed university degrees accounted for 20.2 percent of the labor force in 1992, up from 17.6 percent in 1988. Workers with advanced technical training accounted for 30.4 percent of the labor force in 1992, increasing from 28.3 percent in 1988.

Structural reforms in the Polish and local economy are profoundly reshaping the labor market. Fast growing sectors such as trade, finance and insurance and services are generating strong demands for highly skilled workers trained in business administration and accounting, marketing, management, finance and logistics. This requires a labor force with vastly different skills than are currently available.

Spatial distribution of population

The overall population of the Warsaw metropolitan area declined by about 7,100 persons between 1988 and 1992. This metropolitan-wide average masks extreme variations in and around the region. Table 4.7 and Map 4.1 illustrate the spatial distribution of population changes in and around the region. Most of the decline was concentrated in the City of Warsaw's central gminas. Srodmiescie, Zoliborz, Ochota and Mokotow have experienced substantial declines in population between 1988 and 1992, falling by 4,984, 1,960, 4,220 and 6,148 respectively. Wola's population increased slightly, rising by 762. On the east side of the Vistula, popula-

Table 4.7
Population changes in Warsaw metropolitan area, 1988-1992

Central Warsaw gminas	1988	1992	Change 1988-1992	Percent of change
Mokotów	369,797	363,649	-6,148	-1.7
Ochota	175,369	171,149	-4,220	-2.4
Praga Pld.	257,813	262,622	4,809	1.9
Praga Pln	237,174	238,409	1,235	0.5
Sródmiescie	158,407	153,423	-4,987	-3.1
Wola	251,027	251,789	762	0.3
Zoliborz	205,434	203,474	-1,960	-1.0
Subtotal Central Area	1,655,021	1,644,409	-10,506	-0.6
Ring	761,113	764,532	3,419	0.4
Total Warsaw Metropolitan Area	2,416,134	2,409,047	-7,087	0.3

Source: Economic Analysis Unit

tion increased, with Praga Pld. and Praga Pln. growing by 4,809 and 1,235 between 1988 and 1992. In percentages, Srodmiescie had the largest decline, -3.1 percent. Praga Pld. had the largest percentage increase, 1.9 percent.

In the Ring outside the City of Warsaw, the population of suburban gmina's grew by 3,419, an increase of 0.4 percent. Map 4.1 illustrates that the fastest growing gminas were located just outside the City to the southwest, and farther out to the south and east. In absolute terms the five biggest Ring area population gains were in: Lomianki (3,216); Karczew (1,588); Kobylka (1,301); Wesola (970); and Piaseczno (753). In percentage terms four of the five areas grew rapidly: Lomianki (23.1 percent); Karczew (11.1 percent); Kobylka (10.0 percent); and Wesola (9.9 percent).

The differential rate of population growth between the central city and the Ring over the 1988-1992 period has led to a gradual decline in the portion of the total regional population living in the central area. In 1992, 68.3 percent of the region resided in the seven central gminas. If economic development and housing construction continues to decentralize, the region's population will continue to decentralize. This is likely to exert significant pressure on the infrastructure of suburban areas.

MAP 4.1

Metropolitan Warsaw
Population Change

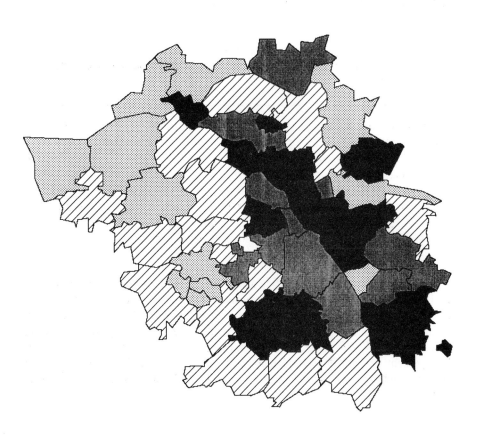

POPULATION CHANGE 1988-1992

- ■ -6200 to -200   (12)
- ▨ -200 to 0   (11)
- ▦ 0 to 400   (16)
- ▨ 400 to 4900   (14)
- ☐ all others (no data) (0)

Household income and expenditures

The Voivodship Statistical Office conducts surveys of household incomes and expenditure of a sample of households in the region. This survey data has been used to estimate aggregate income and expenditures of Metropolitan Warsaw's households for 1992. Table 4.8 presents aggregate estimates of total 1992 household income for the Warsaw Metropolitan area.

Table 4.8
Estimated total household income in Warsaw metropolitan area, 1992

	PLZ
Weighted Average Per capita Monthly Income (Dec.1992)	1,522,560
Average Household Size	x 2.49
Average Monthly Household Income	3,791,174
Total Warsaw Households 1992	x 967,500
Total Estimated Monthly Income (000,000)	3,667,961
Total Annual Household Income (000,000)	44,015,530

Source: Statistical Bulletin, Warsaw Statistical Office, 1993.

The Voivodship Statistical Office also conducts detailed assessments of household expenditure patterns. Table 4.9 presents this data. On average, the typical household spends about 91 percent of its income, saving 8.7 percent. In 1992, about 10 percent of household income was devoted to housing, including rent, maintenance and furnishings. The largest budget category is food, accounting for 38.1 percent of total household income. Utility costs run about 8.4 percent of income, covering cooking fuel, electricity and heat. Clothing accounts for 8.3 percent of total income.

Conclusions

This chapter has reviewed trends in population, households, labor force, the spatial patterns of population distribution and change, and has reviewed household income and expenditures. The picture described is an aging population, decreasing in absolute numbers and household size. Labor supply is declining as the population diminishes and as older displaced workers withdraw their services from the market. Labor force characteristics are shifting as the economic structure of Warsaw changes, and overall labor quality is increasing despite declining state support for education.

Modest population growth is occurring in the suburbs in selected areas near the City of Warsaw. If population and housing development increases in suburban areas, the region will face significant pressures for infrastructure improvements.

Warsaw's nearly one million households make up a large and powerful retail spending base. In 1992, the region's households spent a total of Plz. 40 trillion (approximately $1.9 billion) on goods and services.

Table 4.9
Estimate of Warsaw region aggregate household expenditures by type of consumption, 1992 (PLZ 000,000)

Expenditure category	Percent of household expenditures	Estimated annual aggregate expenditures
Food	38.1	16,769,917
Alcohol Beverages	1.5	660,233
Tobacco	1.5	660,233
Clothing, Footwear	8.3	3,653,289
Dwelling, Furnishing Maintenance	9.8	4,313,522
Electric, Fuel, Heating	8.4	3,697,305
Personal Hygiene, Medical Care	4.9	2,156,761
Education, Recreation	7.6	3,345,180
Transport plus Communication	5.5	2,420,854
Other	5.7	2,508,885
Total Expenditures	91.3	40,186,179
Savings	8.7	3,829,351
Total	100	44,015,530

Source: Statistical Bulletin, Warsaw Statistical Office, 1993.

5 Warsaw property market assessment

Introduction

This chapter reviews current trends in the Warsaw metropolitan region's urban land use and property sector. The first section of the chapter covers general land use and land ownership patterns in the metropolitan region and identifies the current supply of vacant land designated for future urban development. The second section reviews trends in housing conditions and housing construction. The third section describes the emerging office sector. The fourth reviews retail activities in the City and region. Sections five and six estimate the current stock of warehousing and industrial facilities. Section seven reviews information regarding hotel accommodations. The final section summaries findings and points out critical development issues facing Metropolitan Warsaw.

Land use and land ownership

The Warsaw Metropolitan area comprises nearly 380,000 hectares. As shown in Table 5.1, 11.3 percent of the total area is urbanized. Another 1.4 percent (5,173 hectares) is vacant and approved for urban development. The remaining area, accounting for over 85 percent of the region, is in open space, agricultural or forest uses or is not developable.

The City of Warsaw, is more intensely urbanized than the surrounding Ring area. Approximately 14,400 hectares are urbanized, about 30 percent of the City's total land area. The City center, Srodmiescie and the Wola gmina, are the most highly urbanized, each with over 50 percent of their surface area developed. Other City of Warsaw gminas have between 20 and 45 percent of their land area developed.

At both the City and regional level, patterns of urban land utilization are well below levels of other comparably sized West European cities. Until 1990, land use planning and development control in Metropolitan Warsaw was highly restrictive.

Table 5.1
Land utilization and availability, 1992

Gmina or area	Total area	Urban-ized land*	Vacant land desig-nated for develop ment	Other land**	Per-cent urban	Per-cent avail-able
Srodmiescie	1,556	996	12	758	51.2	0.8
Mokotow	11,600	2,839	1,089	7,672	24.5	9.4
Ochota	4,753	2,094	105	2,554	44.1	2.2
Wola	4,451	2,251	409	1,791	50.6	9.2
Zoliborz	4,060	1,500	172	2,388	36.9	1.6
Praga North	10,956	2,150	540	8,266	19.6	4.9
Praga South	12,119	2,765	493	8,861	22.8	4.1
City of Warsaw	49,495	14,595	2,820	32,290	29.9	5.9
Gminas outside Warsaw	330,252	28,336	2,353	299,563	8.6	0.7
Total	379,747	42,931	5,173	331,853	11.3	1.4

Source: Gmina provided land use survey, 1992

* Including road
** Land in parks, open space and undevelopable land.

The centerpiece of development control was the master plan, which provided the precise specification of uses and areas. The former master plan, adopted in 1982, restricted development to five main corridors. Development in these areas was limited, permitting population densities of about 70 persons per hectare. For example, approximately 36 percent of the land areas of the Ochota and Mokotow gminas were zoned for agricultural use. The combination of low development densities and a "wedges and corridors" plan has resulted in the rapid outward expansion of the City, and an increase in transportation and energy costs. Besides severely limiting development to the five corridors, the prior master plan froze the development of over 2000 parcels of land scattered throughout the City by stipulating precise uses which were either economically unfeasible or unwanted [World Bank, 1990].

As Table 5.1 clearly illustrates, a very limited supply of land is designated as being available for development — approximately 5,000 hectares. To help promote more economic development and attract more investment, the supply of land available for urban development should be expanded, especially in the central areas.

Fortunately, the City of Warsaw's new master plan moves a considerable distance toward the recommendations of the World Bank and others by encouraging the urban planning framework to be more market oriented and efficient. The new master plan relies on a much more flexible set of development controls. The plan designates six general urban development focus areas and issues: 1) the central area; 2) housing and services; 3) technical and industrial development; 4) services and warehousing; 5) green areas; and 6) corridor areas targeted for environmentally friendly activities.

While these new initiatives are a step in the right direction, additional actions are needed to promote redevelopment activity in older and largely derelict industrial areas surrounding the City. New policies which will promote infill development of serviced but under-utilized parcels, should be undertaken.

Another land development constraint facing the City of Warsaw concerns land ownership. In the central area of Warsaw, generally corresponding to the urbanized area of the pre-World War II city, land was nationalized, and most of the land in this area is in public ownership. As Table 5.2 illustrates, virtually all of the land in Srodmiescie and over 80 percent of the land in Wola and Zoliborz is in public ownership. In the outlying areas, most urbanized and vacant land approved for development is in private ownership.

Because of the limited supply of developable and privately owned land, many developers and investors are bypassing the City of Warsaw and seeking out sites for development in suburban areas of the metropolitan region. This tendency is likely to cause an abnormal amount of decentralization of development and limit the

Table 5.2
Land ownership patterns, 1992

Gmina or area	Hectares			
	Total area	Public area	Private area*	Percent private
Srodmiescie	1,556	1,556	0	0.0
Mokotow	11,600	7,929	3,671	31.6
Ochota	4,753	3,080	1,673	35.2
Wola	4,451	3,830	621	14.0
Zoliborz	4,060	3,323	737	18.2
Praga North	10,956	6,542	4,414	10.3
Praga South	12,119	6,539	5,580	46.0
City of Warsaw	48,095	31,399	16,696	34.7
Gminas outside of Warsaw	330,252	132,654	197,598	59.8
Total Warsaw Metropolitan Area	378,347	164,053	214,294	56.6

Source: Gmina provided land use survey forms, 1992

* Includes cooperative land

102

ability of the Metropolitan Warsaw economy to generate agglomeration economies. To counter this trend, the City must try to attract a greater share of projects by providing more sites with clear titles and development designation.

Housing conditions and trends

Similar to other Central European capitals, Metropolitan Warsaw's housing market is tight and vacant or newly constructed units are in short supply. The region's tight housing market is a result of a lack of housing finance credit and an increase in the demand for units by new households. Table 5.3 illustrates trends in the region's housing from 1988 to 1992. The stock of occupied housing has increased from 734,718 in 1980 to 826,918 in 1992, an annual average increase of 1 percent. Since 1988, the metropolitan region's housing stock has been increasing by about 8,000 units per year. This rate of production is only about 80 percent of the annual increase in households in Metropolitan Warsaw, and as a result, many households are forced to double up. In 1992, there were about 1.17 households per occupied dwelling. Fortunately, since the average size of households is falling, declining from 2.57 to 2.49 persons between 1988 and 1992, the average number of persons per dwelling unit is gradually declining, going from 2.96 in 1988 to 2.85 in 1992 (see Table 5.3).

Compared to other Central European capitals, the age of the housing stock is relatively young — the median age is about 27 years. This reflects the fact that over 80 percent of the metropolitan area's housing stock was constructed after the Second World War. Table 5.4 shows the age of housing stock in the region in 1992. Despite the relaaively slow rate of housing production (averaging about 1 percent of the occupied stock), housing conditions are improving. The size and quality of new units is rising, and housing cooperatives and communal units are refurbishing flats. Table 5.5 provides some aggregate measures of housing quality. Since 1980, the percentage of flats with water, toilets, private baths, gas hook-ups and central heating has greatly increased. The average size of dwelling units is increasing, rising from 46.6 square meters in 1980 to 51 square meters in 1992.

Most housing production is carried out by housing cooperatives — accounting for some 67 percent of construction in 1992. Tables 5.6 and 5.7 present data on housing construction and ownership. Private sector construction makes up about 20 to 35 percent of the market, and it can be expected to increase in the future when housing finance is available. In terms of ownership, housing cooperatives are the largest form of ownership, accounting for 41 percent of the stock in 1992. Communal ownership is the second largest, comprising 30 percent.

Despite the improvements evident in the housing market, there are some signs of distress. As Table 5.8 illustrates, in 1992, nearly 38 percent of households were in arrears on their housing payments (rents or mortgages) and nearly 9 percent were more than three months late. While these high rates of arrears reflect a permissive legal system (for most housing occupants, eviction is nearly impossible), there are signs that the low- and moderate-income households are having financial difficulties.

Table 5.3

Trends in housing stock, Warsaw metropolitan area, 1980-1992

Year	Total occu- pied stock	Average size usable m2	Average rooms per unit	Average per- sons per unit
1980	734,718	46.6	2.90	3.07
1988	797,100	50.0	3.06	2.96
1990	811,348	50.5	3.07	2.91
1991	819,014	50.7	3.08	2.95
1992	826,918	51.0	3.09	2.85

Source: WUS Statistical Yearbooks, 1988-1993

Table 5.4

Age of housing stock, Warsaw metropolitan area, 1992

Age	Units	Percent of total
0-5	29,800	3.6
6-13	117,400	14.2
14-21	160,900	19.5
22-31	201,300	24.3
32-17	171,200	20.7
48-74	113,800	13.8
over 74	32,500	3.9
Total	826,900	100.0

Source: Economic Analysis Unit

Table 5.5

Housing quality indicators, Warsaw metropolitan area, 1980-1992

Year	Total	Water	Toilet	Private bath	Gas hook-up	Central heat
			Percent of dwelling units with			
1980	734,718	84.8	80.8	77.1	69.0	74.5
1988	797,100	91.8	88.3	85.3	79.3	83.8
1990	811,348	92.0	88.6	85.6	79.5	84.2
1991	819,014	92.1	88.7	85.8	79.7	84.9
1992	826,918	93.3	89.9	87.0	81.6	86.4

Source: WUS Statistical Yearbooks, 1988-1993

Table 5.6
Trends in housing construction, Warsaw metropolitan area, 1980-1992

Year	Comple-tions	Percent built by				Average size m2
		Com-munal	Coopera-tive	Enter-prise	Private	
1992	8,150	1.5	67.3	9.9	21.3	77.2
1991	7,916	0.9	56.8	17.3	25.1	77.0
1990	5,740	1.7	48.3	14.6	35.3	85.3
1988	9,255	1.9	56.6	18.3	23.2	68.8
1980	11,950	0.0	72.1	12.8	16.1	61.2

Source: WUS Statistical Yearbooks, 1988-1992

Table 5.7
Housing stock by form of ownership,
Warsaw metropolitan area, 1992

	Dwelling units	Percent
Private Owner, Others	175,900	21.3
Housing Cooperative	336,200	40.7
Enterprise Owned	71,500	8.6
Communal Owned	243,300	29.4
Total	826,900	100.0

Source: WUS Statistical Yearbooks, 1988-1992

Table 5.8
Housing rental and mortgage arrears,
Warsaw metropolitan area, 1992

Ownership type	Percent of households in arrear	Percent of households in arrears over 3 months
Housing Cooperative	44.6	8.0
Enterprise	14.1	4.1
Communal	35.3	10.6
Total	37.8	8.5

Source: WUS Statistical

City of Warsaw's emerging office sector

Since 1989, demand for high quality office space has increased dramatically. Given the limited construction response to demand, office rents, especially those in "Class A" facilities have surged and now match and even surpass rents found in Western Europe and North America. As in most cities, Metropolitan Warsaw's top office location is in the central business district. There Metropolitan Warsaw's highest rents can be found, reaching $55 USD per month per square meter. Map 5.1 illustrates the pattern of office rents in the Warsaw Central Business District.

Based on the estimated stock of office space in 1992 of 2.7 million square meters and an average space per worker of 25 square meters (the low end for international space standards), the City of Warsaw's office employment was about 110,000 employees. Finance and insurance, the dominant office using sector accounted for 23 percent of total office use.

In 1989, the City of Warsaw's total supply of office space stood at 2,480,000 square meters. Of this amount, 2,320,000 square meters was constructed for government and state enterprise units, and is not suitable for multi-tenant occupation. The remaining stock, 160,000 square meters was "Class A" and suitable for foreign and domestic private enterprises. Between 1989 and 1992, approximately 120,000 square meters of new Class A office space was added to the City of Warsaw's stock. Table 5.9 provides an estimate of private and public office and service building construction activity in Metropolitan Warsaw. Since the pace of construction activities has been so low, especially private sector activity, the office market has been very tight, with overall vacancy rates in the City estimated to average around 2 percent.

The City of Warsaw's Development Promotion Department estimates that office space completions averaged 30,000 square meters during 1993 and 1994. In 1995, a second wave of office completions will hit the market, and annual supply increases will rise to over 50,000 square meters per year. While these additions will relieve market pressure, demand for space is expected to continue to outpace supply.

The annual demand for modern office space averaged 10,000 square meters in 1989 and rapidly increased to 70-80,000 square meters by 1992. Given the rapid growth of the Polish economy, estimated to average 4 percent per year over the next five years, and the enormous structural changes under way in the economy, the demand for office space is likely to grow enormously over the next five years.

Employment and establishment trends provide a clear record of the growing demand for office facilities. Table 5.10 presents tabulations of employment in the major office oriented sector — finance and insurance. As the table illustrates, between 1988 and 1992 employment in finance and insurance increased by nearly 16,000 workers, a 107 percent increase in four years. The number of finance and insurance establishments increased nearly 400 percent increasing from 114 to 569 establishments. In 1988 the average size of a finance and insurance firm was 129 employees. In 1992, the average size was 53, less than half, indicating that the new

MAP 5.1

Office Rent Patterns in Warsaw's Central Business District

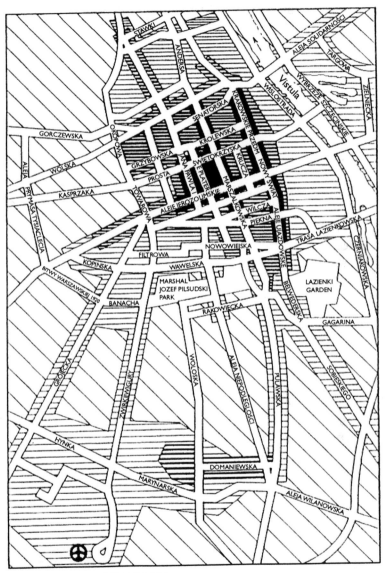

RENTS PER SQ. M. PER MONTH

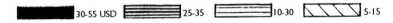

30-55 USD   25-35   10-30   5-15

Table 5.9
Private and public sector construction activities
in the Warsaw metropolitan area,
office and service buildings, 1980-1992

Year	Square Meters		
	Private	Public	Total
1980	25,000	64,000	84,000
1990	21,000	66,000	87,000
1991	17,000	22,000	39,000
1992	30,000	42,000	72,000

Source: Economic Analysis Unit

Table 5.10
Trends in employment and establishments in finance and insurance,
Warsaw metropolitan area, 1988-1992

Year	Employment	Percent change	Establishments	Percent change
1988	14,700	—	114	—
1990	27,600	43.90*	195	35.5*
1991	22,400	-18.80	323	65.6
1992	30,400	35.70	569	76.2

Source: Economic Analysis Unit

firms are smaller. While many of the new firms may not succeed, those that do will expand and require larger office accommodations. This will fuel office demand.

Another indicator of Metropolitan Warsaw's strong office demand is the growth in foreign trade and foreign joint venture firms. Table 5.11 provides a tabulation of private sector domestic and foreign firms established in Metropolitan Warsaw between 1988 and 1992. It is abundantly clear that private firms are expanding at a very rapid rate in Metropolitan Warsaw. Foreign firms, which are likely to take up office space in the City, have increased from literally nothing in 1988 to nearly 3,000 establishments in 1992. This suggests that they are an important force driving the demand for office space in the City.

As found in most other cities, Warsaw's prime office facilities are concentrated in the central business district. Establishment data for the central Srodmiescie gmina and the City of Warsaw, in 1992, indicate that about 30 percent of finance and insurance companies and 37 percent of foreign private sector firms are located in Srodmiescie (see Table 5.12). As of that year, the City of Warsaw contained nearly 40 percent of finance and insurance firms and over 90 percent of foreign companies.

Retail trade

Trade (both retail and wholesale) has been one of the fastest growing branches of economic activity in the Warsaw metropolitan area. Between 1988 and 1992, total employment in trade increased from 116,200 to 136,700, an increase of 20,500. Table 5.13 reports trade employment in the region. Most of the gain in trade employment took place in the center of Warsaw, 83 percent.

In 1989, with the launching of economic reforms, private shops mushroomed, increasing in number from 8,280 in 1988 to 14,386 in 1990. Retail expansion continued and by 1992, 25,412 formally registered shops (and many more kiosks, and informal traders) sprang into operation (see Table 5.14). As a result of the rapid expansion of small shops and the decline of large state-owned facilities, the average size of shops (in terms of square meters fell by more than 50 percent, from 119 square meters in 1988 to 69 square meters in 1992.

Employment in retail trade increased from 110,400 in 1988 to 123,000 in 1992. While in 1988, the average number of employees per shop was over 13 persons, by 1992 it fell to under 5 workers. Nearly 50 percent of retail trade employment (61,400) and space (872,800 square meters) is located in the central gmina of Srodmiescie, and 85 percent of the region's total retail employment and space is located in the City of Warsaw. This high level of concentration of retail activities is starting to change as more retail facilities are established in Warsaw's suburban areas (see Table 5.15).

Despite the substantial increase in retail sales between 1988 and 1992, financial trends indicate that retail activities may be over supplied. In 1992, retail sales in shops and restaurants averaged Plz. 33,000,000 per square meter per year. According to the City of Warsaw's Development Promotion Department, rents in shops let by gminas range from Plz. 1.44 to 7.2 million per square meter per year. On the free market, retail annual rents for a well-located shop run Plz. 10.8 to 14.4 million.

Table 5.11

Trends in domestic and foreign private sector establishments, Warsaw metropolitan area, 1980-1992

Year	Private sector establishments			Percent change		
	Domestic	Foreign	Total	Domestic	Foreign	Total
1980	3,132	8	3,140	—	—	—
1990	25,595	454	26,049	358.6*	2,787.5*	364.8*
1991	47,267	1,310	48,577	84.7	188.5	86.5
1992	77,048	2,857	79,905	63.0	118.1	64.5

Source: Economic Analysis Unit

*Annualized

Table 5.12
Finance and insurance and foreign companies located Srodmiescie, City of Warsaw and Warsaw metropolitan area, 1988-1992

| Year | Finance and insurance companies | | | Percent share | | |
	Srodmiescie	City of Warsaw	Warsaw metro. area	Srodmiescie	City of Warsaw	Warsaw metro. area
1988	44	57	114	38.6	50.0	100.0
1990	82	142	195	42.1	72.8	100.0
1991	144	260	323	44.6	80.5	100.0
1992	241	492	569	29.1	39.5	100.0

| Year | Foreign companies | | | Percent share | | |
	Srodmiescie	City of Warsaw	Warsaw metro. area	Srodmiescie	City of Warsaw	Warsaw metro. area
1988	0	5	8	0.0	62.5	100.0
1990	147	400	454	32.4	88.1	100.0
1991	479	1,184	1,310	36.1	90.4	100.0
1992	1,061	2,623	2,857	37.1	91.8	100.0

Source: Economic Analysis Unit

Table 5.13
Trade employment, Warsaw metropolitan area, 1988-1992

Year	Total trade employment	Employment in retail trade*
1988	116,200	110,400
1990	122,300	113,100
1991	129,600	118,300
1992	136,700	123,000

Source: Economic Analysis Unit

*Retail employment is estimated to be 90 percent of total trade employment in 1992, 91.25 in 1991, 92.5 in 1990 and 95 percent in 1988.

Table 5.14
Retail shops in Warsaw metropolitan area, 1980-1992

`Year	Retail Shops	Total Floor Area m2	Average Size of Retail Shops
1980	6,995	810,100	115.8
1988	8,280	985,600	119.0
1990	14,386	1,601,600	111.3
1991	18,725	1,233,800	65.9
1992	25,412	1,748,400	68.8

Source: Economic Analysis Unit

Table 5.15
Distribution of retail employment and retail space, 1992

Gmina	Employment	Retail space (m2)	Percent of distribution
Mokotow	9,100	129,400	7.4
Ochota	5,200	73,900	4.2
Praga North	11,600	164,900	9.4
Praga South	4,600	65,400	3.7
Srodmiescie	61,400	872,800	49.9
Wola	8,200	116,600	6.7
Zoliborz	4,500	64,000	3.7
City of Warsaw	104,600	1,487,000	85.0
Rest of Voivodship	18,400	261,400	15.0
Total Voivodship	123,000	1,748,400	100.0

Source: Economic Analysis Unit

Given these rents, shops may find it difficult to turn an adequate profit. Financial data provide by the Voivodship Statistical office indicate that retail trade activities have suffered from declining profitability. Retail gross margins, the ratio of profit to sales, have dramatically declined since 1988. According to the Voivodship Statistical Office, gross margins fell from 29 percent in 1990 to 0.6 percent in 1992. As will be discussed in a later chapter, retail growth will be much slower in the near future as the sector goes through a period of consolidation.

Wholesale trade

No sector of the Metropolitan Warsaw economy is going through as fundamental a change as wholesale trade. Prior to the economic market reforms of 1989, most wholesale distribution was handled through large state production or trading companies. Because of the inefficiencies of the distribution system and the almost complete lack of third party private wholesalers, most retailers were forced to either provide a limited selection of goods or take on the burden of stocking and warehousing inventory.

Surveys of retail shops and manufacturing facilities reveals that in 1993, there is still considerable storage of inventory in both retail and production facilities. Despite high rents and operating costs, retail shops in Warsaw devote an average of 35 percent of their total leased space to warehousing and storage. This is more than double the typical rate found in Western Europe and North America. A similar pattern is found in industrial facilities. Approximately 20 percent of industrial facilities are utilized for storage of materials and products. The patterns indicate the lack of a well-developed wholesale distribution system. Over time as the retail sector stabilizes and as industrial and trading firms develop their markets, wholesaling activities will grow.

In 1992, Metropolitan Warsaw had a total of 2,434 warehouses. It is estimated that in 1992, 10 percent of total trade employment was devoted to wholesale trade, up from 5 percent of total trade employment in 1988. In terms of actual employment, these percentage estimates translate into 13,700 workers in 1992 and 5,800 in 1988 (see Table 5.16). In terms of total regional employment, wholesale trade employment accounted for less than 1 percent in 1988 and nearly 1.5 percent in 1992. Over time as Poland's private sector warehousing and distribution system develops, employment will increase. As one indication of how the sector might grow, consider the fact that in North American cities, wholesale trade employment accounts for between 20 and 30 percent of trade (wholesale and retail) employment and between 4 and 8 percent of total employment in metropolitan areas,

Table 5.16
Wholesale employment in Warsaw metropolitan
area, 1988-1992

Year	Wholesale	Number of
1988	5,800	—
1990	9,200	—
1991	11,300	—
1992	13,700	2,434

Source: Economic Analysis Unit

areas of similar size to Warsaw. If warehousing was to mirror the structure of these North American cities, 1992 employment in the sector would range between 37,000 and 75,000, about three to five times more.

Because of the relative infancy of most private wholesale distribution companies and the abundant supply of vacant industrial buildings, most warehousing companies use old industrial buildings. Based on surveys of warehousing activities in Metropolitan Warsaw, warehouses have an average of 140 square meters of storage space per worker. Given the estimated total wholesaling employment of 13,700, Metropolitan Warsaw's total stock of warehousing/wholesaling facilities is estimated at 1,900,000 square meters. Table 5.17 presents estimates for the City of Warsaw, the Ring, and the entire metropolitan area.

Table 5.17
Distribution of warehouse facilities, 1992

	Wholesale employment	Wholesale warehousing space* (m2)
City of Warsaw	10,300	1,425,000
Ring	3,100	475,000
Warsaw Metropolitan Area	13,700	1,900,000

Source: Economic Analysis Unit Estimates, 1994

*Based on estimate of 140m2 per worker.

Distribution of warehousing space is based on the distributions of manufacturing facilities between City of Warsaw and Warsaw Metropolitan Area

Detailed information on the locational patterns of warehousing in the region is not available. However, given the fact that most warehousing is located in vacant industrial buildings, we have estimated the spatial distribution of vacant or converted industrial facilities and have used this distribution to estimate the location of warehousing establishments. Using this distribution, it is estimated that 75 percent of the region's supply of warehousing facilities are located in the City of Warsaw (1,425,000 square meters) and the remainder are located in outlying gminas (475,000 square meters).

Not all industrial buildings are well-suited for warehousing and storage. Buildings should have goods access to highways, have ample parking for trucks, have truck-high loading docks, high ceilings, be secure and in some cases provide heat-

113

ing. Buildings which meet these limited criteria and are located on or near main roads currently command $10 a square meter per month, other buildings of lesser quality rent at $6 to 8 per square meter per month.

In terms of the demand for warehousing and distribution space, the big question is how much of the growing supply of vacant industrial space will be converted and used for warehousing facilities and how much new space will be constructed expressly for warehousing and distribution operations. To help answer this question, the next section examines trends in the industrial sector.

Industrial activity

Historically, the backbone of the Metropolitan Warsaw economy was manufacturing. Employment in the industrial sector averaged around 30 percent of total employment. Since the launching of economic reforms and the radical shifts in trade patterns, Metropolitan Warsaw's industrial base has been in decline. In 1988 total industrial employment stood at 352,000. By 1992, employment had fallen to 234,500 a decline of 34 percent. Table 5.18 reports trends in industrial employment. Estimates of future employment trends indicate that even under the most optimistic scenario, manufacturing employment in Metropolitan Warsaw will remain constant over the next five years. It is more probable, however, that manufacturing employment will actually continue to decline.

Table 5.18
Trends in industrial employment, Warsaw
metropolitan area, 1988-1992

Year	Industrial employment
1988	352,600
1990	293,230
1991	282,504
1992	234,500

Source: Economic Analysis Unit

Industrial activity in Metropolitan Warsaw peaked during the 1980s, giving the region a substantial stock of industrial facilities. Given the decline in industrial activity and employment, it is estimated that industrial vacancies have risen to over 40 percent of the industrial stock of space. As Table 5.19 illustrates, the stock of industrial space in the region stood at approximately 24,000,000 square meters in 1992. Over this time, it is estimated that the stock of actually utilized industrial space

114

Table 5.19
Estimates of industrial space, metropolitan Warsaw, 1988-1992

Year	Employment	Actively used industrial space (m2)	Estimated stock of facilities (m2)	Vacant or converted space (m2)
1988	352,600	21,200,000	23,500,000	2,300,000
1990	293,200	17,600,000	23,700,000	6,100,000
1991	282,500	17,000,000	23,800,000	6,800,000
1992	234,500	14,000,000	24,000,000	10,000,000

Source: Economic Analysis Unit

has fallen from 21,200,000 square meters in 1988 to 14,000,000 square meters in 1992, a decline of over 7,000,000 square meters. At present approximately 42 percent of the Warsaw region's industrial buildings are either vacant or have been converted to other uses, e.g. warehouses, offices, or sports facilities. Over the next five years, it is likely that even more space will become vacant as the industrial sector continues its restructuring.

Most of the vacant space is located in the City of Warsaw. As Table 5.20 illustrates, nearly 80 percent of the decline in industrial employment between 1988 and 1992 was centered in the City of Warsaw (91,400 lost jobs). Ring area industrial employment fell by 26,700. This pattern of industrial decline suggests that declines in industrial space utilization are concentrated in the center. As Table 5.21 illustrates, of the City of Warsaw's 17,700,000 square meters of industrial space, only 10,200,000 square meters, 58 percent is actively used. It is estimated that 7,500,000 square meters of industrial space is either vacant or has been converted to some other use. In the Ring area, slightly more than 60 percent of the total industrial space is currently used for industrial activities.

Table 5.20
Distribution of industrial employment, Warsaw metropolitan area, 1988-1992

Year	City of Warsaw	Suburban gminas	Warsaw metro. area
1988	261,500	91,100	352,600
1990	240,200	53,000	293,200
1991	221,900	60,600	282,500
1992	170,100	64,400	234,500

Source: WUS Statistical Records, 1988-1992

Table 5.21
Distribution of occupied and vacant or converted industrial space,
1992

	Actively used industrial space m2	Vacant or converted space m2	Total stock of space
City of Warsaw	10,200,000	7,500,000	17,700,000
Ring	3,800,000	2,500,000	6,300,000
Total	14,000,000	10,000,000	24,000,000

Source: Economic Analysis Unit

The massive declines in industrial space pose an enormous challenge for the City and the region. What can be done with these derelict industrial areas? Are there other uses which can be housed in these old structures? What kinds of significant environmental hazards remain in these industrial areas which will make redevelopment more difficult? These issues will be addressed in the concluding section.

Lodging

The final area covered in this property assessment is the lodging industry. The Warsaw metropolitan region has about 32 hotels totaling 6,775 beds. In comparison to other cities this is adequate, yet most of the supply caters to the end of the price range. As the economy expands, a wider price range of accommodations will be needed. Table 5.22 presents trends in hotel accommodations for the 1988 to 1992 period.

Table 5.22
Hotel accommodations by type, Warsaw metropolitan area, 1988-1992

Quality	1988 Hotels	Beds	1990 Hotels	Beds	1991 Hotels	Beds	1992 Hotels	Beds
Five Star	1	585	1	585	2	1,322	2	1,145
Four Star	9	3,814	10	4,517	11	4,566	9	2,559
Three Star	13	2,185	11	1,973	12	2,180	15	2,954
Motels	3	96	3	95	4	72	3	58
Pensions	6	148	6	152	3	54	3	59
Total	32	6,828	31	7,322	32	8,194	32	6,775

Source: WUS Statistical Records, 1988-1992

116

The spatial distribution of hotels within the region indicates a strong concentration in the central city. In 1992 in Srodmiescie, the central gmina of Warsaw, 14 hotels accounted for 4,916 beds, an average of 351 per hotel. The remaining City of Warsaw gminas accounted for 7 hotels and 1,443 beds, an average of 206 per hotel establishment. In the outlying areas of the region there were only 11 hotels accounting for 416 beds, an average of 38 rooms per establishment. Table 5.23 reports lodging availability by area of the region. These patterns indicate that there may be opportunities for hotels in suburban locations along highways and near the airport.

Table 5.23
Hotel accommodations by location, 1988-1992

Location	1988		1990		1991		1992	
	Hotels	Beds	Hotels	Beds	Hotels	Beds	Hotels	Beds
Srodmiescie	14	5,306	13	5,835	15	6,772	14	4,916
Other Warsaw Gminas	4	953	5	926	5	962	7	1,443
Ring	14	569	13	561	12	460	11	416
Total	32	6,828	31	7,322	32	8,194	32	6,775

Source: WUS Statistical Records, 1988-1992

Conclusions about property development

This chapter has reviewed trends and patterns in the Warsaw region's property market. Relying on estimates of employment and spatial utilization surveys, estimates have been made of the housing stock, office space, retail space, warehouse facilities, industrial space and lodging. While the projections are preliminary, they provide a useful starting point for assessing the patterns of urban development within the region.

The housing market is reasonably close to equilibrium. Despite the fact that there is a credit crunch and little new housing is being constructed, housing conditions are generally good. Housing services have improved over time and overcrowding is declining (the average number of persons per room is decreasing). In the future, as credit for housing becomes available, more residential construction can be expected, most of which will take place in suburban areas.

The office market is still highly constrained, and supply is not matching demand. This has led to an increase in office rents, raising them to Western European levels. While there are a number of office projects which will come on line over the next three years, more sites for modern office projects are needed. Apparently, the biggest obstacle to office development is the lack of clarity over property rights and the very slow development review and approval process. The City of Warsaw is increasingly aware of these problems and steps are starting to be taken to improve developer access to land for commercial development.

In some districts, such as Wola, Ochota and Mokotow, there are under-utilized industrial areas which would be suitable for office development. The City and the gminas should create redevelopment plans for these areas and design land management programs to insure that parcels suitable for office projects can be made available for development.

The retail sector has expanded dramatically since 1989 and there is ample evidence that private retailing is spreading throughout the City. On major streets, ground floor space has been converted to retail activities, and local authorities are leasing space to private entrepreneurs. There seems to be little sign of constraints toretailing and the City has permitted the widespread siting of kiosks in the central area of Warsaw to provide retail facilities. Over time these facilities should be eliminated, especially from the Palace of Culture area as they have a blighting influence.

A few suburban shopping centers have been developed on the periphery of Warsaw. These modern facilities will provide residents with convenient shopping, but they may undermine the retail dominance of the central city. Here planners might be advised to manage the development of suburban shopping facilities to ensure the long-term vitality of the city center.

Private wholesale and distribution activities are just starting to emerge in Metropolitan Warsaw. Wholesale employment in 1992 was estimated to be about 13,700, accounting for less than 2 percent of the region's total employment. Over time, warehousing and distribution activities will expand and reach levels where 4 to 8 percent of the region's total employment is devoted to such activities. Such an expansion implies that warehousing and distribution facilities will dramatically expand, increasing by up to five times their present space. Until recently, most of the increasing requirements for warehousing facilities has been met by converting vacant industrial space. This pattern is likely to continue in the future but there will be an increase in the construction of new modern facilities. This gradual shift will be driven by two factors. First, not all industrial facilities can be efficiently used for warehousing activities, and the supply of adaptable space will decline. Second, as trade patterns continue to shift, favoring large Western European suppliers, the demand for large-scale and modern warehousing and distribution facilities will increase.

Again, the implications are important for the future urban development of the Warsaw region. Older industrial zones in and around the City will need to be redeveloped, especially those along major west-bound corridors. Large warehousing and distribution facilities (20-100 hectares) and will require large land assemblies. Here again land management policies will be needed to facilitate the development of such projects.

Metropolitan Warsaw's industrial sector is in decline and is expected to continue its downward trend for some time. In some ways Metropolitan Warsaw will follow the former paths of Manchester, Birmingham and Glasgow in the UK and Pittsburgh in the U.S. The declines in economic activity will leave vast areas of the region derelict. The challenge for the City is to develop a program to revitalize these areas and make them suitable for redevelopment. In some cases, buildings can be converted to office or other "post-industrial" activities, but in most cases areas will need to be cleared, toxic wastes removed and land assembled for development. This will require effective land management, especially powers of eminent domain, where the City can compulsorily purchase land for redevelopment.

The City is well served with lodging accommodations. Additional space in three star hotels and other affordable accommodations are needed. Also, hotel accommodation is far too concentrated in the City center, as the City's economy transforms, business travel will increase dramatically. Lodging facilities near the airport and along major corridors should be successful.

Finally, the most significant issue related to urban land development is the vast under-utilization of land in the City of Warsaw. In comparison to other Western European cities, land use patterns are grossly inefficient. Over the next decade, as the Warsaw economy transforms itself from a manufacturing-oriented to a services and trade-oriented economy its requirements for urban facilities, buildings and infrastructure will change as well. In making this transformation, the City faces two basic options, it can attempt to make the transition by re-utilizing vacant and under-utilized land in already developed and equipped areas, or new development can simply move to the outer edges (mainly outside the current boundaries of the City). The former approach will lead to a more compact city and will likely require less money to upgrade and equip the area with modern infrastructure. The second approach will lead to a sprawling city and require far more money for infrastructure development. To help clarify this issue, the next chapter assesses the City of Warsaw's current infrastructure system.

6 An assessment of the city of Warsaw's infrastructure system

Introduction

Infrastructure plays a critical role in promoting the economic growth of cities and nations. Infrastructure reduces the cost of production, affects profitability, and levels of output and employment. Modern infrastructure systems, particularly telecommunications, enable businesses to use more modern technology. Increased transport investment reduces congestion and boosts labor and business productivity. Improvements in water quality, sewerage treatment, solid waste disposal and central heating enhances environmental quality and improves health conditions. Infrastructure improvements facilitate the redevelopment and modernization of older urban areas, providing the basis for new investments in buildings.

Given the significant structural changes taking place in Metropolitan Warsaw's economy, demands for infrastructure support are changing rapidly. Demand for telecommunications, short haul transport, and air freight are increasing; while demand for rail transport, and industrial waste disposal are declining. As Metropolitan Warsaw's economy changes, so must its infrastructure system. In order to attract capital and stimulate economic development, Metropolitan Warsaw must upgrade its old and outmoded infrastructure systems.

This chapter assesses infrastructure conditions in the City of Warsaw. It provides an overview of water and wastewater treatment, district heating, municipal transportation, roads, solid waste collection, telecommunications, electric and gas services.

Water supply and waste-water systems

This section discusses Warsaw's water supply and waste-water systems. Warsaw's Central System of Waterworks draws water from three intake points, illustrated in Map 6.1.

MAP 6.1

Warsaw's Water Supply System

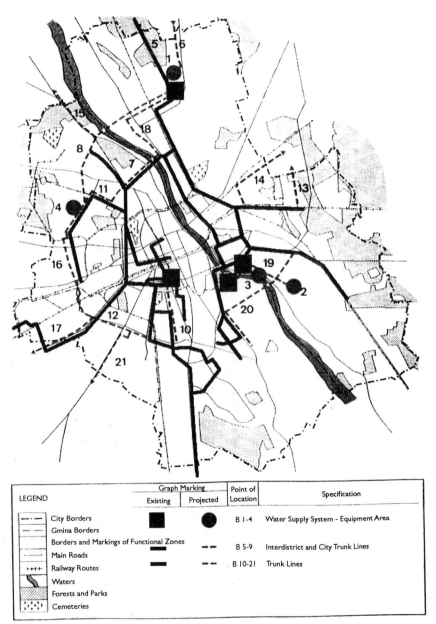

LEGEND	Graph Marking		Point of Location	Specification
	Existing	Projected		
–·–·– City Borders	■	●	B 1-4	Water Supply System - Equipment Area
–··–··– Gmina Borders				
———— Borders and Markings of Functional Zones	▬	– –	B 5-9	Interdistrict and City Trunk Lines
———— Main Roads	▬	– –	B 10-21	Trunk Lines
++++ Railway Routes				
〰 Waters				
░ Forests and Parks				
⋮⋮⋮ Cemeteries				

The Central Waterworks, takes surface water from the Vistula River; it consists of an intake point with a pumping station at ul. Czerniakowska, six raw (untreated) water transit pipes and a filter station at ul. Koszykowa. These waterworks have been servicing the city for over 100 years. The filter station has two water treatment systems: one, used since the waterworks was opened, is ancient, the other was installed in the 1970's, and relies on more modern chemical treatment technologies.

The Praga Waterworks takes infiltrated ground water from the Vistula, and purifies it at a rapid filter station at ul. Brukselska. This waterworks was brought on line in 1964.

The Northern Waterworks takes surface water from the Zegrzyski reservoir. Water treatment at the filter station in Wieliszew is similar to the system installed at the Central Waterworks in the 1970's. Next, the water is pumped to the area station in Bialoleka and after additional disinfection, is brought into the municipal water system through a pumping station.

The Central System Waterworks serves both the City of Warsaw and a significant part of the Warsaw metropolitan region. Table 6.1 presents a breakdown of the distribution of water production by each waterworks, for 1988 to 1993.

The process of transferring facilities located in the metropolitan region over to individual local authorities began in 1992. In 1992 eight plants were separated out from the management of the Municipal Enterprise for Water Supply and Sewage Treatment (MPWiK) and transferred to local authorities. Work is under way to transfer additional water supply facilities. Currently the Central Waterworks System (CSM) services 1,554,000 persons, 64.5 percent of Metropolitan Warsaw's population.

Except for a few areas, the municipal waterworks network is an open system, i.e., working in rings enabling users to be supplied from two sides. However, not all elements of the ring network have been implemented which means that some areas of the city are supplied only from one side. These areas are Ursynow-Natolin, Wochy and Ursus, Praga Polnoc and Zoliborz.

Due to the variation in elevation of the city (exceeding 20 meters in some locations), the waterworks network is divided into two zones of differing pressures, the so-called low zone and the high zone. The low zone is supplied from the Praga and Northern Waterworks and covers the areas under the escarpment of the left bank of Warsaw and Praga Polnoc and Praga Poludnia. The high zone is supplied from the Central and Northern Waterworks and covers the districts of: Wola, Ochota, Ursus, Gorne, Srodmiescie, Pruszkow, and Piaseczno.

The total water distribution system is 2,404 kilometers in length. Of this amount, 345 kilometers (14.4 percent) is comprised of mains of over 300 mm, sub-mains comprise 1,517 kilometers (63.1 percent), and laterals total 542 kilometers (22.5 percent). About 10 percent of the total system has been constructed or replaced since 1989, most of the system is quite old and as discussed below, breaks occur frequently.

The production capacity of Warsaw's Central Supply Works ranges from 700,000 to 950,000 cubic meters per day, depending on environmental conditions.

Table 6.1 (part 1 of 2)
Water production and its structure according to source in Warsaw, between 1988-1993

Plants	1988 Cubic Meters (000's)	1988 Structure %	1989 Cubic Meters (000's)	1989 Structure %	1990 Cubic Meters (000's)	1990 Structure %
1 General production which includes:	278,610	100.0	271,588	100.0	257,749	100.0
2 Central Water Supply System Plant	134,652	48.3	128,725	47.4	123,602	48.0
3 Praga Water Supply System Plant	82,186	29.5	78,172	28.8	62,296	24.1
4 Northern Water Supply System Plant	55,431	19.9	58,054	21.4	65,103	25.3
5 Water Supply System, Sewage & Drilling Plant in Otwock	3,570	1.3	3,724	1.4	3,905	1.5
6 Water Supply & Sewage System in Pruszkow	2,770	1.0	2,913	1.1	2,843	1.1

Source: Economic Analysis Unit

Production capacity of the Northern Waterworks could be increased by 50 to 75 percent if the through-flow of distribution mains running from the system could be expanded. The ratio of production capacity utilization in unfavorable conditions is almost 100 percent, and in favorable conditions it is at a level not exceeding 70 percent. It is assessed that the current production reserves in springs should be sufficient for at least a twenty year period of development. Water consumption per inhabitant is relatively high, amounting to 237 l/d. Therefore, consumption growth is likely to be limited.

Description of waste-water treatment system

There are two independent sewage systems functioning in the City of Warsaw on the east and west banks of the Vistula. The older sewage system on the west bank dates back to the early 1800s. A combined collection sewage system functions over most of the area of the city on both sides of the Vistula. Due to the flat and low layout (in relation to the Vistula) of most of the City, the sewage system is pump and gravitation operated. On the west bank of the Vistula, only the southern part of Mokotow, the western part of Ochota and Ursus have a storm sewage system. On the east bank of the Vistula, only Targowek Przemysowy, Zacisze, Elsnerow

Table 6.1 (part 2 of 2)
Water production and its structure according to source in Warsaw,
between 1988-1993

Plants	1991 Cubic Meters (000's)	1991 Struc-ture %	1992 Cubic Meters (000's)	1992 Struc-ture %	1993 Cubic Meters (000's)	1993 Struc-ture %
1 General production which includes:	251,521	100.0	241,300	100.0	235,200	100.0
2 Central Water Supply System Plant	119,238	47.4	113,344	47.0	120,536	51.2
3 Praga Water Supply System Plant	60,880	24.2	63,296	26.2	52,724	22.4
4 Northern Water Supply System Plant	64,664	25.7	60,880	25.2	61,940	26.3
5 Water Supply System, Sewage & Drilling Plant in Otwock	6,739	2.7	3,780	—	—	—
6 Water Supply & Sewage System in Pruszkow	—	—	—	1.6	—	—

Source: Economic Analysis Unit

and Brodno have a separated sanitary and storm sewer system. Map 6.2 presents the City's system of waste-water collection and treatment. The combined sewage system for the east bank ends at the "Czajka" sewage treatment plant, which was brought on line in 1989. Sewage produced on the west bank of the Vistula flows directly into the river. The entire network serves 1,499,000 inhabitants, about 90 percent of the population of Metropolitan Warsaw. The total collection system is 2,022 kilometers, of which 560 kilometers (27.7 percent) is made up of main collectors, 965 kilometers made up of sub-mains (47.7 percent) and 497 kilometers (24.6 percent) is comprised of laterals. Less than 7 percent of the total system was constructed within the past five years.

Table 6.2 illustrates the distribution of water and waste-water treatment services to end-users. City of Warsaw users account for over 90 percent of the total production; the other 10 percent is losses due largely to stolen service. Domestic users account for the largest share of water consumption, approximately 73 percent. The table also illustrates that industrial and commercial water consumption is declining. From 1988 through 1991, industrial water usage fell from 74,800,000 m^3 to 50,600,000 m^3, a 32 percent decline. In 1992, however, industrial water consumption increased to 53,800,000, a 6 percent increase. Residential consumption is falling as well, declining 14.5 percent from 167,500,000 m^3 in 1988 to 143,200,000

MAP 6.2

Warsaw's Sewage and Waste-water Treatment System

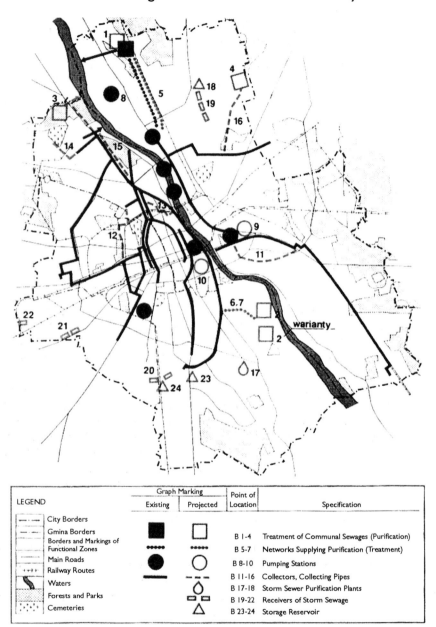

LEGEND	Graph Marking		Point of Location	Specification
	Existing	Projected		
⸺·⸺ City Borders				
⸺ ⸺ Gmina Borders	■	☐	B 1-4	Treatment of Communal Sewages (Purification)
Borders and Markings of Functional Zones				
⸺ Main Roads	●●●●●	○○○○○	B 5-7	Networks Supplying Purification (Treatment)
+++ Railway Routes	●	○	B 8-10	Pumping Stations
Waters	⸺	⸺ ⸺	B 11-16	Collectors, Collecting Pipes
Forests and Parks		◇	B 17-18	Storm Sewer Purification Plants
Cemeteries	▭	▭	B 19-22	Receivers of Storm Sewage
		△	B 23-24	Storage Reservoir

Table 6.2
Distribution of water production and treatment of waste-water
by type of consumer, in Warsaw, 1988-1992

	1988		1989		1990		1991		1992	
	Millions of cubic meters	Structure of Warsaw (%)	Millions of cubic meters	Structure of Warsaw (%)	Millions of cubic meters	Structure of Warsaw (%)	Millions of cubic meters	Structure of Warsaw (%)	Millions of cubic meters	Structure of Warsaw (%)
Total water	278.6	100.0	271.6	100.0	258.1	100.0	215.1	100.0	197.0	100.0
Sold to domestic users	167.5	60.1	168.5	62.0	171.9	66.6	164.5	76.5	143.2	72.7
Sold to other users	74.8	26.8	72.3	26.6	68.7	26.6	50.6	23.5	53.8	27.3
Water not sold	36.4	13.1	30.8	11.3	17.4	6.7	—	—	—	—
Wastewater produced	267.7	100.0	266.4	100.0	261.9	100.0	228.4	100.0	220.6	100.0
Domestic users	164.1	61.3	164.4	61.7	167.6	64.0	160.5	70.3	139.8	63.7
Other users	103.6	38.7	102.0	38.3	94.3	36.0	67.9	29.7	80.8	36.6
Treated wastewater	—	—	29.8	11.2	104.4	39.9	98.8	43.3	95.4	43.3

Source: Economic Analysis Unit

m³ in 1992. In both cases, economic pressures and higher rates appear to be reducing consumption.

Unaccounted for water use, due to leakage and unauthorized connections, is declining, as line losses are minimized and connections better monitored. In 1988, losses were 36,400,000 m³, representing 13.1 percent of total water production. In 1990, losses declined to 17,400,000 m³, accounting for 7.2 percent of total water production.

Trends in waste-water treatment are similar. Domestic consumption accounts for between 61 and 70 percent of total waste-water treatment. In 1992, waste-water treatment from domestic users was 139,800,000 m³, a decrease of 15 percent from 1988 levels. Industrial waste-water treatment declined dramatically between 1988 and 1992, going from 103,600,000 m³ in 1988 to 80,800,000 m³ in 1992. The share of waste-water receiving treatment has increased. Between 1989 and 1992, the percent of waste-water being treated rose from 11.2 to 43.3 percent.

Water supply and waste-water treatment problems and issues

Water supply reserves are only sufficient for the purposes of the daily equalization of unequal distribution of water in the network (ensuring a reserve of water for about 8.5 hours assuming an average level of water consumption, or 6.5 hours assuming maximum demand). However, water supply reserves are not sufficient to cover a major breakdown in the system.

Repair and upgrading of the water distribution system has been quite slow over the past five years, reflecting a lack of financial resources. Between 1989 and 1991, an average of approximately 100 pieces of defective pipe were replaced per year. In 1992, repair work picked up, and over 1500 defects were corrected.

With regards to the capacity of the network there are constraints in the trunk pipe at ul. Modlinska, supplying water from the Northern Waterworks, which is currently taking on a significant role in supplying water to a large part of the City of Warsaw. Network impedance restricts the utilization of production from the Northern Waterworks to about 60 percent of output.

Water production in the older subsystems of the Central Waterworks and Praga are being modernized. The Southern Waterworks entered into use several years ago and is thus relatively young. The physical condition of the water intake stations is generally satisfactory.

The condition of the water distribution network is poor and is reflected in the high number of breakdowns. The average number of breakdowns per kilometer per day of network, is 0.6. The frequency of these breakdowns is also significant; the average daily number of breakdowns is between 4 and 5 (as reported in statistical data from recent years).

One of the most serious infrastructure problems facing the City of Warsaw is the very low quality of its drinking water. The greatest problems connected with the quality of water occur in the Central Waterworks, which takes surface water from the Vistula. Water taken for communal purposes should be of class I purity, however water from the Vistula is of far lower quality, rated at class II or III, and in some instances its quality is so low it is unclassifiable.

The most common water quality problem encountered is high ammonia levels. Its presence causes harmful secondary substances to arise (chloroform will arise as a result of chlorine gas treatment), as well as negatively influencing the taste and aroma characteristics of the water. The present water purification technology used by the Central Waterworks does not guarantee the removal of ammonia.

The program for the modernization of Warsaw waterworks, in place at present, is aimed at improving water quality. The program intends to move away from the taking of surface water by building underground infiltration water intake points. Water from these intakes will have significantly lower levels of ammonia present. An under-bed infiltration water intake was brought on line in January 1993. This unit is called PW-1, with an output of 50-60 thousand m^3/d, it supplies water to the ul. Czerniakowska pumping station, where it is then pumped onto the Central Waterworks filter station. Another identical intake with a similar output capacity is to be completed in 1994, and a third well is under construction. Work is also under way to replace the current chlorine gas treatment system with a chlorine dioxide based process which will eliminate the possibility of harmful secondary substances arising in the water.

Another important water quality problem is the significant level of salt in the water of the Vistula which speeds the corrosive processes affecting industrial pipes. Current water purification methods do not reduce salt content. One of the possible

127

means of improving the situation is a reduction in the level of saltiness of the Vistula itself.

Water from the Praga and Northern Waterworks has significantly higher quality parameters. The best results achieved in this respect are at the Praga Waterworks where filtration is based on biological methods. Here chlorine gas is currently being replaced with chlorine dioxide. The purification process at the Northern Waterworks has been improved, replacing aluminum sulfate with iron sulfate. Also under construction, in cooperation with the French company "Trailgaz", is a preliminary installation for the ozonization of water, which will further improve the purification processes.

Many additional problems affect the sewage treatment equipment. Most of the arteries on the west bank of the Vistula are several dozen years old, which given the corrosive attributes of the water, has resulted in numerous failures. Most problems occur in those parts of the network which use steel pipes placed in service between 10 and 45 years ago. Due to financial limitations, the pace of pipe replacement has lagged and breaks continue.

There is significant overloading of the main drains and pumping station in the sewage system both on the east and west banks of Vistula, limiting the possibility of the further development of the City. The most serious of these is the overloading of the main drain serving the Ursynow-Natolin band (the southern part of Mokotow). Capacity constraints in this drain prohibit development of the southern part of the City.

The overloading of the main drain, receiving sewage from the "Powile" pumping station, results in the dumping of excess sewage into the Vistula at the center of the City. This practice significantly degrades the river's sanitary condition. The overloading of the main drain at Al. Krakowska and the "Ochota" pumping station is preventing the further development of Ochota and the "Okecie" airport region.

There are also capacity constraints in secondary main drains and local networks. On the east bank of the Vistula, the capacity of the "Saska Kepa" pumping station is insufficient and constitutes a barrier to the development of the Praga district to the South. Sewage drains from Gocaw are directed with the aid of three local temporary pumping stations. In this area of the City, overloading is also occurring at the pumping station and main drain in Rado. This area also suffers a lack of sewage treatment equipment and appliances.

Sewage produced in the eastern part of the City of Warsaw is led off to the "Czajka" sewage treatment works. "Czajka" has a capacity of 400 thousand m^3/d, although it currently accepts about 250 thousand m^3/d of household and industrial sewage (62.2 percent of capacity). "Czajka" is a mechanical and biological sewage treatment plant with the ability to reduce primary pollution indices by more than 90 percent. These results are nearly achieved, with a reduction of suspended solids by 89 percent, and biochemical oxygen demand by 95 percent.

The physical condition of the City of Warsaw's sewage collection and treatment system is far worse than its water treatment and distribution system. As already mentioned above, capacity overloading occurs in first and second grade drains of the sewer system. Furthermore the advanced age of the sewage collection network and treatment system make it difficult for the system to manage the current level of effluent. In recent years, the lack of resources has limited modernization and upgrading programs, further exacerbating system deficiencies.

Water supply investments

The primary concern at this point is the water intakes for the Central Waterworks. Complete elimination of the taking of surface water from the Vistula is anticipated; to be replaced by under-bed water taken with the aid of bank wells. The estimated future water requirements in the area of the Central Waterworks is 600 thousand m^3/d. Since the average capacity of one well is 50 thousand m^3/d, 12 wells must be constructed. Five of ten wells shall be located on the west bank of the river and the remaining 7 on the east bank. With the aim of completing a full ring water supply system, it is still necessary to construct about 20 more sections of primary network, with a total length of about 60 km. At least half of this should have a diameter of 800 mm and greater. The most important of these sections are:

- the main artery for Ursynow-Natolin from ul. Ondraszka-Chodkiewicza from ul. Raclawicka, and then to ul. Marynarska — partially commenced;

- the main artery for Wochy and Ursus from ul. Hynka and Lopuszaska from Al. Zwirki-Wigury to Al. Jerozolimskie and then to Ursus — also already commenced;

- the main artery from ul. Modlinska, enabling the full utilization of production capability of the Northern Waterworks;

- the main artery from ul. Powiecka-Patriotow which shall enable the development of the so-called Otwock band (currently no possibility exists for connecting new users).

It is also necessary to increase reserves of water in retention reservoirs. For this purpose reserves at the area station in Bialoleka must be doubled, from 60 to 120 thousand m^3. In addition the construction of the "Bemowo" area station with a retention reservoir having a capacity of 200 thousand m^3 must begin. The total reserves of water would then amount to about 460 thousand m^3 and would protect inhabitants against the effects of a system breakdown, as well as improve normal usage. Due to the high breakdown rate, the rate of replacements and repairs should also be increased.

Undoubtedly the most essential investments in waste-water collection and treatment is the construction of a sewage treatment plant for the west bank of the river. Plans call for building two independent sewage treatment systems. Completion of the project is expected in five years time. In phase I the throughput capacity will be 112 thousand m^3/d, though the final target throughput has still not been decided. Future projections call for an expansion of the system up to 160 to 230 thousands m^3/d.

For the northern part of the City the "Pancerz" treatment works is being planned, together with a 3 km extension of the Burakowski main drain and the construction of an overflow main drain from the treatment plant to the Vistula. A water treatment plant must also be constructed at Potok Sulewiecki to provide cleaning of storm-water runoff.

Additional pumping houses and main drains are needed to remove overloading problems. Currently, work is under way on the construction of a combined main drain along the Trasa Aninska, as well as in the region of "Okecie" airport. The construction of a second main drain is essential at Powile, directing sewage from the pumping station to the Burakowski main drain as well as taking some of the burden off the main sewage drain at ul. Patriotow in the Otwock area.

Moreover on the east side of the City it is essential to implement the following projects: the "Nowodwory" pumping station with a system of main drains, and the "Saska Kepa II" pumping station with main drains, reducing the load on the "Kondratowicz" main drain. The capacity of the pumping stations and main drains will enable the further development of the east bank of the Vistula, and the southern part of the City of Warsaw. These system additions will also help improve general sanitary conditions in the City.

Financial performance of water and water-water systems

The extent to which new investments in water and waste-water can be financed depends on the resources of the utility. This section examines the financial performance of the utility. As is the case in most countries, tariffs for water and wastewater are regulated. Fortunately, in constant prices, revenues to the MPWiK, the water and waste-water utility for the City of Warsaw, have increased dramatically between 1988 and 1992, rising by 121 percent. Table 6.3 presents MPWik revenues in constant 1988 prices. Water revenues account for approximately 55 percent, waste-water collection and treatment accounts for about 40 percent and the remaining 5 percent comes from revenues earned from supporting activities.

With the advent of reforms, more emphasis is now placed on generating revenues from water and waste-water treatment activities. In 1992, tariffs from users accounted for 98.5 percent of total operating revenues. Between 1988 and 1990, the portion of total revenues from domestic consumers increased from 40.1 to 47.3

Table 6.3

MPWiK revenues by source, 1988-1992, in constant 1988 PLZ (000,000)

	1988		1989		1990		1991		1992	
	PLZ	Strc (%)	PLZ	Strc (%)	PLZ	Strc (%)	PLZ	Strc (%)	PLZ	Strc (%)
Water Revenues	4,729	55.0	3,743	56.9	5,620	53.7	11,983	54.0	10,447	55.0
Wastewater Revenues	3,261	38.0	2,240	34.0	4,182	39.9	9,729	43.8	8,259	43.0
Other Revenues	606	7.0	599	9.1	672	6.4	478	2.2	289	2.0
Total	8,596	100.0	6,582	100.0	10,474	100.0	22,190	100.0	18,995	100.0

Source: Company Reports

percent, reflecting the decline in industrial users and a realignment of residential rates.

Between 1989 and 1992, the real cost of water production and distribution and waste-water collection and treatment increased by 51 percent. Costs of water and waste-water services are reported in Table 6.4. In 1989, water and waste-water revenues totaled Plz. 6,582,000,000 while total costs were Plz. 10,719,000,000. By 1992, revenues reached Plz. 18,995,000,000 and costs Plz. 16,168,000,000. The utility has successfully obtained sufficient rate increases in the past few years, allowing them to cover operating expenditures.

Historically, water and waste-water tariffs only covered between 60 and 70 percent of the costs of production. As illustrated in Table 6.5, the average price of a cubic meter of water has increased from Plz. 21.1 in 1988 to Plz. 57.7 in 1992 (1988 prices). In 1988 this was sufficient to cover 66 percent of the cost of water production. In 1990, tariffs increased and as a result nearly 85 percent of the actual cost of water production was recovered from rates. A similar pattern is exhibited for waste-water rates and costs. Recent trends in revenues and expenditures for 1991 and 1992, reveal that costs are now fully recovered. As illustrated in Table 6.4, charges for capital amortization have been doubled and rates have been moved upward to cover these higher charges.

Central heating

Like other cities in Central Europe, heat and hot water are provided by a central heating system. The City of Warsaw's system of five plants and distribution net-work of nearly 1400 kilometers is the largest in Poland, and one of the biggest in Central Europe. Current assessments indicate that the system does not provide an adequate level of energy to meet current demands. As of 1992, the production deficit is estimated to reach 8 percent of demand. The system is under considera-

Table 6.4
Cost of water and waste-water services (MPWiK), 1989-1992, in constant 1988 PZL (000,000)

Material Cost	1989	1990	1991	1992	Percent change 1988-
Amortization	1,553	4,670	6,512	4,797	208.9
Variable Costs	1,392	1,540	1,459	1,415	1.7
Energy	1,339	1,907	1,748	1,528	14.1
Transport	63	62	91	35	-44.4
Repairs	878	403	2,846	2,124	141.9
Other	535	390	475	394	-26.4
Subtotal	5,760	8,972	13,092	10,293	78.7
Non-Material Cost					
Wages and Salaries	2,509	1,569	2,305	2,419	-24.6
Wages Taxes	1,384	959	1,412	1,043	-24.6
Social &Housing Benefits	33	18	43	55	66.7
Other Special Funds	76	131	—	—	—
Bank Services	483	445	2	1	-99.8
Service Trips	11	18	15	11	0
Other	462	1,033	1,885	2,346	407.8
Subtotal	6,330	4,174	5,661	5,875	-7.2
Total Costs	10,719	13,145	18,754	16,168	50.8

Source: Company reports

ble stress and requires massive upgrading. This section describes the system, identifies critical problem areas and reviews financial performance.

Description of Warsaw's central heating system

The heating system in Warsaw has been in operation since 1953. The centralized heating system (SSC), is supplied from 5 basic sources: four district heating and power plants: District Heating and Power Plant (DHPP) Powile, DHPP Zeran, DHPP Siekierki, DHPP Kawczyn and one district heating plant — DHP Wola. The oldest heat source is the Powile condensation power station. As early as the 1950's DHPP Zeran was commissioned and in the 60's DHPP Siekierki came on line. The construction of DHP Wola was completed in 1982; DHPP Kawczyn was completed in the 1980s as well. Outside the City of Warsaw in the Ring of the metropolitan region, DHPP Pruszkow was constructed, supplying heat to the so-called Western

Table 6.5

Table 6.5
MPWiK estimated revenues and cost per cubic meter of output,
in 1988 constant PLZ

	1988	1989	1990	1991	1992
Water Produced (000,000) m3	223.6	222.7	221.9	197.9	181.2
Water Revenues (000,000)	4,729.0	3,743.0	5,620.0	11,983.0	10,447.0
Revenue / m3	21.1	16.8	25.3	60.6	57.7
Water Cost	7,155.0	6,013.0	6,590.0	—	—
Cost / m3	32.0	27.0	29.7	—	—
Cost Recovery %	65.9	62.2	85.2	—	—

	1988	1989	1990	1991	1992
Wastewater Produced (000,000) m3	23.3	242.2	238.1	207.8	200.7
Wastewater Revenues (000,000)	3,261.0	2,240.0	4,182.0	9,729.0	8,259.0
Revenue / m3	13.0	0.2	17.6	46.8	41.2
Wastewater Cost	4,623.0	3,245.0	4,905.0	—	—
Cost / m3	19.0	13.4	20.6	—	—
Cost Recovery %	70.5	68.7	85.4	—	—

Source: Company Reports

belt, Ursus, Piastow and part of the district of Wola. Heating is also provided in limited areas by the natural gas distribution system, though the vast majority of residents and establishments are served by the central heating system.

In the framework of these five main heat sources, five area subsystems were designated (see Map 6.3). During the extension of the heating system, network links were created improving supply and allowing the decommissioning of some sources during the summer period. Thus, during the heating season the system functions in five regions, and in the summer period hot water is only prepared at DHPP Zeran and DHPP Siekierki. However, the network is not a bi-directional ring, as is the water supply network. Thus it is not possible to have a so called "open system" with the sources operating in a shared network. This more flexible type of arrangement has been proposed for some time.

An additional element in the heat production system comes from industrial boiler houses which distribute excess heat to local residential buildings and institu-tions.There are also boiler houses run by housing cooperatives, schools, hospitals and other institutions and plants. Typically these are small boiler houses with limited range, and are not covered in the statistics. Given the decline in industrial activity in the region, the number of boilers providing waste heat has been falling, placing more demand on the principal heat system. For example, between 1990 and

MAP 6.3

Warsaw's Central Heating System

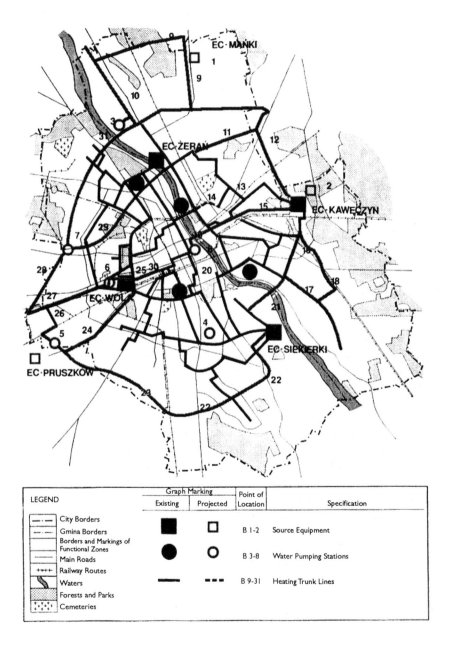

LEGEND	Graph Marking		Point of Location	Specification
	Existing	Projected		
—·— City Borders				
—··— Gmina Borders	■	□	B 1-2	Source Equipment
Borders and Markings of Functional Zones				
—— Main Roads	●	○	B 3-8	Water Pumping Stations
++++ Railway Routes				
Waters	——	---	B 9-31	Heating Trunk Lines
Forests and Parks				
Cemeteries				

1992, the number of boiler houses declined from 174 to 133. Boiler house declines have particularly adverse consequences for cities adjacent to Warsaw, such as Legionowo, Otwock, Karczew, Pruszkow, which have heavily relied on waste heat from industrial boilers.

The heat delivery system is operated by the Metropolitan Thermal Power Enterprise (SPEC). It purchases heat produced in the five DHPP's for resale. It exercises supervision over the local boiler houses and manages the municipal heating network.

The geographical range of the heating industry is assessed using data on cubic space and the number of buildings heated and included in the heat distribution network (hot water). These data are presented in Table 6.6. It is generally assessed that the City's heating system supplies about 1,680,000 inhabitants.

Table 6.6
Warsaw's central heating system, 1988-1993

	1988	1989	1990	1991	1992	1993
Produced Heat GJ	50,956.0	50,627.0	50,135.0	53,341.0	50,980.0	—
Percent to Residential	53.0%	50.8%	51.8%	54.6%	54.6%	—
Percent of Heat Loss	7.0%	6.9%	6.9%	—	—	—
Maximum Demand (MW)	—	—	6,854.9	6,778.6	6,582.6	6,488.8
Length of Heating Network (km)	—	—	1,422.5	1,428.2	1,389.8	—
Trunk Lines (km)	—	—	247.1	251.7	251.0	—
Distributor Lines (km)	—	—	576.0	566.0	546.3	—
Connectors (km)	—	—	599.4	610.5	592.5	—
Number of Boilers Used	—	—	174.0	164.0	133.0	—
Total Heat Supply Points	22,792.0	—	23,902.0	24,165.0	25,111.0	—
Cubic Space Heated (000)	199,000.0	201,728.0	204,114.0	203,920.0	199,388.0	—
Surface Area Heated (000)	38,600.0	39,192.0	39,801.0	39,924.0	38,731.0	—
Heat Deficit % of Average Demand	—	—	—	—	8.0	—

Source: Company Reports

The total length of the network supervised by SPEC amounted, at the end of 1992, to 1389.8 km, which includes the trunk network — 251.0 km. With the aim of maintaining the correct pressure parameters for the water in the network, there are three pumping stations. Satisfying the requirements of the general population for heat should be reviewed with respect to maintaining the heating parameters in premises (20 C$^\circ$) and the temperature of hot water (55 C$^\circ$).

The total heating power capacity of the five power plants, is 5,297 MW. Outside this system, heat is supplied by local boiler houses, providing 68.6 MW. The combined output level of these sources has been consistent in recent years. The amount of thermal energy supplied is utilized for heating and ventilation of premises (central heating); end-user hot water; and production purposes. Utilization by end-user is divided as follows: residential premises 58.5 percent; general and service premises 19.3 percent; industrial end-users and technical support 20.2 percent; and other end-users 2.0 percent.

The central heating requirements, dependent on external temperatures, comprise somewhat over half of the thermal energy sold. The thermal balance shows a deficit of thermal power in 1992 (see Table 6.6). Total average demand for the City amounted, in 1992, to 5,535 MW which suggests a deficit of around 8 percent. If calculated using maximum demand estimates, then this deficit would be even greater, 22.9 percent.

This deficit is not broken down by specific supply sources, however, there are several areas of the City which are poorly served. To correct this problem it is essential to construct new trunk pipes or reconstruct the existing ones. The next section surveys system level problems and issues.

Central heating problems

When compared to Western European levels, Warsaw's standard of heating services can only be regarded as poor. This is largely due to both the low efficiency of the system and the unjustified and artificially elevated demand for heat. Assessments of the system reveal the following problems:

- the City's heat generation system relies on old inefficient equipment and utilizes dirty fuels, leading to the high levels of harmful emissions produced by district heating plants;

- poor quality of water used in the heating system causes rapid corrosion and frequent breakdowns in the network;

- distribution system breakdowns, heat losses and aging production equipment lead to high production and distribution cost;

- the lack of meters limits the possibilities for regulating end-user demand; and

- the low level of thermal insulation in most buildings.

In general, Warsaw's heating system can be described as inflexible and highly ineffective. In addition, the system is old and not well maintained. Indicators of the system's physical condition are presented in Table 6.7. Capital investment is not taking place fast enough, and the condition of heat generation and distribution facilities is declining. Given the rate of network section replacement, the number of years it will take to completely overhaul the system ranges from 25 to 31 years. Given the problems with corrosion, this rate is far too slow, has resulted in the high rate of network breakdowns (2,100 to 3,200 per year). The relatively low rate of replacement has led to an increase in the age of the heating system's capital stock — the ratio of depreciated to total asset value has increased from 31.6 percent in 1988 to 37.5 percent in 1992, a 19 percent increase.

Table 6.7

Indicators and physical condition of Warsaw central heating system

	1989	1990	1991	1992
Length of New Network Constructed (km)	3.8	9.2	4.0	6.4
Length of Replaced Network (km)	51.2	51.3	46.0	55.0
New and Replaced Network to Total (%)	3.9	4.7	3.5	4.4
Replacement Cycle (years)	28.0	25.0	31.0	25.0
Number of Breakdowns / year	2,810.0	3,235.0	2,846.0	2,124.0
Breakdowns / km Network	2.0	2.3	2.0	2.0

Source: Company Reports

Upgrading the central heating system

The forecasts developed by the City of Warsaw's Development Department predict a continued deficit in thermal power supply. It is estimated that the deficit in the next few years will amount to about 1,350 MW. Heating planners fully recognize the scope and magnitude of problems and are now taking steps to correct them. A project to implement new sources of energy is currently under development by experts from Denmark and Germany, in cooperation with Warsaw's Energoprojekt. Initial acceptance has been gained for the construction of new power units at DHPP Kawczyn and DHPP Pruszkow II. Three power plants are scheduled to be built: between 1995-1998 — a power unit will be built at DHPP Kawczyn with an electrical output of 150MW and thermal power of 300 MW; during the 1997-2000 period a power unit will be constructed at DHPP Kawczyn; and after the year 2000, a power unit will be built at DHPP Pruszkow. These massive modernization and upgrading projects may threaten supply continuity. Upgrading projects scheduled between 1993-1998 at DHPP Zeran and DHPP Siekierki will significantly reduce power availability and widen the demand-supply deficit.

Improving overall hot water quality will be expensive, requiring the installation of water treatment equipment and the redesign of water intakes. It is estimated that total network modernization will cost approximately $1,000,000,000. A loan granted by the World Bank of 100 million US dollars is assessed as satisfying about 10 percent of the real network requirements.

In addition to new investments in thermal power generation, better system-level management is needed, including a system of quantitative control for heating factor throughput. Investments in thermal power sources must be accompanied by corresponding actions to improve the supply and delivery of thermal power to end-users. Distribution runs should be optimized and upgraded, using corrosive-resistant pre-insulated pipes.

Currently only 31 percent of the maximum on-line power is distributed to metered end-users. The remaining 69 percent of power is sold according to the volume of buildings (heat) and number of inhabitants (hot-water). Energy conservation activities should be undertaken, particularly the metering of the amount of heat flow supplied. With this in mind all supply points should be equipped with measuring meters. This should result in a reduction in network demand and utilization. The following measures should be taken to correct end-user demand and improve efficiency within the system:

- thermal junctions should be automated;

- metering of all end-users;

- unification of supplies (thermal exchange type junctions);

- modernization of the internal systems; and

- installation of radiator valves.

Financial situation

Table 6.8 presents operating costs of the Metropolitan Thermal Power Enterprise (SPEC) for 1988-1992. Real costs increased by 12 percent between 1988 and 1992. Real non-material costs declined and material costs increased by 14 percent. Generally it can be stated that during the period there were no fundamental changes in the structure of costs despite the rise in the level of costs due to inflation. The cost of thermal energy, which the enterprise acquires mainly from commercial suppliers, accounts for about 75 percent of total costs. The enterprise fulfills the functions of energy delivery and distribution, and largely avoids the realm of energy production.

The financial performance of SPEC is presented in Table 6.9. SPEC is quite profitable when compared to other communal utilities. In 1993, SPEC's profitability fell due to the introduction of strong restrictions on energy prices by the Ministry of Finance. Given the scale of modernization projects needed to upgrade the City's central heating system, Ministry of Finance limitations on tariffs suggest that either the investments will be stalled or central government subsidies must rise.

Municipal transport services

By international standards, Warsaw has one of the best urban transportation systems in Europe. The ratio of transit trips to the population, is very high averaging nearly 1:1. The transportation system is extensive, with 1.65 meters of network per capita. The extent of the network, along with a low vehicle ownership level (192 vehicles per 1000 persons), has kept the transit trip ratio high. The ratio is set

Table 6.8
Central heating costs, in constant 1988 prices, 1988-1992

Costs according to type	1988 mil-lions of zlotys	1988 per-cen-tage	1989 mil-lions of zlotys	1989 per-cen-tage	1990 mil-lions of zlotys	1990 per-cen-tage	1991 mil-lions of zlotys	1991 per-cen-tage	1992 mil-lions of zlotys	1992 per-cen-tage
Amortization	3,307	5.4	1,587	3.1	3,530	4.9	5,096	6.5	3,732	5.5
Materials and consumables	3,068	5.1	1,751	3.5	3,336	4.6	4,160	5.3	3,491	5.1
Energy	46,204	72.9	35,502	0.7	55,042	76.2	59,651	75.5	51,771	76.1
Outside services	—	—	0	0.0	0	0.0	5	0.0	8	0.0
Transport services	228	0.4	135	0.3	255	0.4	641	0.8	568	0.8
Renovation services	1,670	2.8	3,026	5.8	3,440	4.8	3,470	4.4	1,799	2.6
Other material services	1,112	1.8	431	0.8	1,515	2.1	1,226	1.5	1,975	2.9
Material costs in total	55,589	91.6	43,667	86.5	67,118	93	7,425	94	63,344	93.1
Wages and salaries	2,731	4.5	3,269	6.5	2,325	3.2	2,571	3.3	2,716	4.0
Income tax and NI contributions	1,523	2.5	1,817	3.6	464	0.6	617	2.0	1,160	1.7
Deductions for social &	—	—	0	0.0	960	1.3	48	0.1	59	0.1
Other deductions for special funds	—	—	0	0.0	0	0.0	0	0.0	0	0.0
Banking services	868	1.4	1,740	3.4	20	0.1	3	0.0	3	0.0
Official travel	—	—	0	0.0	264	0.4	17	0.0	34	0.0
Taxes & other non-material services	—	—	0	0.0	0	0.0	504	0.6	701	1.0
Non-material costs in total	5,122	8.4	6,827	13.2	5,083	7.0	4,704	6.0	4,673	6.9
Total costs	60,711	100	50,467	100.	72,201	100	78,954	100	68,017	100

Source: Company Reports

Table 6.9
District heating profit and loss, 1988-1992, in constant 1988 (000,000) zlotys

	1988	1989	1990	1991	1992
Total Revenues	63,369	61,536	83,286	93,529	75,667
Total Costs	60,711	50,493	70,990	76,910	65,894
Accumulation of Capital	4,658	11,042	12,296	16,619	9,773
Subsidies	318	366	456	366	127
Accumulation of Capital with Subsidies	4,976	11,408	12,752	16,985	9,900
Balance of Extraordinary Profits & Loss	30	33	280	-1,538	-183
Value of Basic Production Sales	—	59,956	81,432	92,576	74,206
Costs	—	48,910	69,218	76,077	64,687
Accumulation of Capital	—	10,971	12,214	16,499	9,519
Subsidies	—	366	456	366	127
Accumulation of Capital with Subsidies	—	11,337	12,670	16,865	9,646
Gross Profit as a % of Total Revenues	7.9	18.7	16.1	16.3	13.0
Net Profit as a % of Total Revenues	2.4	9.4	6.4	5.7	7.3

Source: Company Reports

139

to decline, as the private vehicle ownership level has been rising rapidly in recent years. Despite the excellent coverage of the City's system, financial pressures are degrading service quality. Fleet age and breakdowns are rising. Subsidies to transit have been cut, and fares have been increased. In 1989, farebox revenues accounted for 56 percent of operating costs, comparable with German cities. By 1992, fares had risen dramatically, covering nearly 80 percent of total operating costs. This section describes Warsaw's transportation system, identifies problems and issues and reviews financial trends.

Description of Warsaw's transit system

Public transport service in the City is currently comprised of three linked subsystems: bus, tramway and trolley-bus lines. Data concerning the public transport network is presented in Table 6.10. A total of 192 lines were operating in 1993. With 153 routes, buses are the main means of transport. The geographical range of bus lines covers the City as well as neighboring districts (gminas). Between 1988 and 1993, the total number of bus routes declined by 30, because of continuous revision of the route structure. Night-time bus service did not decline during the period under discussion.

There are 26 tram lines operating in the City. Most of the lines parallel heavily trafficked main routes. The number of tram routes declined by four between 1988 and 1992, reflecting the conversion of some routes to bus lines.

Trolley-bus transport plays a minor role in the City. There is only one 12.9 km long trolley-bus line connecting Dworzec Poludniowy with the town of Piaseczno. No changes are planned in this portion of the system.

One underground line, extending from the southern district of the City (Ursynow-Natolin) to the center is under construction. It is expected that when the underground line is put into service in 1994, certain bus lines will be withdrawn.

The Municipal Transport Managing Board (Zarzad Transportu Miejskiego, ZTM) coordinates the management of public transport services. The Municipal Transport Company (MZK), formerly a state company which used to be the key unit in the structure of the Municipal Transport Managing Board (ZTM), was transformed into a state budget establishment in mid-1992. On April 1st, 1994 the Municipal Transport Company (MZK) was divided into two companies — the Municipal Bus Service Company (including the trolley-bus line) and Warsaw Trams (TW). This division was undertaken so that the bus company may be privatized.

Since 1992, 24 private buses running along 5 peripheral lines have been providing services to the population. Carriers compete for contracts through competitive tenders. This year proposals were invited for an additional 50 buses. Further tenders will be invited to operate 80 buses in the years 1995-1997. Tenders invited by City Authorities can be submitted by the Municipal Bus Service Company (MZA) as well as by private carriers. Should demand for bus services rise, additional private tenders will be needed.

Table 6.10 (part 1 of 2)
City communications network of Warsaw in 1988-1993

	1988		1989		1990	
Type of Lines	Num	Strc (%)	Num	Strc (%)	Num	Strc (%)
Number of Lines	226	100.0	222	100.0	221	100.0
Bus Lines (Day)	183	81.0	177	79.7	175	79.2
Bus Lines (Night)	12	5.3	12	5.4	12	5.4
Tram Lines	30	13.3	32	14.4	32	14.5
Trolleybus Lines (Day)	1	0.4	1	0.5	1	0.5
Trolleybus Lines (Night)	—	—	—	—	1	0.5
Length of Lines (km)	2,717	100.0	2,721	100.3	2,764	100.0
including: bus routes	2,281	84.0	2,250	83.0	2,291	82.9
Tram Routes	432	15.9	458	16.9	460	16.6
Trolley routes	13	0.5	13	0.5	13	0.5
Length of Routes in Use (km)	918	100.0	932	100.0	942	100.0
including: bus routes	794	86.5	803	86.2	814	86.4
Tram Routes	111	12.1	116	12.4	115	12.2
Trolley routes	13	1.4	13	1.4	13	1.4

Source: Company Reports

Transit fleet data are presented in Table 6.11. Over the past five years, Warsaw's transportation fleet has declined from 2,766 to 2,623, a 5.2 percent decline. The bulk of the decline has been in the bus fleet, decreasing from 1,826 in 1988 to 1,684 in 1993. Trams have decreased from 908 to 900, and trolley buses have increased from 32 to 39.

Two measures of distance covered by the fleet are presented in Table 6.11. The first measure records the actual kilometers traveled per vehicle per year. The second measure weights kilometer distance traveled according to the level of occupancy. The standard occupancy of 80 passengers is set as the norm. Vehicles with more than 80 passengers are proportionately credited with greater distance. For example, a vehicle with 120 passengers traveling 10 kilometers is credited with 15 kilometers.

Regardless of the measure used, vehicle kilometers traveled has declined on all routes between 1988 and 1993. This has been caused by many factors, among them: the impoverishment of society, rising unemployment, and the increase in the price of tickets (making personal means of transport more economically competitive).

Table 6.10 (part 2 of 2)
City communications network of Warsaw in 1988-1993

Type of Lines	1991 Num	1991 Strc (%)	1992 Num	1992 Strc (%)	1993 Num	1993 Strc (%)
Number of Lines	209	100.0	193	100.0	192	100.0
Bus Lines (Day)	165	78.9	156	80.8	153	79.7
Bus Lines (Night)	12	5.7	11	5.7	11	5.7
Tram Lines	30	14.4	24	12.4	26	13.5
Trolleybus Lines (Day)	1	0.5	1	0.5	1	0.5
Trolleybus Lines (Night)	1	0.5	1	0.5	1	0.5
Length of Lines (km)	2,777	100.0	2,693	100.0	2,715	100.0
including: bus routes	2,304	83.0	2,253	83.7	2,289	84.3
Tram Routes	460	16.6	427	15.9	413	15.2
Trolley routes	13	0.5	13	0.5	13	0.5
Length of Routes in Use (km)	938	100.0	944	100.0	938	100.0
including: bus routes	810	86.4	812	86.0	806	85.9
Tram Routes	115	12.3	119	12.6	119	12.7
Trolley routes	13	1.4	13	1.4	13	1.4

Source: Company Reports

Technical and operational indicators

Table 6.12 illustrates trends in the operational readiness of the fleet. A figure of 100 would mean that all vehicles are ready for service. A level of 85 percent means that 15 percent of the fleet is out of service.

The indicator of technical readiness of transport stock is treated as a measure to evaluate the performance of technical back-up facilities of the company, that is workshops and depots. The shorter it takes to wait for repairs and the faster they are carried out, and the better the quality of these repairs — the higher the index. Figures presented in Table 6.12 show that indicators of technical readiness of transport stock for buses and trams have remained at a reasonably high, constant level, and for trolley-buses, conditions have improved. The condition of transport stock can also be measured by means of the number of cars withdrawn from service per 10,000 km of service (failure frequency). This indicator is the lowest for trams, and generally shows a decreasing tendency. In 1993, buses had the highest failure rate.

Another technical and operational indicator, the indicator of transport stock utilization, makes it possible to get an idea of what percentage of carriages are in service and what percentage has come to a standstill. Apart from standstills caused by repairs and damage mentioned above, it also includes standstills caused by lack of demand (irregularity) or lack of operating personnel. This indicator is consistently lower than the indicator of technical readiness for the fleet. Except for trolley-buses, the utilization factor showed a slight rising tendency during the 1988 to 1993 period. The intensity of work performed by public transport stock can also be measured by the indicator of the average daily "in service" time of fleet vehicles, expressed in hours. This indicator is approximately the same for all routes and remained quite stable during the period analyzed, averaging between 14 and 15 hours per day.

The "operational speed" indicates the intensity of work of the traffic stock enroute. It's level depends on the technical condition of transport stock, distance between stops, duration of parking at final stops, and most of all, traffic on particular routes. The speed achieved in suburban zones is higher than in the center of the City, and that is why the highest indicators are observed on trolley-bus lines. Generally, owing to the worsening conditions enroute and rising overcrowding of streets, a constant fall in average operational speed is observed during the 1988-1993 period. The sharpest fall during the period was on trolley-bus lines. Despite conditions in speed, punctuality has improved. Between 1992 and 1993, the percentage of buses, trams and trolley-buses arriving at stops on time increased by over 40 percent.

Generally speaking, both favorable and negative trends took place in the period analyzed. Favorable trends include the improvement of the technical readiness, transport stock utilization, and punctuality indicators. The most obvious negative trend was the fall in average operational speed, making the average duration of a ride longer.

Future investment needs

In Warsaw, bus transport is based mainly on Hungarian IKARUS buses. In the years 1992-1993 the purchase of Polish buses built by JELCZ was resumed. The acquisition of new transport stock has been insufficient for a long time. The demand for new units, 10 percent of inventory transport stock, amounts to 160-170 buses in the case of the Municipal Transport Company (MZK). The actual purchase of transport stock (see Table 6.13) does not exceed 40 percent of demand, which results in cars being kept in service for 11-12 years or longer, increasing the average age of transport stock. Trends in real investments in rolling stock indicate that fleet purchases are declining. In constant 1988 prices, purchases declined by 43 percent between 1988 and 1992.

To make the best of a poor situation, MZK undertakes other activities in order to maintain the level of transport services. For example, in 1992 the company bought 30, brand-new coachworks for buses and 10 coachworks for articulated buses which are used in all-car repairs (general overhauls). Parts from these coachworks will help prolong the service life of repaired cars. Due to high customs duties this method was abandoned in 1993. However, in 1993 new spare parts for

Table 6.11 (part 1 of 2)
Fleet inventory and kilometers traveled in Warsaw, 1988-1993

Type of Fleet	1988		1989		1990	
	Num	Strc (%)	Num	Strc (%)	Num	Strc (%)
State of Fleet Inventory as of December 31	2,766	100.0	2,731	100.0	2,670	100.0
Buses	1,826	66.0	1,793	65.7	1,732	64.9
Tramways	908	32.8	908	33.2	908	34.0
Trolley buses	32	1.2	30	1.1	30	1.1
Number of Real Traveled km per car, overall in millions	155.9	100.0	144.2	100.0	147.7	100.0
Buses	110.3	70.8	98.9	68.6	102.0	69.1
Tramways	43.1	27.6	43.6	30.2	43.7	29.6
Trolley buses	2.2	1.4	1.5	1.0	1.7	1.2
Outside Fleet	0.3	0.2	0.2	0.1	0.3	0.2
Number of Traveled km per car according to MZK calculations overall in millions	250.2	100.0	234.1	100.0	240.3	100.0
Buses	180.1	72.0	164.1	70.1	169.9	70.7
Tramways	67.2	26.9	68.0	29.0	68.2	28.4
Trolley buses	2.9	1.2	2.0	0.9	2.2	0.9
Estimated number of transported passengers in millions					1,312.4	

Source: Company Reports

buses were purchased from the Hungarian company IKARUS. These parts were used to assemble 60 buses and several articulated buses. This enabled a savings of about PLZ 650 million per bus and about Plz. 1 billion per articulated bus.

Tram transport is based on 13N and 105N type carriages produced in Poland by the production plant "Konstal" in Chorzów. The service life of tramway stock is 16.7 years (the annual rate of depreciation — 6 percent). The 64.2 percent of the stock which was mentioned above has exceeded its service life. Maintaining present service levels, which are currently insufficient to satisfy demand, will mean that some of 13N type carriages will have to be kept in service until the year 2000. At that point they will be 40 years old, and will have exceeded the deprecation period by three times. Between 1990 and 1992, deliveries of new stock did not keep pace with withdrawals from service. Estimates prepared by MZA and Warsaw Trams indicate that in order to maintain and upgrade their fleets, 90 buses, 30 articulated

Type of Fleet	1991 Num	1991 Strc (%)	1992 Num	1992 Strc (%)	1993 Num	1993 Strc (%)
State of Fleet Inventory as of December 31	2,636	100.0	2,593	100.0	2,623	100.0
Buses	1,696	64.3	1,654	63.8	1,684	64.2
Tramways	908	34.4	900	34.7	900	34.3
Trolley buses	32	1.2	39	1.5	39	1.5
Number of Real Traveled km per car, overall in millions	137.0	100.0	140.6	100.0	140.2	100.0
Buses	95.7	69.9	98.4	70.0	98.5	70.3
Tramways	39.2	28.6	39.8	28.3	39.6	28.2
Trolley buses	1.7	1.2	1.9	1.4	1.9	1.4
Outside Fleet	0.4	0.3	0.5	0.4	0.2	0.1
Number of Traveled km per car according to MZK calculations overall in millions	221.9	100.0	226.0	100.0	224.4	100.0
Buses	158.5	71.4	161.6	71.5	160.4	71.5
Tramways	61.2	27.6	62.0	27.4	61.8	27.5
Trolley buses	2.2	1.0	2.4	1.1	2.2	1.0
Estimated number of transported passengers in millions	1,210.4		1,232.0		1,222.0	

Source: Company Reports

buses, and 40 tram cars need to be purchased. As of 1993, costs for these units are Plz. 392 billion for MZA and Plz. 180 billion for Warsaw Trams.

Financial resources allocated in 1993 enable the company to purchase about 70 buses and about 23 tramway cars. Thus a little more than 50 percent of demand can be met. A similar situation applies to major repairs (general overhaul) of tramway track. About 20 km of single track needs repairing and the cost of the repair is evaluated at Plz. 227 billion. Financial resources allocated make it possible to repair only 12 km of track.

Financial situation

Repair and maintenance expenses constitute the biggest share of total costs. As far as buses are concerned, the cost of repairs and maintenance makes up approximately

Table 6.12
Exploitation ratios of the city (MZK) transportation fleet, 1988-1993

Kinds of Ratios	1988	1989	1990	1991	1992	1993
Ratio of Technical Preparedness of the Fleet						
Buses	0.857	0.863	0.87	0.879	0.871	0.864
Tramways	0.804	0.82	0.835	0.816	0.836	0.831
Trolley buses	0.764	0.719	0.861	0.915	0.877	0.924
Ratio of Utilization of the Fleet						
Buses	0.669	0.653	0.718	0.693	0.733	0.732
Tramways	0.658	0.683	0.705	0.656	0.68	0.678
Trolley buses	0.587	0.437	0.61	0.603	0.539	0.568
Number of Repairs and Breakdowns						
Buses	5.1	4.9	4.4	4.4	3.7	4.1
Tramways	3.2	1.6	1.6	1.6	1.4	1.5
Trolley buses	7.1	7.7	3.3	4.4	3.6	3

Source: Company Reports

one-third of total cost. In the case of trams and trolley-buses it amounts to even more — about 50 percent of the total cost. Table 6.14 presents the transit cost structure.

Between 1988 and 1992 the cost of one-carriage-kilometer for particular vehicles has undergone change. In 1988-1993 the cost of one-carriage-kilometer in tram service was the highest, which was related to the high failure frequency of this system. Unit costs for buses and trolley-buses are lower and similar to each other (see Table 6.15). The lowest unit cost is observed in the case of outside track, as private carriers do not bear administrative costs and very often do not have technical or repair back-up facilities. In real terms, transport costs are rising. Bus service costs per kilometer have increased by 21 percent between 1988 and 1992. Tram costs are up by 17 percent. Trolley-bus service increased by 4.2 percent between 1990 and 1992.

MZK's need for budget subsidies is declining. The ratio of subsidies from city budget system expenses is going down, as tariffs are raised. Table 6.16 reports ffinancial performance of MZK. In 1989 subsidies constituted 79.0 percent of operating costs, and by 1992 that percentage had fallen to 30.4. The year 1993 witnessed the balance of general costs and incomes, and subsidies granted were small.

Roads

On the basis of an agreement made June 4, 1993 between the Warsaw Voivodship and the City of Warsaw, the City took over responsibility for roads and traffic control in the administrative boundaries of the City of Warsaw. In particular, local

Table 6.13

Fixed assets and investment in transportation fleet, in constant 1988 zlotys

Specification	1988	1989	1990	1991	1992
Gross Value of Fixed Assets in mld zloty	44.8	18.6	38.0	66.5	58.6
Net value of fixed assets in mld zloty	23.8	10.9	19.8	30.6	26.3
Depreciation Ratio in %	46.9	41.1	47.8	54.0	55.1
Overall Investment Expenditures in mln zloty	4.6	6.3	1.8	2.5	2.1
Buses	2.5	3.3	0.7	1.0	1.3
Tramway and Trolley Buses	2.1	3.0	1.1	1.6	0.8
Relation of Investment Expenditures to Gross Value of fixed Assets = Renewal co-factor in percentage	1.0	3.4	0.5	0.4	0.4
Overall Quantity of Purchased Fleet	131.0	180.0	128.0	98.0	48.0
Buses	94.0	136.0	90.0	52.0	17.0
Tramways	37.0	32.0	38.0	38.0	12.0
Trolley buses		12.0		8.0	19.0
Overall Costs of Fleet Purchases in mln zloty	2.1	2.7	3.1	2.7	1.2
Buses	1.5	2.0	2.3	1.5	0.8
Tramways	0.6	0.5	0.8	1.0	0.3
Trolley buses		0.1	0.0	0.1	0.1

Source: Company Reports

traffic control was extended to national and regional roads. To carry out its new tasks, the City set up a government body called the Bureau of City Roads (ZDM).

The total length of roads under the administration of ZDM is 675 kilometers, of which 203 kilometers (30 percent) constitute national roads, and 472 kilometer (70 percent) are regional (voivodship) roads. Detailed data is presented in Table 6.17. Nearly all these roads are paved. Their total surface area is 7,877,000 square meters, 3,444,500 square meters of which belong to national roads (43.7 percent) and 4,432,500 square meters to regional roads (56.3 percent). Map 6.4 outlines the road network of the Warsaw metropolitan region.

MAP 6.4

Warsaw's Road and Street System

LEGEND	Graph Marking		Point of Location	Specification
	Existing	Projected		
City Borders			A 1	Motorway
Gmina Borders			A 2-6	Express Routes
Borders and Markings of Functional Zones			A 7-16	Main Transit Routes
Main Roads			A 17	Main Area Routes
Railway Routes			A 18-40	Cumulative Transit Streets
Waters			A 41-81	Cumulative Area Streets
Forests and Parks				
Cemeteries				

Table 6.14
Cost structure of basic Warsaw transit operations, 1988-1992, in percent

Elements of costs	1988	1989	1990	1991	1992
Buses	100	100	100	100	100
Fuel	17.5	15.3	19.3	16	16.5
Repair & Upkeep	32.2	32.8	32.6	32.5	34.4
Wages & Surcharges	21	27.9	20.8	25.4 *	26.8
Departmental Costs	6.8	6.6	5.8	8.5	10
Plant-wide Costs	7.3	7.4	6.5	4.5	3.7
Amortization	7.3	3.6	6.6	4.2	
Remaining Costs	6.9	6.3	8.2	8.9	8.6
Tramways	100	100	100	100	100
Energy	13.6	15.4	22.2	15.5	13.7
Repair & Upkeep	57.1	53.1	48.8	56.7	61.6
Wages & Surcharges	11.4	16.1	10.8	12	13
Departmental Costs	3.9	3.9	3	4.7	5.1
Plant-wide Costs	7.1	7.4	6.6	3.8	2.9
Amortization	4.9	2.2	5.8	3.5	
Remaining Costs	2.1	1.9	2.8	3.8	3.7
Trolley buses	100	100	100	100	100
Energy	7.8	8.3	15.3	12.3	10.6
Repair & Upkeep	53.5	52	46.1	45.9	48
Wages & Surcharges	12.9	17.6	13.8	18.7	22.1
Departmental Costs	4.1	4.3	3.9	7.2	8.7
Plant-wide Costs	7.4	7.3	6.6	4.5	3.7
Amortization	8.3	4.5	9	5.8	
Remaining Costs	6	6	5.3	5.16	6.9

Source: Company Reports

* with a bonus for fuel savings

The Bureau of City Roads (ZDM) is furthermore responsible for 233 structures, including: 31 bridges; 73 viaducts; 37 pedestrian passages; 25 breakwaters; 51 pedestrian bridges; 2 exit ramps; 13 tunnels; one escalator and 30 public squares.

In accord with the agreement, ZDM also took control of property that has until now been used by the Directorate of Voivodship Urban Roads. This property con-

Table 6.15
Cost structure of the Warsaw transit system, 1988-1992, in percent

Type of Costs	1988	1989	1990	1991	1992
Buses	100.0	100.0	100.0	—	—
Variable Costs Depending on No. of km Traveled per Car	55.8	53.9	58.0	—	—
Fixed Costs Depending on No. of Hours in Usage per Car	36.1	42.3	34.2	—	—
Fixed Costs Depending on No. of Cars in Fleet	8.1	2.8	7.8	—	—
Tramways	100.0	100.0	100.0	—	—
Variable Costs Depending on No. of km Traveled per Car	72.3	70.2	73.1	—	—
Fixed Costs Depending on No. of Hours in Usage per Car	22.4	27.4	20.4	—	—
Fixed Costs Depending on No. of Cars in Fleet	2.8	1.4	3.3	—	—
Fixed Costs Depending on the Length of Routes in Use	2.5	1.0	3.2	—	—
Trolley buses	100.0	100.0	100.0	—	—
Variable Costs	66.2	66.0	65.6	—	—
Fixed Costs Depending on No. of Hours in Usage per Car	23.9	29.3	24.4	—	—
Fixed Costs Depending on No. of Cars in Fleet	4.4	2.4	2.0	—	—
Fixed Costs Depending on the Length of Routes in Use	4.3	2.3	8.0	—	—
Cost of 1 km Traveled per Car in zl per Car-km	178.0	175.6	170.5	193.9	211.7
Buses	170.0	171.1	167.8	183.2	200.9
Tramways	177.0	170.4	176.1	219.7	240.2
Trolley buses	262.0	275.9	201.0	221.2	197.8
Outside Fleet	—	—	124.8	120.4	129.9

Source: Company Reports

sisted of 16 bases, on the grounds of which were located 77 buildings, mainly in poor condition.

Roadway conditions

In general, the condition of roads in the City of Warsaw is highly unsatisfactory. According to ZDM's estimates: only about 2.4 million square meters, or about 30 percent of the overall road surface is in good to excellent condition and is not in need of repair. About five million square meters, 64 percent of the total roadway system must be completely rebuilt because of its high level of deterioration. The remaining 0.5 million square meters of roads are in need of general repairs.

The condition of roadway structures is similarly bad. Of the 233 structures mentioned above: eleven are dangerous and require immediate repair; ten are rapidly deteriorating and need to be secured; four elements are obsolete and require constant monitoring and repair; and seven elements pose traffic hazards due to their poor condition. All together, therefore, 32 structures — mainly bridges and viaducts — need substantial expenditures to upgrade their condition. The remaining structures need substantial expenditures for ongoing utilization.

Table 6.16
Financial performance of MZK operations for 1989-1992,
in constant 1988 PLZ (000,000)

Specification	1989	1990	1991	1992
Total Revenues	18,409	21,359	23,852	29,251
Total Expenditures	32,977	32,761	32,727	36,622
Total Gross Income	-14,568	-11,402	-8,874	-7,371
Subsidy Received	20,057	17,011	9,290	8,874
Total Gross Income & Subsidies	5,761	5,750	304	1,503
Balance of Unforeseen Losses & Profits	-10	-121	-161	-296
Revenues from Operations	9,638	12,298	16,942	22,061
Total Operating Costs	25,398	25,196	26,557	29,174
Gross Operating Income	-15,761	-12,897	-9,614	-7,698
Subsidy Received	20,057	17,011	9,290	8,874
Gross Operating Incomes & Subsidies	4,296	4,114	-811	1,176
Subsidy as a Percent of Operating Costs	79.0%	67.5%	35.0%	30.4%
Subsidy as a Percent of Total Expenditures	60.8%	51.9%	28.4%	24.2%
Revenues per km of Services (PLZ)	67	83	124	157
Operation Costs per km of Services (PLZ)	176	171	194	208

Source: Economic Analysis Unit

Table 6.17
Lengths and surface areas of national and voivodship roads in Warsaw,
by type of surface, 1993

Type of surface	National		Voivodship	
	Length km	Area sq.meters ('000)	Length km	Area sq.meters ('000)
Hard-surface roads, including:	203.0	3,444.5	469.0	4,432.5
Road-metal	—	—	0.3	1.4
Cobble-stone	—	—	5.5	32.3
Concrete	0.1	0.4	0.4	8.0
Mixed mineral-asphalt				
All together	199.1	3,403.7	450.3	4,267.2
Poured asphalt only	77.7	1,096.8	210.1	1,917.2
Paving bricks, stone-concrete	3.8	40.4	12.5	123.6
Dirt roads, including:	—	—	3.0	905.0
Improved (cinder, gravel, etc.)	—	—	2.3	6.7
Unimproved (natural)	—	—	0.7	2.8
Total	203.0	3,444.5	472.0	4,442.0

Source: Economic Analysis Unit

The ZDW, as a government body, is closely tied to the City's budgetary plans. In 1993, it received 441,709 million zlotys for its activities: 208,950 million zlotys (47.3 percent) for upkeep and repair of streets, and 232,759 million zlotys (52.7 percent) for investment projects. In addition, ZDM earns revenue from various activities, which in 1993 totaled 13,410 million zlotys. This revenue was handed over to the City. Of the ZDM's budget, only Plz. 3,380,000,000 came from parking and lease income in 1993.

The relatively short period of time during which ZDM has functioned does not allow a more complete evaluation of its operations. In general, however, it should be stated that the scale of neglect and needs in the area of repair work and investment projects is enormous. Substantially more resources need to be generated to cover the costs of repairs and upgrading.

Sanitation services

The City of Warsaw has responsibility for city cleaning, including:

- collecting, removing, and disposing of solid waste;

- removing liquid waste from areas not served by sewers and pouring it into the sewer system; and

- maintaining cleanliness and order in public areas (streets, squares, and parks).

These services are rendered by the City Sanitation Works (MZO) (since July 1, 1991 — a government body belonging to the City), as well as by a number of private firms.

MZO removes solid wastes from premises as well as from streets and squares. The share of waste from premises exceeds 90 percent of the total amount of waste removed. Somewhat over half of the areas covered by waste removal services are residential sections of the City. Map 6.5 illustrates the waste collection system of the Warsaw metropolitan region. The MZO's service area is declining as private vendors increase their level of activity in the region.

Refuse is collected in various types of containers, the number of which continually changes, and is thus difficult to ascertain. A specialized fleet of vehicles is used to remove refuse from premises, and a general vehicle fleet is used for removal from streets and squares.

According to MZO data, about 470 to 500 thousand metric tons of solid waste is removed from Metropolitan Warsaw every year. This amount is systematically rising. Research conducted in three districts of Warsaw — Zoliborz, Northern Praga, and Mokotow — indicate that the rate of waste collection increased during the period 1991 to 1992 from 1.1 cubic meters per resident per year to 1.55 cubic

MAP 6.5

Warsaw's Waste Collection System

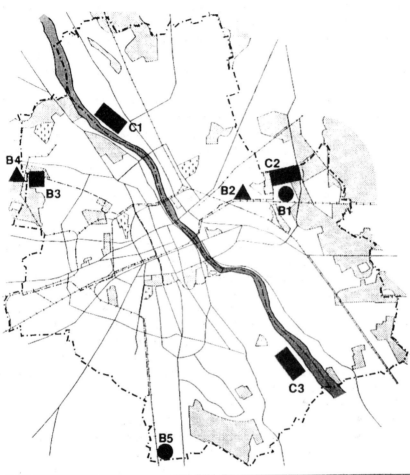

LEGEND	Graph Marking	Point of Location	Specification
— · — City Borders	■	B 3	Solid Waste Composting Stations
— · · — Gmina Borders	●	B 1,5	Overloading Stations
------- Borders/Markings of Functional Zones	▲	B 2,4	Incinerating Plants
——— Main Roads	▬	C 1-3	Storage of Thermal-Electric Power Plant Wastes
+++ Railway Routes			
Waters			
Forests and Parks			
Cemeteries			

meters. According to estimates made by the Dutch firm, Haskoning, the amount of solid waste collected will increase 3 percent a year until the year 2000.

Solid waste is transported by MZO to Lubna (36 kilometers from the city center), where the only operational municipal garbage dump is located. This garbage dump occupies an area of 14 hectares. Conditions there have been growing steadily worse over the last few years, because of the exhaustion of its holding capacity and associated harmful environmental effects. In its present form, it will be usable for only another three to four years. The situation is ameliorated, somewhat, by the fact that private waste removal firms make use of existing garbage dumps in Pruszkow and Wolomin.

A further problem is the proper disposal of solid waste. Owing to the fact that refuse in Warsaw contain large amounts of organic substances and has low fuel value, the most advantageous current method of neutralizing the waste is composting. At present, about 12 percent of the garbage produced in Wola and Zoliborz is composted. In 1992, a total of 1,380 metric tons of enhanced compost was produced, 200 tons of which was given away, and 1,100 tons of which was sold at the price of 60,000 zlotys a ton. Tests indicate that the compost is of good quality and does not contain heavy metals. Nonetheless, there are problems with selling it. Moreover, the use of DANO waste processing technology leaves behind about 30 percent which is not fit for composting, and must be taken to appropriate waste sites. The neighboring garbage dump at Radiowo is used for this purpose.

In the City of Warsaw, the organized removal of water-borne pollutants covers all residential and other buildings not connected to the sewer system and that have sealed collection tanks. The removal of the waste, carried out by MZO vehicles, has declined between 1988 and 1992, due to growing competition from private firms and from the growth of the sewer system. In 1992, about 60 percent of water-borne wastes were removed by MZO, while the remainder was removed by private firms. About 160,000 residents — over 6 percent of the total population of the City — were served in this fashion.

Water-borne wastes are poured into three filtration stations located in various points on the periphery of the City of Warsaw. There are too few of these points, however, resulting in long transport distances. Moreover, the condition of these points is so bad that they should not be utilized. Programs aimed at improving condition, have been planned for many years, but have not been realized because of a lack of funds.

MZO also renders services in the area of year-round cleaning of streets and squares, maintenance of public toilets, and the removal of automobile wrecks. The total street and square surface area cleaned by MZO has remained consistent over the past five years. The street cleaning process is conducted by mechanical equipment. The problem of removing automobile wrecks has not yet been solved. MZO does not have the necessary transportation equipment. There is also a lack of presses for crushing wrecks before sending them to steel plants.

MZO's service capacity depends to a large degree on the quantity of vehicles it possesses and the degree of wear and tear on those vehicles. Table 6.18 provides

Table 6.18
MZO fleet description, 1989-1992

	1989		1990		1991		1992	
	Num	Struct %	Num	Struct %	Num	Struct %	Num	Struct %
Waste Collection Vehicles	1520	100	1491	100	1402	100	990	100
Solid Waste	478	31.4	509	34.1	493	35.2	386	39
Fluid Waste	335	22	326	21.9	290	20.7	143	14.4
Index of technical readiness of vehicles								
For the collection of solid waste	0.692		0.736		0.764		0.753	
For the collection of fluid waste	0.661		0.676		0.647		0.564	
Index of vehicle utilization								
For the collection of solid waste	0.511		0.553		0.553		0.53	
For the collection of fluid waste	0.48		0.459		0.402		0.392	

Source: Economic Analysis Unit

an overview of MZO's fleet. The size of the fleet systematically declined between 1988 and 1992, unfortunately effecting specialized equipment (garbage compactor trucks) in particular. In the context of systematically increasing amounts of waste, this is a troublesome development.

Indices of utilization of the fleet and its readiness are low. This is a result of the high level of wear and tear of MZO's fixed assets and the exclusion from use of a large part of the fleet due to breakdowns. The average age of the fleet's vehicles is close to 8 years, which is considered the maximum utilization period. Almost half of the fleet's units have been utilized for over 10 years. The ratio of wear and tear of MZO's fixed assets in 1991 was nearly 60 percent. Purchases of new vehicles does not cover losses connected with retirement of old units. Also, MZO's support facilities are in poor condition and they suffer shortages of service-repair workers and spare parts.

In general, sanitation services in the City are considered to be catastrophic, requiring immediate and radical action. The situation to some extent will be improved by private firms; however, these firms will not be able to make up for the neglect of years past.

Sanitation investment needs

Investment needs are enormous and stem in part from anticipated growth in demand in the future, as well as from substantial neglect of this area over the past five years. The expansion of the garbage dump in Lubna to an area of 39.96 square hectares, in accordance with the placement decision made in 1972, is anticipated. This expansion is slated for realization by 1995. In the course of negotiations, a municipal agreement was made with the township of Gora Kalwaria (about 30 kilometers south of Warsaw) to expand and utilize Kalwaria's garbage dump.

The composting/disposal facility at Radiowo is now being expanded to reach a capacity of 290 metric tons per day. This stage is to be completed by the end of 1993. When completed, Radiowo's total compost processing capacity will then be 580 metric tons per day, accounting for about 25 percent of waste produced in the City.

A waste disposal site in Praga is also underway. This facility, to be called "Wschod" (East), will have a capacity of 500 tons per day. This investment project is being realized by the EKO Company, a joint venture with a foreign partner, and is to be completed in 1995.

Action has already been undertaken in connection with the construction of a compacting station located southwest of the City of Warsaw. At this station, waste would be compacted and then transported to the garbage dump at Lubna. The establishment of a joint venture company with foreign participation is anticipated. However, plant siting issues are holding up action.

In the area of water-borne waste removal, it is essential to find suitable locations for the construction of modern filtration plants, and get them built promptly.

Financial situation

Changes in sanitation revenues and expenditures are presented in Table 6.19. Comparing oparational costs with revenues shows that MZO's operations are unprofitable. In avaluating each of the services that MZO renders, street-cleaning is the only service where tariffs cover all actual costs. The remaining services were loss-

Table 6.19
Profit and loss account from sanitation activity, 1988-1992,
in constant 1988 plz (000,000)

	1988	1989	1990	1991	1992
Total value of sales	11.2	10.6	7.8	6.7	4.8
Total costs	11.8	10.9	8.0	6.6	4.9
Accumulation of capital	-591.0	-0.3	-0.2	0.1	-0.1
Subsidies	1.5	2.5	1.5	0.9	0.9
Accumulation of capital with subsidies	876.0	2.0	1.3	1.0	-4.5
Balance of extraordinary profits & loss	50.0	79.9	15.9	-18.4	14.5
Balance sheet profit	926.0	2,193.3	1.3	1.0	10.0
Value of basic production sales	—	10.1	7.4	6.4	4.6
Costs	—	10.5	7.7	6.4	4.7
Accumulation of capital	—	-0.4	-0.3	0.0	-0.1
Subsidies	—	2.5	1.5	0.9	0.1
Accumulation of capital with subsidies	—	1.7	1.1	0.9	0.0

Source: Economic Analysis Unit

making, requiring the City to subsidize MZO's operations. Besides enormous investment needs (discussed above) it is also essential to reorganize MZO in the direction of greater economic and legal independence. It would seem appropriate for the City to consider privatizing MZO's operations and to exploit methods of full cost recovery where possible.

Telecommunications

As a result of organizational and legal changes initiated in December 1991, the Polish Mail, Telegraph, and Telephone (Polska Poczta, Telegraf i Telefon) state enterprise was converted into a joint stock company owned entirely by the state treasury and renamed Polish Telecommunications Joint Stock Company (Tele-komunikacja Polska Spóka Akcyjna). Telecommunication services were separated out on January 1, 1992. At the same time, ten managing district offices were set up, which are responsible for the supervision and coordination of operations and investment within their districts. Furthermore, it is noteworthy that the 1990 law on Communications abolished the state's monopoly in the area of telecommunications services by permitting others to set up networks. Map 6.6 presents an overview of Warsaw's telecommunications system.

The majority of local telephone switching boards are unapproved systems produced after World War II, as well as newer digital systems. International telephone connections are made through an automatic switchboard located in the City of Warsaw (type 5ESS, with a capacity of 3,500 connections). This switchboard also facilitates semi-automatic and manual calls. Fiber-optic cables relay automatic calls to 23 European countries and 9 locations outside of Europe.

In the telegraph network, the switchboard in the City also functions as an international switching station for telexes and telegraphs. Moreover, the hub of the Polpak tele-information is located in the City of Warsaw and functions as an international switching station. The overall capacity of this network is 1,328 lines.

The capacity of the City's switchboards in 1990 was close to 500,000 lines, constituting 12.5 percent of the capacity of local telephone switchboards in the country (about 4 million lines). Current usage in the nation is nearly at capacity (93 percent).

The generally accepted measure for evaluating the state of telecommunications is the number of subscribers of connections per 1000 inhabitants. At the end of 1990, it was 189.1 in the City of Warsaw, which substantially exceeded the national average at this time: 93.3 (131.6 in cities). In contrast, Western European cities such as Vienna, Copenhagen and Milan have 566, 698 and 952 lines per 1000 respectively.

Similarly, the level of modernity of Polish telecommunications also receives low ratings in comparison with other countries. The variety of simultaneously offered services testifies to this. In Poland (including Warsaw) only basic services: telephone and telegraph have been offered until recently. Telefax and office fax services were only introduced in 1988, and electronic mail in 1991.

MAP 6.6

Warsaw's Telecommunications System

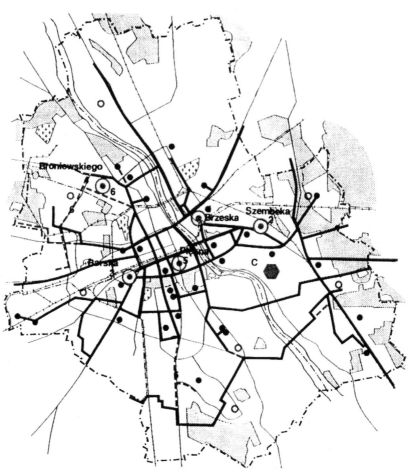

LEGEND	Graph Marking		Point of Location	Specification
	Existing	Projected		
─·─· City Borders	●	⊙	B 1-5	Transit Exchange
─··─· Gmina Borders				
─── Borders and Markings of Functional Zones	●	○		City Exchange
─── Main Roads				
++++ Railway Routes	───	─ ─	B 6	Main Telecommunications Lines
⌇ Waters				
▦ Forests and Parks	⬡		C	Preferred Localization of Sending Center
⁙ Cemeteries				

Assessments by foreign technicians indicate that the efficiency of the Polish network is low. The age and condition of the transmission systems provide the basis for this poor performance. The inter-city network is technologically obsolete and does not provide good quality transmission and audibility. Moreover, the general condition of the local network is poor, experiencing frequent break-downs.

The construction of a modern telecommunications network, comparable to the networks of developed European countries, is expected after the year 2000. This requires, among other things, modernizing the assortment of services.

The general plan for the development of the Warsaw Telecommunications Hub (WWT) has been accepted by the Polish Telecommunications Joint Stock Company and is being implemented by the Warsaw District Managing Office. The plan's objective is to double the number of subscribers in the City by the year 2000 from 415,000 in 1991 to about 700,000 in 1995 and about 1 million in the year 2000. This plan is to be implemented in the following phases:

Phase I: the installation of 8 digital transistorized switchboards (ALCATEL type); this stage was already completed in November 1992. The size of the switchboards and their capacity should suffice until 2010.

Phase II: the installation of a new international switchboard; this stage is currently being implemented. An EWSD central switching system is being installed by Siemens. It is to be one of 12 switching systems of this type, which will create the foundation for modernizing the domestic inter-city network.

Phase III: the replacement of the most worn out gear-based switchboards with digital switchboards produced by ALCATEL and SIEMENS; the implementation of this stage has already begun, although it is anticipated that it will last the longest.

Phase IV: the elimination of the gear-based inter-city switchboard; it will be implemented after Phase II is completed.

Phase V: the completion of the entire process of modernizing the telecommunications network with the introduction of uniform seven-digit numeration in the WWT by about the year 2000.

The CENTERTEL cellular phone network was recently established in the City of Warsaw. This network is based on the Scandinavian standard NT-450. The CENTERTEL network is in operation in several of the largest cities in Poland and has 10,000 subscribers, the majority of which are in the City of Warsaw. When completed, this network will be able to accommodate 100,000 subscribers. These services, however, are more expensive than those of a purely public network, and are mainly meant for business users.

A condition that must be met if the investment program is to succeed is a substantial increase in financial resources. Telecommunications modernization costs for the City of Warsaw are estimated at Plz. 8 billion over the 1993-2000 period. Telecommunication services are highly profitable, which means that the financial resources necessary for modernization will come mainly from income for services. In the next 5 to 8 years it is anticipated that foreign and domestic loans will also be drawn for this purpose.

Electric power

The City of Warsaw is supplied with electric power from the following sources:

- Zeran Heat and Power Plant (in service since 1954)

- Siekierki Heat and Power Plant (in service since 1961)

- Powile Heat and Power Plant (in service since 1904)

These plants are owned by the Warsaw Heat and Power Complex, and cover close to two-thirds of the overall demand for electric power in the City of Warsaw. The remaining portion of electric power is bought from the Polish Electric Power Network Company, and is supplied to Warsaw through 4 main supply points. Map 6.7 outlines the major electrical power sources in the region.

The Warsaw electric power system is administered by Stoleczny Zaklad Energetyczny S.A. (Capital City Energy Works Joint-Stock Company), which covers the entirety of the City of Warsaw — 485 square kilometers. The combined installed power in Warsaw power plants is 915 MW. The combined available power, however, is 640 MW in the winter. Powile power plant is the oldest in Warsaw; and with the lowest capacity and efficiency it is used only during the winter. The overall available power in Warsaw's power plants is lower than peak demand in the City and must be supplemented with power from the national system. In general, however, the level of service is considered to be good. Shortages in electric power supply do not occur.

Demand for electric power is highly uneven over the course of the year. Demand for power during peak hours varies from 370 MW in July to 990 MW in December 1992. Average monthly demand, on the other hand, varied from 130 GWK in July to 580 GWK in December of that year. Over the course of the last few years, this amount has not significantly changed.

Industry and large consumers account for 41.3 percent of total consumption. Residential users consume 32.8 percent of the supply. Other non-residential users account for 19.3 percent. The remaining 6.8 percent goes to the transportation sector and street lighting.

Technical conditions

The overall langth of the network serviced by Stoleczny Zaklad Energetyczny S.A. is 9,344 kilometers which consists of 494 kilometers of 110 and 220 kV high-tension networks; 4790 kilometers of medium-tension networks; and 4080 kilometers of low-tension networks.

High-tansion power lines transfer electric power within the national power network to supply points. Most of these lines are above ground, and underground cables for 110 kV only exist in short sections. A portion of the medium-tension net-

MAP 6.7

Warsaw's Electric Power System

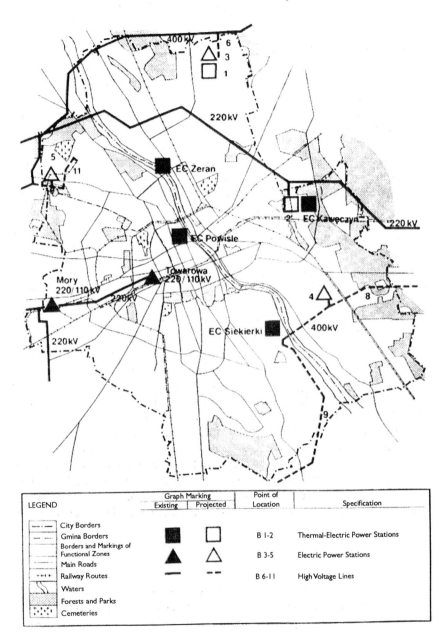

LEGEND	Graph Marking		Point of Location	Specification
	Existing	Projected		
⋅—⋅— City Borders				
—⋅— Gmina Borders	■	□	B 1-2	Thermal-Electric Power Stations
Borders and Markings of Functional Zones				
Main Roads	▲	△	B 3-5	Electric Power Stations
+⋅+⋅+ Railway Routes	—	– –	B 6-11	High Voltage Lines
Waters				
Forests and Parks				
Cemeteries				

works, which constitute the basic building block of the electric power supply system, date back to the pre-World War II era. Beginning in 1952, this network additions were made using new technology developed by Warsaw Polytechnic University. The prewar portion was to have been replaced as this network was expanded. Because of the significant increase in usage during the post-war period, the existing distribution network is not sufficient in all locations. This is most evident in the downtown district and Praga. The energy power supply system, given its age and the quality of materials installed in the past, should be renovated and replaced. The condition of the network is not satisfactory; the increase in breakdowns and excessive electric power loss testify to this.

The overall amount of electric power supplied — thanks to the national power supply network — is sufficient for the needs of Warsaw. Problems crop up only in connection with the distribution of the electric power around the City.

The situation in Mokotow is considered to be good on account of the fairly large power supply reserves at the regional supply points located in the district. The anticipated development of the district, however, will require the construction of additional regional supply points.

In Ochota power reserves are considered to be adequate, though increases in power demand by Okecie airport will require the construction of a new regional supply point.

In downtown power reserves are considered to be sufficient only on the periphery of the district. The large and growing demand for power in the center of the district requires a new regional supply center.

In Wola, power supply is limited. The needs of residential consumers are fully satisfied, but if industrial demands increase, additional capacity will be needed. Zoliborz has a good power supply situation and there will be no limitations in the next few years in the distribution of power to new consumers.

In Praga South, existing power supply reserves are at the exhaustion point. Conditions are particularly difficult in residential areas on the eastern and southern periphery of the district. In Praga North, additional supply is needed.

Overall, the construction of 9 new regional power supply points is anticipated. Taking into account needs for the construction of new 110 kV power lines above the ground, transformers, and other equipment, anticipated expenditures necessary for the satisfaction of current and future needs are estimated at Plz. 957 billion (in 1992 prices). This sum does not cover the costs of building a distribution network and associated equipment such as city transformer stations and sending-receiving points.

Gas supply

Since 1978, consumers in the City of Warsaw have been supplied with high-methane natural gas with a fuel value of 35 MJ/cubic meter. The percentage of the population using the gas supply network is close to 90 percent. The gas supply network reaches across the entire country. Warsaw is connected to the Mazowiecki District Gas Works, which is one of six macro-regional gas suppliers.

A closed ring of high-pressure gas pipelines has been built around Warsaw with a length of 121 kilometers. It is supplied with gas from three different directions and sources. This creates a certain, unfailing gas supply system for the City. From the gas pipeline ring around Warsaw, natural gas is pumped to the City by 12 reduction stations, which reduce the pressure of the gas and add a characteristic odor to it. Map 6.8 illustrates the metropolitan regions gas distribution system.

The gas distribution system includes: main gas lines connecting the reduction stations with each other, which can withstand high pressure loads in case of accidents; medium-pressure distributor gas lines which bring gas to industrial consumers; and low-pressure distributor gas lines which bring gas to buildings.

The overall length of the distribution network is 2,020.3 kilometers, and the number of building connections is 44,639. The total consumption of gas was 562 cubic hecto-meters in 1992. With 567,500 consumers, that yields an amount of 996.1 cubic meters per consumer.

The current distribution system is at maximum capacity. Current demand for gas, which is highly uneven, is somewhere in the area of 60,000 cubic meters/h during the summer and 120,000 cubic meters/h during the winter. Further growth in demand may lead to shortcomings in the system.

In order to improve the current state of the gas distribution system, investment projects connected with the construction of reduction stations and distribution networks should be undertaken. If further growth in demand for gas occurs in Warsaw, the possibility of more serious investment projects for high-pressure gas pipelines running around the City and bringing gas to reduction stations should be considered. This requires, however, an analysis on a scale larger than Metropolitan Warsaw.

Recent estimates put the cost of expanding system capacity by an additional 20,000 cubic meters of gas at Plz. 115 billion (1992 prices). This cost does not cover associated needs in the area of expanding the distribution system.

Because of the high cost of system expansion, proposals to replace downtown Warsaw's central heating system with an independent gas system are unrealistic. Making the switch would increase the demand for gas by 128,000 cubic meters/h, which is an amount somewhat higher than the current demand for gas by all Warsaw consumers during the winter. A two-fold increase in demand would require the construction of a new high pressure distribution ring around the city, more reduction stations, main pipelines, etc.. Moreover, in order to bring such a large amount of gas to Warsaw, it would be necessary to fundamentally rebuild gas supply pipelines. Given the high costs, most experts regard such proposals as unrealistic.

Summing up Warsaw's infrastructure needs

This chapter has reviewed the physical and financial conditions of the City of Warsaw's major infrastructure systems: Water supply and waste-water collection

MAP 6.8

Warsaw's Gas Supply System

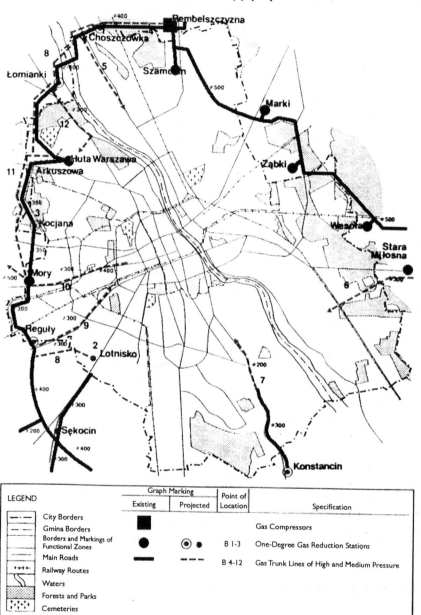

LEGEND		Graph Marking		Point of Location	Specification
		Existing	Projected		
—·—·—	City Borders	■			Gas Compressors
—··—··—	Gmina Borders				
————	Borders and Markings of Functional Zones	●	◉ ●	B 1-3	One-Degree Gas Reduction Stations
————	Main Roads	▬	─ ─ ─	B 4-12	Gas Trunk Lines of High and Medium Pressure
+++++	Railway Routes				
	Waters				
	Forests and Parks				
	Cemeteries				

and treatment, central heating, municipal transportation, roads and bridges, sanitation, telecommunications, electric power and gas. In nearly all cases, conditions range from poor to very poor, reflecting years of deferred maintenance. In some cases, service capacity has not kept pace with increased levels of demand.

Overall physical conditions

While gross water supplies are adequate to meet overall demands, water quality is poor, especially supplies coming from the central waterworks. Treatment technologies need to be modernized at older facilities, and water distribution systems need refurbishment and expansion (in the North Waterworks service area).

Waste-water treatment is deficient in many respects. First and foremost, only 43 percent of waste-water is treated, and substantial volumes of untreated sewerage flow into the Vistula. The principal cause of the low treatment level is the overloading of existing sewerage treatment plants. Treatment capacity has not kept pace with demands.

In the case of central heating, the current system is extremely inefficient and cannot produce the levels of energy required. The current deficit amounts to about 8 percent of average demand. During peak periods, the supply-demand gap exceeds 20 percent. Heat and hot water production systems are a major source of air pollution. The system does not adequately treat the water used to provide heat and hot water, and the system is plagued with extensive failures from pipe corrosion. The system has few meters to register demand and usage and as a result, there are few opportunities to control inflated demand. A final problem is that most buildings are poorly insulated, reflecting the gross underpricing of heating services.

Warsaw's extensive transportation system operates reasonably well, providing buses, tram and trolley-bus service. In comparison to other Western European cities, Warsaw's transit operator receives a very high percentage of its revenues from the farebox. Subsidies account for about 30 percent of direct operating costs. Major problems center on the lack of financing for fleet replacement.

The condition of Warsaw's roads, bridges and viaducts, is an entirely different story. Here conditions are extremely bad, reflecting decades of poor maintenance. Over 60 percent of the City's road surface needs total restoration (new construction of roadbeds). Nearly 10 percent needs surface repairs. Conditions of bridges, viaducts, pedestrian passages, breakwaters and other facilities are in a similar poor state.

Sanitation and solid waste removal is facing a number of challenges. First and foremost, the generation of solid waste is increasing rapidly, at about 3 percent per year. The City's principal landfill is nearing capacity. Disposal of liquid waste from septic tanks is inadequate, typically dumped in overloaded treatment plants. The lack of proper tariffs, has lead to the underfinancing of sanitation services. This is mostly reflected in the lack of an adequate fleet of vehicles. On the positive side, the private sector has shown interest in providing sanitation services.

Telecommunication service levels are very poor, but improving. Warsaw's level of telephone service is about one-fourth to one-fifth of the levels found in other

Western European cities. Fortunately, the sector has been restructured and rates are rising to help finance system improvements. Private capital is expected to support telecommunication upgrading.

Electric power service is adequate to good. Deficiencies exist primarily in distribution to districts. Assessments of the sector suggest that about nine regional power supply points are needed to provide adequate service. Downtown power demand is likely to grow if office development increases, and this will require additional capital investments to upgrade and expand the distribution system.

Gas for cooking and heating is supplied by the national grid system. Warsaw is quickly approaching a major capacity constraint since the regional distribution network is at capacity. Increasing capacity will require a major project to build a second main pressure line around the metropolitan area. As more new development seeks to provide independent heating and hot water, the demand for gas is likely to increase.

While Warsaw's infrastructure system is in poor condition, there is reason for much optimism. Economic and financial reforms have lead to the liberalization of rate setting for infrastructure services. This has led to relatively strong financial performance in the sector and over the long term provides options to finance improvements with tariffs.

However, in some sectors, full cost recovery tariffs will be quite high, if adequate charges are levied for upgrading and depreciation. In the case of central heating, the Ministry of Finance has limited rate increases because residential heating charges have risen rapidly. Households now typically pay 8.4 percent of their income for heating, electricity and gas. This is about double the level paid in other countries.

In Chapter 9 we will consider the overall financial implications of modernizing Warsaw's infrastructure system.

7 Forecast of economic activity for Warsaw and the Warsaw metropolitan area

Introduction

This chapter begins with an analysis of three economic development forecasts for Poland. Two of the forecasts predict economic trends to 1997, and the other, to 1999. Each forecast relies on assumptions formulated as the result of an assessment of the economic situation of the country and the conditions of its development. The remainder of the chapter provides insight into possible economic development scenarios and forecasts for the Warsaw metropolitan region.

Review of economic development forecasts for Poland

The first national economic forecast to be considered was made in the third quarter of 1993 by "The Economist Intelligence Unit" (EIU). The forecast assumes that the economic policy that has been followed so far will be continued. The economy's return to growth in 1992 and its acceleration in 1993 have created a foundation for continued growth. Factors contributing to this growth will be: increasing investment activity, export trade, and private consumption. The projected average rate of growth in the gross domestic product in the period between 1993 and 1997 will be 3.7 percent. The dynamics of individual macroeconomic indices for this period, as predicted by the EIU, are presented in Table 7.1.

The authors of this forecast have also concluded that the following trends will take place in this period. They anticipate interest rates will fall along with inflation, which in 1997 will approach single-digit levels. The value of the zloty in comparison with hard currencies will tend to insure the competitiveness of Polish exports. The government will aid exports. Energy prices will be on par with world levels. The budget deficit will remain under strict control. Increases in industrial production will be about 5 to 6 percent per year.

Table 7.1

Table 7.1
Economic growth in Poland, 1993-1997, in percent

Growth in %	1993	1994	1995	1996	1997
GDP	2.5	3.7	4	4.2	4.2
Private Consumption	1.5	3	3.5	3.8	3.8
Public Consumption	2.7	3	3	2	3
Gross Investment Outlays	3	4	4.8	5.2	5
Exports	4	6.8	7.2	7.7	7
Imports	6.5	7	7.5	8	7.5
Domestic Demand	2.1	3.2	3.7	3.8	4

Source: Country Forecast: Poland 3d Quarter 1993. The Economist Intelligence Unit Limited, 1993.

The second forecast, worked out by Jan Rajski of Poland's Institute of Finance, makes use of an inter-sectoral flow model of the economy. He concludes that, internal conditions are not favorable for the country, because a substantial budget deficit and public debt limit resources available to the private sector and create a heavy fiscal burden. As a result, a transfer of accumulated capital from the economic sector to the banking and budgetary sector will take place, and will seriously limit resources for productivity improving investments. There are also unfavorable external conditions affecting the development of the Polish economy, which are linked mainly to the weakness of world-wide markets. The author presents two forecast scenarios, one optimistic and the other pessimistic. GDP growth in the optimistic scenario is:

1993	1994	1995	1996	1997
3.0%	5.5%	6.5%	7.5%	6.0%

and in the pessimistic scenario:

2.2%	3.8%	3.8%	4.0%	3.7%

The pessimistic scenario is similar to EIU's forecast, with differences lying between 0.1 and 0.5 percentage points.

The third forecast, to 1999, has been made by a team at the Institute of Econometrics and Statistics at Lodz University (W. Florczak, M.M. Kazimierska-Zato, and W. Welfe). The authors assume that economic policy will change in order to fight the recession and increase effective demand (primarily investment and foreign demand). Policy changes include tax breaks, cheaper credit, risk insurance, government guarantees, and other measures.

Another important assumption of the Lodz forecast is that automatic economic growth mechanisms will function more and more efficiently as the public sector is increasingly commercialized and the private sector expands. In February 1994, the authors released a new version of the forecast which, in comparison with the earlier September 1994 version, takes into account the modest changes in economic policy carried out by the new government. The government's new program is a compromise between a continuation of the policy of stabilization, while making efforts to step up exports and increase the pace of investment.

A comparison of the above economic development forecasts for Poland suggests that despite the different assumptions and goals held by the authors, the predicted trends and pace of growth in the Polish economy are, with the exception of J. Rajiski's optimistic forecast, startlingly similar. This similarity may testify to the accuracy and realism of these forecasts. The remainder of this chapter will make use of a somewhat modified version of the most recent February 1994 Lodz forecast. Table 7.2 presents the main indicators for this forecast, through 1997. This forecast predicts somewhat faster GDP growth, a substantially higher pace in investment expenditures, and falls between the pessimistic and optimistic forecasts of J. Rajski.

Table 7.2
Projections of Poland's economic growth, 1993-1997

Change in %	1993	1994	1995	1996	1997
GDP (Total)	4.1	4.4	4.5	4.7	4.5
in Industry	4	3.7	4.2	4.1	4
in Construction	6.1	6.9	5.2	6.5	6.1
In Agriculture & Forestry	1.4	6.3	4.7	5.6	6.1
in Other Branches of National Economy	4.8	3.7	4.4	4.5	3.9
Investment Outlays	5.2	7.9	7.3	6.7	8.4
Exports	1.4	7.8	7.6	7.7	7.8
Imports	9.3	4.3	3.4	3.8	3.3
Private Consumption	5.1	2.2	2.6	2.7	2.8
Public Consumption	2.7	2.3	2.3	2.2	2.4
Real Wages	-1.7	3.2	2.6	2.6	2.8

Source: Economic Analysis Unit

Anticipated goals of economic growth in Poland

The economic situation in Poland is very problematic and complicated: unemployment has reached 16 percent of the active work force, government debt and foreign indebtedness are growing, and there is a high foreign trade deficit. External conditions are similarly disadvantageous: sluggish growth and economic protectionism in the European Union is limiting the expansion of Polish exports. A brighter point on the international horizon is the recent reduction of part of Poland's debt to commercial banks in the London Club. Despite the reduction in Poland's debt including an earlier forgiveness by the Paris Club, debt service will absorb increasingly large sums, reaching $8 billion USD in 2008.

Signs of an economic upturn appeared last year in the European Union's economy. If such improvements become an ongoing trend, a reduction of limitations on Polish imports can be anticipated. Increases in Polish exports to the European Union will mainly depend upon the economic situation in Germany, which is now the nation's largest trade partner. An improvement in the world economic situation could ease the economic problems facing Poland, but won't solve them. Thus, the creation of domestic economic and social-political conditions stimulating a high rate of lasting economic growth is essential.

The internal and external conditions affecting Poland's economy largely determine the long-term goals for its development. Limiting unemployment to reasonable levels will require the creation of an appropriate number of jobs — thus steps must be taken to insure a high rate of investment. On the other hand, in order to service the foreign debt, high growth in exports resulting in a substantial surplus over imports is essential. For these reasons, the middle-term social-economic program for 1994-1997, prepared by the government's Central Planning Office (CUP), takes as its main goal the assurance of permanent and balanced economic growth. The CUP anticipates GDP growth for the period to total 21.8 percent, or 5.1 percent per year. The main factors behind this expected economic growth will be: investments (which are to grow by 40 percent, or 8.9 percent per year), and increases in foreign trade. Consumption is to increase by 15 percent over this period, and real income per capita by 13 percent. Finally, the unemployment rate is expected to fall to 14 percent, and inflation to the same figure.

This is undoubtedly a very difficult program to realize, because many conditions must be fulfilled for it to become reality. With mounting pressure for wage increases and the persistence of relatively high inflation, it will not be easy to assure such high growth in investment. Economic figures for the first quarter of 1994 provide a certain basis for optimism, though this is too short a period to be able to speak of the appearance of permanent signs of an accelerated growth.

In order to meet the challenges of assuring growth, Poland must continue reforms leading in the direction of a modern market economy. This means the continued privatization of the economy, which not only strengthens market mechanisms, but which also constitutes one of the more important factors behind increasing foreign investment. In order to gain the trust of foreign investors and encourage them to invest in the country, the creation of mutually advantageous economic conditions, a generally favorable economic climate, and political stability are essential. It is also essential that reform of the banking sector be continued, so that it can become a stabilizing element of the economy.

The continuation of reform and the introduction of elements stimulating growth (investment incentives, loan guarantees, etc.) should set in motion internal growth mechanisms, which could become the most important element in Poland's economic growth. Substantial effects could also be achieved in connection with an improvement in economic conditions in the former member states of COMECON, especially Poland's eastern neighbors.

Economic development scenarios for Warsaw

A previous analysis and assessment of ongoing trends and the internal and external conditions behind the growth of individual sectors and branches of the economy, provides a basis for elaborating development scenarios. Assessments of existing development potential inherent in local labor, capital, and environmental resources, together with assessments of possibilities for mobilizing and activating them, are also of crucial importance.

This analysis and the conclusions drawn from it have led to three development scenarios for the economic development of Metropolitan Warsaw. These scenarios will later assist in creating forecasts for Metropolitan Warsaw's economy.

Scenario I is based on the assumption that trends in the period 1988-1992 will continue through 1997. This means a further decline in production and employment in industry and transportation, production stabilization and employment losses in construction, a rapid drop in employment in science, applied science, scholarship, culture, art, etc., and rapid employment growth in finance and insurance, trade, and communications. If economic processes proceed according to this scenario, the result will be an excessive decline in employment in some sectors of Metropolitan Warsaw's economy and excessive employment growth in other sectors. As a result, large disproportions would appear, causing waste in local resources, especially labor. This is a pessimistic scenario, which should be treated as a warning. However, a continuation of these trends is unlikely. Expansion in trade has already come up against the barrier of limited demand; and the continuation of the recent tempo in the development of communications, and finance and insurance, also seems unrealistic, for the same reason. Another scenario is needed which will take into account differentiated conditions and possibilities for growth in individual sectors of Metropolitan Warsaw's economy.

Scenario II is the scenario of differentiated sectoral growth. It assumes that employment in industry will not increase before 1997 because, as analysis showed, labor in this sector of the economy is not being fully utilized. Thus the potential for a significant increase in production exists without increase in employment. Construction could also increase production mainly by making better use of factors of production, that is, through growth in the productivity of labor. As a result, growth in construction employment will be insignificant. The work force in agriculture and forestry will decline, because agricultural land in Metropolitan Warsaw will shrink rather than expand.

Transportation also has a certain amount of reserve capacity at its disposal owing to the substantial decline in demand for such services. Thus, increases in the utilization of transportation services will yield no more than insignificant increases in employment. Communications, one of the fastest-growing sectors of the Warsaw economy, will not be able to maintain its recent (1988-1992) rate of growth. The industry will eventually reach a saturation point.

Wholesale and retail trade in Metropolitan Warsaw is approaching its saturation point, as illustrated by both the fall in its rate of growth after 1990 and the decline in its profitability. Further growth will depend upon increases in effective consumer demand. Communal services have significant potential for growth stemming not only from the development of the City, but also from efforts to make up for past and continuing neglect in investments from a quantitative as well as qualitative (modernization) point of view. Such investments, however, will tend to decrease employment.

In turn, the growth in employment in the residential service sector will be insignificant. A long period of time is required before this sector overcomes the crisis it is currently in. Despite the government's declared intention to significantly increase expenditures on education by 1997, a break-through in this area should not be anticipated. Growth in education will also be very modest, because the number of children is declining, which will be an unspoken argument in favor of limiting funds for this sector. True, there exists an urgent need to improve classroom conditions, especially to reduce the student/teacher ratio, but social pressure to do so will be attenuated by the development of private schools, which children from the richest social groups will attend. In addition, it is difficult to assume that in so short a period of time, real salaries in science and scholarship will become competitive in the eyes of young educated persons. Thus employment growth in this sector will be insignificant.

If culture and art maintain current levels of employment and expenditure until 1997, that in itself will be a success. Health care services are at very low levels, and there is nothing to indicate that they will radically improve during the period under discussion, though demand will increase due to the aging of the populace of the region. This is another reason why growth in employment will be insignificant.

Finance and insurance will not continue to expand at their recent rate. Accelerated consolidation of banks should be anticipated, because the majority of small and weak banks will not be able to withstand the competition of large, strong ones; they will have to choose between going bankrupt and merging with stronger partners. That's why employment increases in this sector will occur mainly in insurance and real-estate firms, rather than in banking. By all indications, government will maintain its current rate of increase in employment, owing to the new administrative division of Warsaw, the possible creation of townships, and the increasing number of tasks of the state administration. In the remaining sectors of the economy in which there are many small but active firms, a certain increase in employment can be expected. However, the small share of such firms in total employment, means that such increases will have little overall effect.

Scenario III is the optimistic scenario, assuming an average growth rate two times faster than that of scenario II. This is not an irrational assumption, because the economic condition of Metropolitan Warsaw is better than that of the country as a whole. Furthermore, Metropolitan Warsaw has comparative advantages stemming from the concentration of numerous functions on its territory and its relatively better infrastructure. The region has the best conditions for attracting various kinds of service-related activity, especially highly specialized financial and trade services, and high- technology development and production activity.

Economic development forecasts for Warsaw

Economic development forecasts are made on the basis of the results of analyses of past trends in particular sectors of the economy and of an assessment of the conditions and possibilities of their future development. Such an assessment was made above in elaborating economic development scenarios for Metropolitan Warsaw. The following section will present accepted indicators of change, and analyze the rate and structure of Metropolitan Warsaw's anticipated economic growth.

Scenario I assumes a continuation of 1988-1992 trends. In drawing up the forecast, the average annual rate of change of work force size during the 1988-1992 period, in individual sectors of the economy, was assumed. The results of these calculations are presented in Table 7.3.

Scenario II was defined as the scenario of differentiated growth, because it takes into account the varied conditions and development possibilities of individual sectors of the Metropolitan Warsaw economy. In drawing up this economic growth forecast for the period through 1997, the following rates of change of employment in individual sectors of the Metropolitan Warsaw economy were assumed:

- industry: 0% growth,

- construction: 20% of the GDP growth rate in nationwide construction,

- transportation: 10% of the GDP growth rate in other sectors of the national economy,

- farming and forestry: reduction of the work force of about 25% by 1997,

- communications: 60% of the 1988-1992 growth rate,

- wholesale and retail trade: 20% of the growth in consumption, which will average 3% a year during this period,

- communal services: 20% of the average ratio of investment expenditures/fixed assets during 1988-1992,

173

- culture and art as well as sports and recreation: 0% growth,

- state administration: 50% of the 1988-1992 growth rate,

- finance and insurance: 10% of the 1988-1992 growth rate,

- housing, science and scholarship, technological development, education, health care, and other sectors of the Metropolitan Warsaw economy: 20% of the GDP growth rate in other sectors of the national economy.

It is necessary to explain the difference between the categories noted as "other sectors of the Metropolitan Warsaw economy" and those noted "other sectors of the national economy". The first category embraces the other branches of material production not counted in any of the other main economic sectors, mainly: publishing and film entities, information service entities, and other branches of material production (environmental research and monitoring centers, testing bureaus, offices of weights and measurements, quality control entities) and other non-material services (hairdresser, cosmetic, photographic, cleaning, equipment rental, etc. services). The second category, on the other hand, embraces economic sectors of the national economy other than industry, construction, agriculture and forestry. The results of calculations for the economic growth forecast based on scenario II are presented in Table 7.4.

Scenario III was described as the accelerated growth scenario, assuming higher, though varied, rates of change. Wherever possible, growth in a given economic sector was made dependent on the main factor influencing that growth. For example, in construction, the growth rate was made dependent upon investment expenditures. The economic development forecast for Metropolitan Warsaw in scenario III was created using the following growth rates:

- industry: 0% growth through 1994, then 20% of GDP growth rate for nationwide industry,

- construction: 50% of the growth rate of investment expenditures,

- agriculture and forestry: as in scenario II (fall of about 25%),

- transportation: 50% of the average growth rate in industry and construction,

- wholesale and retail trade: 50% of the growth rate of consumption,

- communal services: 30% of the average ratio of investment expenditures/fixed assets for 1988-1992,

Table 7.3 (part 1 of 2)
Projection of employment in Warsaw and the Warsaw metropolitan area, in 1993-1997 (in '000)
Scenario I — Continuation of trends from years 1988-1992

Branch of Economy	1992		1993		1994	
	City of Warsaw	Warsaw metro. area	City of Warsaw	Warsaw metro. area	City of Warsaw	Warsaw metro. area
Total	725.1	970.1	720.3	956.3	719.1	947.7
Industry	170	234.5	159	218.3	148.6	203.2
Construction	76	94.2	73.3	89.9	70.7	85.9
Agriculture & Forestry	21.3	74.1	21.3	74.1	21.3	74.1
Transport	27.5	39.7	26	37.9	24.5	36.2
Communication	13.4	16.4	13.7	16.9	14.1	17.5
Wholesale & Retail Trade	105	136.7	110	142.3	115.3	148.2
Other Branches of Material Prod.	17.2	—	15.5	—	13.9	—
Communal Services	35.3	41.6	38.3	44.1	41.5	46.9
Housing	17.1	19.7	15.8	18.0	14.6	16.5
Science & Technical Develop.	25.8	27.0	23.1	24.0	20.7	21.4
Education	62.3	78.5	62.7	77.4	63	76.4
Culture & Art	15.3	17.0	14.6	16.0	13.9	15.1
Medical Care	48.2	64.0	48.8	63.6	49.5	63.4
Sports & Recreation	9.2	9.7	8.5	8.9	7.8	8.1
Other Non Material Services	21.5	—	24	—	27	—
State Administration	28.1	34.5	29.7	36.3	31.4	38.2
Finance & Insurance	26.5	30.4	31.5	35.6	37.5	41.9

Source: Economic Analysis Unit

- housing: 30% of the GDP growth rate in the other sectors of the national economy,

- science, scholarship, and technological development: 50% of the GNP growth rate in the other sectors of the national economy,

- health care: 40% of the above growth rate,

- education: 40% of the growth rate in other sectors of the national economy,

- culture and art, as well as sports and recreation: 20% of the growth rate in consumption,

- state administration: 50% of the 1988-1992 growth rate,

- other sectors: 40% of the GDP growth rate in other sectors of the economy.

Table 7.3 (part 2 of 2)
Projection of employment in Warsaw and the Warsaw metropolitan area, in 1993-1997 (in '000)
Scenario I — Continuation of trends from years 1988-1992

Branch of Economy	1995 City of Warsaw	1995 Warsaw metro. area	1996 City of Warsaw	1996 Warsaw metro. area	1997 City of Warsaw	1997 Warsaw metro. area
Total	721.7	943.7	728.2	944.6	738.8	950.9
Industry	139	189.2	130	176.2	121.5	164.0
Construction	68.2	82.1	65.9	78.6	63.6	75.2
Agriculture & Forestry	21.3	74.1	21.3	74.1	21.3	74.1
Transport	23.1	34.5	21.8	32.9	20.6	31.5
Communication	14.4	18.0	14.7	18.5	15.1	19.1
Wholesale & Retail Trade	120.8	154.3	126.6	160.7	132.7	167.5
Other Branches of Material Prod.	12.5	—	11.3	—	10.2	—
Communal Services	45.1	50.0	48.9	53.5	53	57.2
Housing	13.5	15.1	12.5	13.9	11.5	12.7
Science & Technical Develop.	18.6	19.2	16.6	17.1	15	15.4
Education	63.4	75.6	63.8	74.9	64.2	74.3
Culture & Art	13.2	14.2	12.6	13.4	12	12.7
Medical Care	50.2	63.2	50.9	63.1	51.6	63.1
Sports & Recreation	7.2	7.5	6.6	6.8	6.1	6.3
Other Non Material Services	30.2	—	33.8	—	37.9	—
State Administration	33.2	40.2	35.1	42.3	37	44.4
Finance & Insurance	44.6	49.2	53.1	58.0	63.2	68.5

Source: Economic Analysis Unit

The economic development forecast created using this scenario III is presented in Table 7.5.

Economic development forecasts must also be made for the area of the metropolitan region which lies outside the City of Warsaw. The City of Warsaw and the Ring surrounding it are co-dependent, linked by numerous functional ties. It should be emphasized, however, that not all of these linkages are positive. In some cases "the better it is in the City of Warsaw, the better in the Ring outside". Some of these linkages are however negative; i.e. "the better it is in the City of Warsaw, the worst in the Ring outside". For example, some sectors of the economy of the Ring outside the City of Warsaw suffered a significantly deeper recession that their counterparts in Warsaw.

The next section analyses the structure and rate of economic growth for both the City of Warsaw and the metropolitan region, up to 1997, according to the particular forecast scenarios. The corresponding data are presented in Tables 7.6 and 7.7.

Table 7.4
Projection of employment in Warsaw and the Warsaw metropolitan area, in 1993-1997 (in '000)
Scenario II — Diversified growth

Branch of Economy	1993 City of Warsaw	1993 Warsaw metro. area	1994 City of Warsaw	1994 Warsaw metro. area	1995 City of Warsaw	1995 Warsaw metro. area	1996 City of Warsaw	1996 Warsaw metro. area	1997 City of Warsaw	1997 Warsaw metro. area
Total	730.2	976.2	735	982.5	740.4	989	745.4	995.6	750.7	1002.3
Industry	170	234.5	170	234.5	170	234.5	170	234.5	170	234.5
Construction	76.9	95.3	77.8	96.5	78.8	97.7	79.7	98.8	80.7	100
Agriculture & Forestry	20.2	73	19.2	72	18.3	71.1	17.3	70.1	16.5	69.3
Transport	27.6	39.8	27.8	40.1	28	40.4	28.1	40.5	28.3	40.8
Communication	13.6	16.7	13.8	17	14	17.3	14.2	17.6	14.4	17.9
Wholesale & Retail Trade	105.6	137.6	106.3	138.8	106.9	139.7	107.5	140.7	108.2	141.8
Other Branches of Material Prod.	17.4	—	17.6	—	17.8	—	18	—	18.2	—
Communal Services	35.8	42.2	36.4	42.9	37	43.6	37.6	44.3	38.2	45
Housing	17.3	19.9	17.4	20	17.6	20.3	17.7	20.4	17.9	20.6
Science & Technical Develop.	26.1	27.3	26.3	27.5	26.5	27.7	26.8	28	27	28.2
Education	63	79.2	63.5	79.7	64.1	80.4	64.6	81.1	65.1	81.7
Culture & Art	15.5	17.2	15.6	17.3	15.7	17.4	15.9	17.6	16	17.7
Medical Care	48.7	64.7	49.1	65.2	49.6	65.8	50	66.4	50.4	66.9
Sports & Recreation	9.3	9.8	9.4	9.9	9.5	10	9.6	10.2	9.7	10.3
Other Non Material Services	21.7	—	21.9	—	22.1	—	22.3	—	22.5	—
Public Administration	28.8	35.2	29.6	36.1	30.4	36.9	31.3	37.9	32	38.7
Finance & Insurance	27.2	31.1	27.8	31.8	28.5	32.5	29.2	33.3	30	34.2

Source: Economic Analysis Unit

If 1988-1992 trends were to continue through 1997, the number of people employed in the economy of the City of Warsaw would increase about 2 percent, while a 2 percent employment loss would occur in the region. Finance and insurance would have the largest growth in employment in both the City and the region (138.5 and 125.3 percent respectively), followed by communal services (50 percent in the City), and state administration (over 25 percent in both areas). The largest decline would occur in science, scholarship, and technological development (43 percent for the region). These deep sectoral changes would be felt similarly in both the City and in the region, and would significantly alter the structure of economy of both areas. Industry's share of total employment would shrink from 23.5 to 16.5 percent in the City, and construction's by 2 percentage points. Finance and insurance's share would increase from 3.1 to 7.2 percent in the region, and that of wholesale and retail trade from 14.5 to 18 percent in the City.

Table 7.5
Projection of employment in Warsaw and the Warsaw metropolitan area, in 1993-1997 (in '000)
Scenario III — Accelerated growth

Branch of Economy	1993 City of Warsaw	1993 Warsaw metro. area	1994 City of Warsaw	1994 Warsaw metro. area	1995 City of Warsaw	1995 Warsaw metro. area	1996 City of Warsaw	1996 Warsaw metro. area	1997 City of Warsaw	1997 Warsaw metro. area
Total	735.8	982.8	746.6	996.4	760.1	1012.2	773.7	1028.4	787.9	1045.3
Industry	170.1	235.1	170.1	235.6	171.5	237.6	173	239.6	174.3	241.5
Construction	78	96.5	81	100.3	84	104	86.8	107.4	90.6	111.9
Agriculture & Forestry	20.2	72	19.2	69.9	18.3	68	17.3	66	16.5	64.5
Transport	27.8	40.3	28.4	41.2	29.5	42.6	30.6	44.1	32	45.8
Communication	13.7	16.8	14	17.3	14.3	17.8	14.5	18.1	14.8	18.5
Wholesale & Retail Trade	106.6	138.8	108.2	140.9	109.8	142.9	111.5	145.1	113	147
Other Branches of Material Prod.	17.6	—	17.9	—	18.2	—	18.5	—	18.8	—
Communal Services	36.1	42.5	37	43.6	37.9	44.6	38.8	45.6	39.7	46.6
Housing	17.4	20	17.6	20.3	17.8	20.5	18.1	20.9	18.3	21.1
Science & Technical Develop.	26.5	27.7	27	28.3	27.6	28.9	28.2	29.6	28.8	30.2
Education	63.7	80.3	64.7	81.7	65.8	83.1	67	84.7	68	86
Culture & Art	15.4	17.1	15.5	17.2	15.6	17.3	15.7	17.4	15.8	17.6
Medical Care	49.3	65.5	50	66.6	50.9	67.8	51.9	69.2	52.6	70.2
Sports and Recreation	9.3	9.8	9.3	9.8	9.4	9.9	9.4	9.9	9.5	10.1
Other Non Material Services	22	—	22.3	—	22.7	—	23.1	—	23.5	—
State Administration	28.8	35.4	29.6	36.4	30.4	37.4	31.3	38.5	32	39.4
Finance & Insurance	27.8	31.7	29.2	33.1	30.7	34.7	32.3	36.3	33.8	37.9

Source: Economic Analysis Unit

Scenario II anticipates employment growth in the City of Warsaw's economy of 25,600 people (3.5 percent), and 32,200 people (3.3 percent) in the entire region, by 1997. The largest increase in the work force occurs in finance and insurance as well as in communal services and communications. Agriculture and forestry suffer employment losses. Changes in the structure of the economy during the 1992-1997 period are insignificant in both the City and the region; changes are less than 1 percentage point in any sector.

As a result of economic growth, scenario III forecasts that the size of the work force would increase by 62,800 people (8.7 percent) in the City, and 75,200 people (7.5 percent) in the region, by 1997. Employment would increase the most in finance and insurance, as well as construction and transportation, while a decline would take place only in agriculture and forestry. Changes in the structure of the economy during the five year forecast period would also be fairly small in both geographic areas, not exceeding 1.5 percentage points.

Table 7.6
Percent change in employment 1992-1997, Warsaw and metropolitan Warsaw, three scenarios (in %)

Branch of Economy	Scenario I—1997 1992=100% City	Metro	Scenario II—1997 `1992=100% City	Metro	Scenario III—1997 1992=100% City	Metro
Total	101.89	98.02	103.53	103.32	108.66	107.75
Industry	71.47	69.94	100.00	100.00	102.53	102.99
Construction	83.68	79.83	106.18	106.16	119.21	118.79
Agriculture & Forestry	100.00	100.00	77.46	93.52	77.46	87.04
Transport	74.91	79.35	102.91	102.77	116.36	115.37
Communication	112.69	116.46	107.46	109.15	110.45	112.80
Trade	126.38	122.53	103.05	103.73	107.62	107.53
Communal Services	150.14	137.50	108.22	108.17	112.46	112.02
Housing	67.25	64.47	104.68	104.57	107.02	107.11
Science & Tech. Dev.	58.14	57.04	104.65	104.44	111.63	111.85
Education	103.05	94.65	104.49	104.08	109.15	109.55
Culture & Arts	78.43	74.71	104.58	104.12	103.27	103.53
Medical Care	107.05	98.59	104.56	104.53	109.13	109.69
Sports & Recreation	66.30	64.95	105.43	106.19	103.26	104.12
State Administration	131.67	128.70	113.88	112.17	113.88	114.20
Finance & Insurance	238.49	225.33	113.21	112.50	127.55	124.67

Source: Economic Analysis Unit

In comparing these three economic development scenarios for both the City and the metropolitan region up to 1997, it appears that the most probable is scenario II. Changes undergone in this scenario, both in employment and in structure, are moderate. It would be difficult, after all, to expect as high a rate in employment growth as in 1988-1992 to continue for another five years. If so, finance and insurance would increase its work force by 36,700 in the City, wholesale and retail trade by 30,800 in the region, and communal services by 17,700 in the City. Scenario I would also lead to problems in the labor market, because unemployment among industrial, construction, and transportation workers would rise, with a short-age of qualified candidates for employment in finance and insurance. In the City, 7,340 additional workers would be needed annually in finance and insurance. Furthermore, such a large increase in state administration (10,000 people in the region) would not be desirable. Undoubtedly, the most desirable scenario is III, which in principle would enable the liquidation of unemployment. It appears, how-ever, overly optimistic, since the factor limiting the Warsaw Metropolitan region's economic growth over the next four years will be the weak growth in household

Table 7.7
Structure of Warsaw and metropolitan Warsaw area for 1992 and three scenarios (in %)

Branch of Economy	1992 City	Metro	Scenario I — 1997 City	Metro	Scenario II — 1997 City	Metro	Scenario III — 1997 City	Metro
Total	100.00	100.00	100.00	100.00	100.00	100.00	100.00	100.00
Industry	23.45	24.17	16.45	17.25	22.65	23.40	22.12	23.10
Construction	10.48	9.71	8.61	7.91	10.75	9.98	11.50	10.71
Agriculture & Forestry	2.94	7.64	2.88	7.79	2.20	6.91	2.09	6.17
Transport	3.79	4.09	2.79	3.31	3.77	4.07	4.06	4.38
Communication	1.85	1.69	2.04	2.01	1.92	1.79	1.88	1.77
Trade	14.48	14.09	17.96	17.61	14.41	14.15	14.34	14.06
Communal Services	4.87	4.29	7.17	6.02	5.09	4.49	5.04	4.46
Housing	2.36	2.03	1.56	1.34	2.38	2.06	2.32	2.02
Science & Tech. Dev.	3.56	2.78	2.03	1.62	3.60	2.81	3.66	2.89
Education	8.59	8.09	8.69	7.81	8.67	8.15	8.63	8.23
Culture & Art	2.11	1.75	1.62	1.34	2.13	1.77	2.01	1.68
Medical Care	6.65	6.60	6.98	6.64	6.71	6.67	6.68	6.72
Sports & Recreation	1.27	1.00	0.83	0.66	1.29	1.03	1.21	0.97
State Administration	3.88	3.56	5.01	4.67	4.26	3.86	4.06	3.77
Finance & Insurance	3.65	3.13	8.55	7.20	4.00	3.41	4.29	3.63

Source: Economic Analysis Unit

income and low enterprise profitability. These factors will make it impossible to attain a development growth rate which would support 15,000 new jobs annually in the region, as scenario III predicts. True, further decentralization in industry, construction, transportation, and wholesale trade should be taken into consideration. Nonetheless, it is unlikely that employment would rise faster than in scenario II.

In closing, it is worth mentioning that even if the economy of the City of Warsaw and the metropolitan region developed in accord with the forecast based on the optimistic scenario III, the region would not restore employment to 1988 levels. In 1997, employment would be lower than it was 9 years earlier by 3,500 people in the City, and 21,100 in the metropolitan region. Structurally, however, employment in 1997 would be considerably different than 1988.

The economic forecasts under discussion correctly characterize the main directions of development in the City of Warsaw and the surrounding region. The anticipated changes illuminate the scale of the tasks that must be undertaken in spatial economic planning, especially infrastructure planning, in order to assure appropriate conditions for development.

8 Future real estate requirements
of the Warsaw region

Introduction

This chapter estimates Metropolitan Warsaw's future real estate development requirements for the period from 1992 to 1997. These future estimates are based on the population and employment projections outlined in chapters 4 and 7. The reader is cautioned to bear in mind that these estimates are tentative and based on impartial information. The projections are best viewed as indicative, order of magnitude measures, useful for motivating policy discussions. Projections are provided for housing, office space, retail establishments, industrial and warehousing facilities.

Housing requirements

Unless there is a significant change in housing finance, a dramatic up-turn in housing construction is not expected. Population growth and rate of household formation in both the City and the metropolitan area is projected to be fairly low over the next five years. Most housing construction will be market rate and targeted at upper income households.

Post-1989 patterns of housing construction will probably continue up until 1997, suggesting that completions will average 6,000 to 8,000 units per year. This means that the metropolitan area will absorb an additional 30,000 to 40,000 dwelling units between 1992 and 1997. The majority of these units will be constructed in suburban areas in and around the City of Warsaw.

Office space

The demand for office space in the Warsaw metropolitan region can be expected to grow strongly over the next five years. Projections of employment growth in economic sectors using office space are very positive. Table 8.1 presents projections

Table 8.1
Employment projections for finance and insurance and administration, metropolitan Warsaw, 1992-1997

Scenario	1992 Employment	1997 Employment	Net change
I	64,900	112,900	48,000
II	64,900	72,900	8,000
III	64,900	77,400	12,500

Source: Warsaw Economic Analysis Unit, 1994

of employment for finance and insurance, and administration. Net new employment in these sectors is projected to increase between 8,000 and 48,000 workers by 1997. Assuming that each office employee requires 25 square meters of accommodation, then the additional demand for office space originating from finance and insurance and administration alone, will range from 200,000 to 1,200,000 square meters between 1992 and 1997. On an annual basis this averages out to 40,000 to 240,000 square meters. Other sectors of the economy will require office space as well. In addition, office-using activities in manufacturing, trade, science and technology, agriculture and personal and communal services will add to the demand for office space.

Given past trends in office space demand, and the likelihood that scenario II employment projections will prevail, it is probable that annual demand for office space will range between 50,000 and 75,000 square meters of space per year. Much of this demand will come from new firms, but a major component of demand will be driven by a move to higher quality accommodation offering advanced telecommunications, modern office layouts and adequate parking. If supply conditions improve and office rental rates start to decline, demand will ratchet upward as more existing firms move up to class "A" modern structures.

The pace of office space construction is rapidly increasing. Table 8.2 presents real investment outlays for buildings in constant prices between 1988 and 1992. The rate of office construction and building refurbishment increased by over 8,000 percent between 1988 and 1992. It is expected that the rate of office construction will increase dramatically over the next five years, as stalled projects get underway. By 1992, the City of Warsaw's stock of office space stood at approximately 2.7 million square meters. Between 1992 and 1997, office space is projected to increase by between 300,000 and 350,000 square meters, an average of 60,000 to 70,000 square meters per year.

Table 8.2
**Finance and insurance investment outlays for building
construction, metropolitan Warsaw, 1988-1992**

Location	Constant 1988 PLZ (000,000)			
	1988	1990	1991	1992
Warsaw	256	5,387	8,650	31,593
Ring	127	619	990	583
Total	383	6,006	9,640	32,176

Source: Economic Analysis Unit

Spatial patterns of office construction

While the preferred location for large class "A" office development projects is in the central business district, the actual location patterns will largely depend on whether developers can get access to prime downtown sites. Problems with titles, and planning permission have slowed or killed many deals. In response many developers have shifted to suburban locations where property titles are clearer, and planning permission quicker and simpler to obtain. Trends in office construction between 1988 and 1992, indicate that most investment in office construction has been within the City of Warsaw. In 1992, 98 percent of office construction outlays were in the City. This may change if some aggressive gminas, can convince investors that tenants will lease space in outlying areas. The European Trade Center Warsaw project is an example of a very large 30,000 square meter mixed use project (retail, office, exhibition space) which is located outside of the City. If such projects are successful and it still continues to be a difficult and time consuming process to secure central city land, then the share of office space construction going to the suburbs will increase, perhaps to 25 percent of total new construction. If Warsaw follows the office development practice of the U.S. and not Western Europe, over the next twenty years, up to 50 percent of the metropolitan area's office space could be located outside of the central business district (Srodmiescie).

Retailing

Metropolitan Warsaw's retail sector has been extremely dynamic, with real retail sales growing at an annual rate of 21 percent between 1988 and 1992. In the early years of economic reform, retail shops proliferated throughout the metropolitan area. The number of shops increased from just under 7,000 in 1988 to over 25,000 in 1992. In the early going retail trade was very profitable, with gross margins averaging 29 percent in 1988. However, the tremendous increase in retail establishments cut into margins and profitability in the sector declined to less than 1 percent in 1992.

Despite the decline in retail trade margins, the sector has a bright future. Household incomes in the metropolitan area are increasing and retail sales volumes are rising. National level projections estimate that real consumption should increase at an annual rate of 3 percent per year. In Metropolitan Warsaw, with higher levels of employment and a more dynamic economy, retail spending is likely to increase at an annual rate of four to five percent.

As of 1992, total trade employment (covering both retailing and wholesaling) stood at approximately 136,700. Projections to 1997 indicate that total trade employment will grow slowly, increasing to a low of 141,800 or to a high of 167,500 (see Table 8.3). Given the structure of the retail sector, particularly the over-supply of small vendors, and the gross under-representation of wholesale activities (discussed below), most of the growth in employment will be in the wholesale portion of the trade sector. Retail employment will fair differently depending upon which economic development scenario, as discussed in the previous chapter, prevails. Total retail employment will probably remain about the same under scenarios II and III. Under the conditions of scenario I, where total trade employment increases to 167,500, retail employment is likely to increase by 12,300 between 1992 and 1997. Much of the increase in employment will be absorbed into existing retail facilities, many of which are under-utilized.

Table 8.3
Projected trade employment, 1992-1997, in the Warsaw metropolitan area

Projection scenario	1997 Employment	1992 Employment	Net increase
I	167,500	136,700	30,800
II	141,800	136,700	5,100
III	147,000	136,700	10,300

Source: Economic Analysis Unit

In terms of retail construction activities, net additional retail space is likely to increase by 50,000 to 100,000 square meters. The high end of the projection, assumes that employment increases in the sector by roughly 10,000 and that many shops, kiosks and poorly sited and equipped facilities upgrade to new shops.

The spatial pattern of retail facilities is starting to decentralize and this pattern will continue over the next five to ten years. For example, prior to the launching of economic reforms, over 90 percent of the region's retail trade activity was located in the city center. Since 1989, investment in retail shops (either new construction, refurbishment or adaptation of existing buildings) is rapidly increasing in suburban areas. Between 1990 and 1992, construction outlays in retail facilities in suburban areas has increased by 135 percent rising in real terms from Plz. 2,951 million in 1990 to Plz. 6,948 million in 1992. Over the same period retail investments in the City of Warsaw increased by 58 percent, rising from Plz. 12,083 to Plz. 19,081. Current trends suggest that about 25 percent of total regional investment in retail construction takes place in suburban areas.

If residential construction picks up in suburban areas, the decentralization of retail establishments to the suburbs will accelerate. By 1997, over one-third of the region's retail construction activity could be located outside the present City of Warsaw boundaries.

Industrial facilities

Economic projections of employment in the industrial sector suggest that continued retrenchment will be the order of the day. Many state-owned factories will be privatized or cease operations. In most cases, privatized firms will be radically reorganized and systematic efforts made to improve labor productivity. This undoubtedly means cutting employment and modernizing facilities. Space utilization requirements (per unit of output) will decline and many older inefficient factories will be closed. Most multi-story facilities will be rejected by foreign investors and if investments are made in new facilities they will mostly take place in suburban areas. Manufacturing will decentralize to suburban areas.

These trends are already clear. Data presented in Chapter 3, examining spatial trends in capital investment, suggests that industrial investment in plants and equipment is rapidly shifting to areas outside of the City of Warsaw. In 1988, 73 percent of the metropolitan area's investment in industrial plants and equipment was located in the City of Warsaw. In 1992, only 57 percent was so located.

Despite the fact that industrial output in the region is projected to increase, because of increases in labor productivity, under the most optimistic scenario industrial employment is projected to increase by only 7,000 (3 percent). Under other scenarios, industrial employment is projected to either decline by 30 percent or remain stable. Table 8.4 reports industrial employment projections under each of the three forecasted scenarios. However, regardless of which scenario, industrial vacancies will climb, as factories close or move to more modern and efficient facilities.

Chapter 5 reported that the total stock of industrial facilities stood at 24,000,000 square meters in 1992, and of this amount, only 60 percent, or 14,000,000 square

Table 8.4
Projections of industrial employment
in the Warsaw metropolitan area

Projection scenario	1992 Employment	1997 Employment	1992-1997 Change
I	234,500	164,000	70,500
II	234,500	234,500	0
III	234,500	241,500	7,000

Source: Economic Analysis Unit

meters was currently used for industrial operations. Despite the vast oversupply of industrial space, a modest amount of industrial space is expected to be constructed over the 1992-1997 period. In fact, between 1990 and 1992, an average of 65,000 square meters of industrial space was constructed annually. This reflects pressure on the sector to modernize and upgrade facilities. Much of the new construction will be stimulated through privatization and foreign investment.

A significant portion of the vacant industrial space is being taken over by warehousing activities. Despite the massive supply of vacant space, well located and adaptable industrial space is relatively scarce. Given the pressures to economize on costs and to increase productivity, industrial space utilization is expected to decline by about 10 percent over the next five years, as new factories drastically cut back on social areas, administrative and storage areas. This suggests that industrial space utilization levels will approach 54 square meters per worker. Table 8.5 presents estimates of industrial space utilization trends between 1992 and 1997 based on the three possible scenarios of future employment. As the table shows, regardless of the scenario used, total industrial space utilization is expected to decline. The range of decline is from 959,000 to 5,144,000 square meters. In the most adverse case, the stock of industrial space will be reduced by nearly 40 percent.

Spatial distribution of industrial space

Given modernization pressures driving the industrial sector, industrial activities are likely to decentralize out of the center to lower cost suburban areas. This is a common pattern found in North America and Western Europe, during the 1950s and 1960s. Tables 8.6 and 8.7 present estimates of industrial employment and facility space for the City of Warsaw and surrounding Ring for 1992 and 1997.

Warehousing and distribution centers

Demand for warehousing and distribution facilities will grow dramatically over the next five years. This is due to several factors. First, the Polish economy will

Table 8.5
**Projections of industrial space
in the Warsaw metropolitan area**

Projection scenario	1992 Space, sq.mt.	1997 Space, sq.mt.	1992-1997 Change, sq.mt.
I	14,000,000	8,856,000	-5,144,000
II	14,000,000	2,663,000	-1,337,000
III	14,000,000	13,041,000	-959,000

Source: Economic Analysis Unit

Table 8.6
**Spatial projections of industrial employment
in the Warsaw metropolitan area**

	1992	Scenario		
		I	II	III
City of Warsaw	170,100	121,500	170,000	174,300
Ring	64,400	42,500	64,500	67,200
Total Region	234,500	164,000	234,500	241,500

Source: Warsaw Economic Analysis Unit, 1994

Table 8.7
**Spatial projections of industrial space in the Warsaw metropolitan area
(square meters)**

	1992	Scenario		
		I	II	III
City of Warsaw	10,200,000	6,561,000	9,180,000	9,412,300
Ring	3,800,000	2,295,000	3,483,000	3,629,000
Total Region	14,000,000	8,856,000	12,663,000	13,041,000

Source: Warsaw Economic Analysis Unit, 1994

continue to expand at a projected rate of 4.0 to 4.5 percent per year, and this growth will be reflected in an increased demand for goods. Second, attracted by strong economic growth and rising consumer income, trade patterns are internationalizing and Western European, North American and Asian distributors are moving into

Poland. As they develop businesses in the nation, warehousing and distribution centers will be in strong demand. Third, the continued privatization of the economy will promote the growth of wholesalers and distributors and they in turn will seek out facilities for storing goods.

In most market economies, wholesale trade accounts for about 6 percent of total employment. However, only about 1.5 percent of the Warsaw metropolitan area's total employment is currently employed in wholesale trade. Metropolitan Warsaw's wholesale trade sector should be about four times larger if it is to match the levels found in western market economies.

Over the course of the next ten years, wholesaling employment in Metropolitan Warsaw will move towards these levels. If wholesaling activities in Metropolitan Warsaw were to move half the distance toward levels found in North America by 1997, then wholesale activities would account for about 4 percent of total employment. Using the 4 percent of total employment as a basis for projecting future wholesale activity, Table 8.8 presents estimates of 1997 employment in wholesaling, using overall estimates of total employment growth.

Table 8.8
Projected future employment in wholesale trade,
in the Warsaw metropolitan area

Scenario	Total Employment	Wholesale Employment
	805,600	32,200
II	992,100	39,700
III	1,027,000	41,100

Source: Warsaw Economic Analysis Unit, 1994

Based on surveys of warehousing facilities in the Warsaw Metropolitan area, it is estimated that warehousing facilities contain an average of 140 square meters of space per employee. By applying this average to the estimates and projections of wholesale employment, estimates of the historical and projected levels of warehousing space can be obtained. Table 8.9 presents estimates of the net demand for warehousing space in 1997. This is based on a 1992 estimated wholesale space of 1,900,000 square meters (13,700 employees times 140 square meters per worker). Estimates provided in Table 8.8 show that the gross demand for warehousing space will range from 4.5 to 5.8 million square meters of space.

This suggests that the total five year net new demand for warehousing and distribution facilities in the metropolitan area will range from approximately 2.6 to 3.9 million square meters. On an annual basis this translates to 520,000 to 780,000 square meters of net new demand.

Table 8.9
Projected demand for warehousing facilities, 1997,
in the Warsaw metropolitan area

Projection scenario	Sq. Mt.		
	1997 wholesale employment	1997 wholesale space requirements*	net new demand for warehousing space**
I	32,200	4,500,000	2,600,000
II	39,700	5,600,000	3,700,000
III	41,100	5,800,000	3,900,000

Source: Economic Analysis Unit

* assumes 140 sq.m. per employee

**net new demand is 1997 requirements minus 1,900,000

Spatial patterns of warehousing demand

Given the abundant supply of vacant or under-utilized industrial space in the Warsaw metropolitan area, most of the current effective demand for space is directed toward well-located industrial facilities which have buildings suitable for goods storage and transfer. Not all industrial buildings are well-suited for warehousing and storage. Buildings should have good access to highways, have ample parking for trucks, have truck-high loading docks, high ceilings, be secure and in some cases provide heating. Buildings which meet these limited criteria and are located on or near main roads currently command $10 a square meter per month, other buildings of lesser quality rent at $6 to $8 per square meter per month.

To date there is little evidence of widespread new construction of warehousing facilities in the region. This is due to the fact that the region has at least 10,000,000 square meters of industrial space which is no longer used for manufacturing. Assuming that all of the 1,900,000 square meters of warehousing space is located in such facilities and that another 1,000,000 square meters in used for other purposes (offices, clubs, retail shops, sports facilities), there is at least 7,000,000 square meters of space available, enough to accommodate the projected net new demand for warehousing facilities for 1997. If the demand for warehousing space is fully met by the stock of vacant industrial space, the spatial pattern of warehousing space demand should reflect the existing diatribution of vacant industrial space. By assessing the location of such manufacturing space, it is estimated that in 1992, 75 percent of the region's supply of warehousing facilities was located in the City of Warsaw (1,425,000 square meters) and the remainder was located in outlying gminas (475,000 square meters). If the ratio remains the same, then the City of

Warsaw should capture 75 percent of the net new demand for space, between 1,875,000 and 3,000,000 square meters.

On the other hand if new construction of warehousing commences and starts to capture a share of the market, the future demand for warehousing and distribution facilities will shift to suburban areas. If new construction captured between 25 and 40 percent of the market and all of the new construction was sited outside the City, then the spatial division of warehousing demand would be about 50 percent — 50 percent between the City of Warsaw and the surrounding ring. Table 8.10 reports the projected 1997 distribution of warehousing facilities.

Table 8.10
Distribution of warehousing space,
metropolitan Warsaw ('000) sq. meters

	1992	1997 Low estimate Share in City		1997 High estimate Share in City	
		50%	75%	50%	75%
City of Warsaw	1,425	2,250	3,375	2,900	4,350
Ring	475	2,250	1,125	2,900	1,450
Total	1,900	4,500	4,500	5,800	5,800

Source: Warsaw Economic Analysis Unit, 1994

Overall summary of future property development activity, 1992-1997

Based on projections of employment and population, a series of "order of magnitude" projections of housing, office space, retail shops and centers, industrial facilities and warehousing and distribution centers, have been constructed. The projections are primarily driven by changes in employment levels. In most cases some additional element of demand for upgrading of space has been factored in, but this is subjective. The estimates provided in Table 8.11 present summary findings of net demand for housing, office, retail, industrial and warehousing space.

Table 8.11
Summary of property development projections, 1992-1997, metropolitan Warsaw

	Projected net demand	
Housing	30,000 to 40,000	dwelling units
Office Space	300,000 to 350,000	square meters
Retail Space	50,000 to 100,000	square meters
Industrial Space	-1,000,000 to -5,000,000 net	square meters
Warehousing & Distribution Facilities	2,600,000 to 3,900,000	square meters

Source: Warsaw Economic Analysis Unit, 1994

9 Conclusions and recommendations

Introduction

This report has assessed current economic, real estate and infrastructure conditions in Metropolitan Warsaw. It has also prepared projections, to 1997, of future economic trends and the resulting demand for real estate and infrastructure services. This chapter summarizes the main findings of the research, and it offers recommendations for addressing Warsaw's future infrastructure development and upgrading needs.

Economic performance

Since 1988, Metropolitan Warsaw's economy been going through fundamental economic restructuring. As Chapter 2 discussed, employment in Metropolitan Warsaw declined from 1,066,400 in 1988 to 969,900 in 1992. Most of the decline took place in the manufacturing sector, where employment declined from 331,400 to 234,500. Other significant declines occurred in construction, transportation, housing services, and science and technology. In contrast, employment grew in the retail and wholesale trade, finance and insurance, agriculture and state administrative sectors.

Metropolitan Warsaw's foreign trade patterns have also undergone deep changes, switching their orientation from the East to the West. The share of exports to countries of the former USSR declined nearly four-fold, and imports from these countries fell 2.5 times.

Shifting demand significantly altered the product structure of exports. At the national level, industrial exports, declined from 75 to 35 percent of total export volume. Construction industry exports similarly fell from 7.7 to 1 percent.

The causes of these changes in the structure of foreign trade are varied. To a significant degree, they were forced by the collapse of the Eastern market. The most important cause, however, is the low competitiveness of Poland's products. Errors in Poland's economic policy have also contributed to the unfavorable situation in foreign trade. Among the most important are: excessive opening of the domestic market, which went beyond the need of creating competition for domestic producers (in the light manufacturing and food industries), faulty exchange-rate policy, and privatization programs not geared toward modernizing the structure of industry.

The structure of the City of Warsaw's and the surrounding metropolitan area's foreign trade, underwent similar though significantly deeper changes than the country as a whole. The entire region experienced a greater decline in the share of industrial exports than the nation, and a dramatic collapse in the construction industry's exports. Despite these declines, Metropolitan Warsaw's share of total national exports is significant, accounting for 12 percent in 1992. The Warsaw metropolitan region does, however, import more than it exports.

Despite the recession in the economy across Poland, investment expenditures are being made. The growth rate of investment has been linked to the level of profitability of particular sectors of the national economy. In both Metropolitan Warsaw and the nation, the most rapidly growing sectors of the economy are communications and retail and wholesale trade. The growth rate in investments, as measured by the ratio of investment expenditures to the value of fixed assets, was higher in Warsaw, with the exception of 1988, than in the country as a whole. As a result, Warsaw's share in total investment expenditures in the national economy increased from 7 percent in 1990 to approximately 10 percent in 1992. It is worth mentioning that these percentages were greater in the suburban ring of Warsaw than in the City, suggesting that investment growth is greater in the suburbs.

Next to its greater investment possibilities, Warsaw's economy is in a more advantageous situation than the national economy thanks to a market that is over 2.5 times greater in terms of per capita income and local governmental fiscal capacity.

The number of companies in Metropolitan Warsaw increased nearly 15 times between 1988 and 1992 (from 5,600 to 83,800). The greatest increase (20 times) occurred in the City of Warsaw gminas outside of the central gmina. The downtown area had the lowest growth rate (8.5 times).

In industry and transportation, the greatest growth in the number of firms took place in gminas adjacent to the City of Warsaw and in gminas located beyond. On the other hand, in the construction sector, the number of firms grew fastest in gminas around the downtown and around the those gminas adjacent to the City. This trend testifies to the appearance of fairly clear signs of decentralization in some sectors of the economy. On the other hand, communications and finance and insurance are concentrating in the city center.

The greatest amount of economic activity took place in wholesale and retail trade, where the number of firms increased over 72 times. This is the result, on one hand, of the relatively high profitability and quick turnover of capital in this sector up until 1990, and on the other hand, of the ease of entry into the market and low start-up costs. Owing to these economic conditions, small firms dominated the trade sector. However, in the near future, a trend toward the concentration of trade activity in larger firms is anticipated.

Important changes also occurred in the spatial distribution of trade firms. The share of firms located downtown fell by about 20 percent, while the share of firms located outside the downtown, but in the City, increased by 23 percent. In the gminas just beyond the City limits, the share of trade firms increased by 2 percent. Beyond these gminas, the relative share of trade firms declined (although in absolute terms they increased by 500 percent). Significant growth in the number of firms outside the downtown, but in the City, testifies to the progressive de-concentration of economic activity in the Warsaw region.

The total value of income (in constant prices) obtained by economic entities in the Warsaw metropolitan area in 1992 slightly exceeded 1988 levels. This occurred thanks to firms located downtown, whose income rose 20.4 percent. The income of economic entities located in other areas was lower in 1992, from as much as 46 percent in the most distant gminas, to 16 percent in those gminas adjacent to the downtown. At the same time, however, the costs of obtaining income significantly increased, by over 45 percent for the region as a whole, and by 97 percent for firms operating in the downtown. Nonetheless, income exceeded costs in all gminas.

The relationships between income and cost trends are significantly differentiated in the particular sectors of the economy. The fall in industrial production and transportation activity is significantly greater than the decline in employment. In construction, however, the opposite occurred — income reached 1988 levels, while employment fell 21 percent. In other words, as opposed to industry and transportation, labor productivity increased.

The most profitable economic sectors in the metropolitan area in 1988 were trade and communications — thanks to this, they developed quickly between 1988 and 1992. On the other hand, in 1992, the highest profitability rates were in communications and communal services, highly monopolized sectors of the economy. Communal services, it should be noted, achieved these relatively good results because of reduced costs. Income, in constant prices, grew by 13 percent, while real costs declined by 13 percent.

The profitability of the City's and the region's economy, though somewhat higher than the national average, is low. In most cases, investors can make a greater return by placing their money in banks. Such a situation does not foster the development of economic activity, especially of a productive character — quite to the contrary, it is a threat to development.

The distribution of fixed assets and of investment expenditures, according to location, essentially confirms the aforementioned trends toward decentralization and de-concentration in several economic sectors in the metropolitan region. These trends could be the harbinger of a process of fundamental transformation in the functional structure of the Warsaw metropolitan region.

Warsaw's future economic prospects

Economic growth forecasts made in this report are based on analysis and evaluation of recent trends and of local and external conditions of growth in particular branches of the regional economy. Three scenarios have been prepared:

I continuation of recent trends (during 1988-1992)

II differentiated growth in particular sectors of Warsaw's economy

III accelerated growth, at a rate nearly twice as fast as that assumed under scenario II.

Scenario I projects that total employment in the metropolitan area decreases from 970,100 in 1992 to 950,900 in 1997. The net decline, masks very significant changes in employment across the various sectors of the economy. The continuation of recent trends would lead to an excessive fall in employment in some economic sectors, especially industry, transportation, science, education and technological development; and to excessive employment growth in other sectors, such as finance and insurance (where employment would grow from 26,500 in 1992 to 63,200 in 1997). This disproportionate growth would result in a significant waste of resources, especially labor.

It is unlikely, however, that these trends will continue, because retail trade has already hit the demand barrier, and any further expansion of this sector will depend on increases in consumption. It also seems improbable that the rate of growth in the finance and insurance sector will continue at its recent tempo. Acceleration in the process of bank consolidation should be anticipated, because the majority of small and weak banks will not be able to withstand growing competition from large and powerful competitors. Communications will also fail to maintain its recent growth rate, even if it attains absolute increases on par with those achieved during the 1988-1992 period. This is due to the same dynamic mechanism in development processes, where a saturation point is reached. Unused production capacity in industry, transportation and construction allow for significant expansion of production with little or no employment growth.

Scenarios II and III, which are believed to be more plausible, estimate that regional employment will increase to between 1,002,300 (II) and 1,045,300 (III). Under both scenarios, the Warsaw region's economy will continue to restructure, but there will be far less retrenchment in industry, science and education and communal services. In the most probable outcome (scenario II) the structure of the economy will shift from primary, to secondary and tertiary activities. As the next sections describes, these changes in the composition of the economy will influence the demand for real estate development and infrastructure investments.

What will it cost to modernize and expand Warsaw's economic base?

The most likely projection (scenario II) estimates that employment will increase from 970,100 to 1,002,300 between 1992 and 1997. This increase in employment and the continuing restructuring of the Metropolitan Warsaw economy will generate a significant increase in the demand for new facilities and supporting infrastructure.

Based upon projections of population and economic activity, it is estimated that 30,000 to 40,000 housing units will be constructed between 1992 and 1997. Office construction activity will range from 250,000 to 375,000 square meters of new buildings. The construction of new retail space will range from 50,000 to 100,000 square meters. The net demand for industrial facilities will decline in aggregate terms, but some limited new construction of modern facilities will occur over the 1992-1997 period. A significant number of warehousing and distribution buildings will be constructed over the five year period. In total, somewhere between 5,200,000 and 7,350,000 square meters of new housing, offices, shops and warehouses will be constructed over the 1992-1997 period (these figures assume an average housing size of 75 square meters).

Economic and population growth in the City will require the expansion of infrastructure systems. Available funding may limit the expansion to lengthening networks and connecting new users where reserves of productive capacity of central equipment, and reserves of capacity in the main transmission networks exist. In areas where such reserves are lacking, growth will require additional investments in infrastructure facilities. Given the fact that much of the City of Warsaw's existing systems of infrastructure are deficient and operating beyond capacity, it is very likely that even modest increments in growth will require major capital expenditures in infrastructure.

To simplify the analysis, Warsaw's future infrastructure requirements can be divided into two kinds: 1) investments and repairs to remove the backlog of deferred maintenance and to upgrade the system to acceptable standards; and 2) investments to support additional growth in population and economic activity.

Very preliminary estimates of the cost of upgrading the current level of infrastructure services range from $1.8 to $2.2 billion US dollars. About half the amount is needed for central heating, water and waste-water treatment, and solid waste disposal systems. The other half is needed for roads, transportation, telecommunications, electric and gas.

The actual impact of new construction on the demand for infrastructure investments will greatly depend on the location of new development. For example, if all new growth is channeled into areas with existing infrastructure capacity (using vacant infill sites, or redeveloping derelict industrial areas), the estimated cost of providing infrastructure service ranges between $670 and $940 million (in 1993 prices). On the other hand if all new development was located in "green-field" areas requiring the expansion of trunk infrastructure systems, the total cost would range between $1.8 and $2.5 billion, about 170 percent more.

Warsaw's total infrastructure investment requirements, for both upgrading and repairing existing systems, and providing new service to growth areas, ranges from $2.5 to $4.7 billion dollars. If all of these improvements are financed through long term debt (over 30 years at 8 percent interest), the annual aggregate debt service payment would range from $222 to $420 million. This works out to $230 to $430 per household, and accounts for between 11 to 21 percent of 1992 average household income. Given these high costs, how can the region can pay for its infrastructure needs? Are there ways to reduce the necessary costs of infrastructure, without stifling economic growth and development?

Local government budgets will not be capable of financing improvements. The total income from budgets of all the districts of Metropolitan Warsaw up to 1997 would not suffice to finance infrastructure investments needed to meet new demands and make up for the investment backlog. Looking just at the City of Warsaw's needs, it will be difficult to finance future new infrastructure costs, since it is currently impossible to earmark more than Plz. 109,000,000 to Plz. 129,000,000 a year from the local budgets for infrastructure. Assuming infrastructure finance was available at 8 percent for 30 years, these set asides would only support Plz. 1.2 to Plz. 1.4 billion in debt. Thus the financing of infrastructure, whether it is for upgrading and maintenance or the provision of service to new customers, constitutes a serious problem which local government will have to confront if the City of Warsaw is to become, in the not too distant future, a modern European city.

There are, however, a number of possible solutions to the infrastructure financing problem. Several of the infrastructure sectors can and will successfully attract private capital to finance improvements and expansion. Telecommunications, electric and gas system improvements can all be financed privately through user charges. More "public" services, such as water supply, waste-water treatment and solid waste disposal can also rely on user charges to help finance investments. Charges for road use should be levied through gasoline taxes and vehicle licenses.

Another option worth exploring is the privatization of public services. As other countries and cities have discovered, it is possible to privatize urban services. Private, or jointly owned public-private entities can provide essential services and achieve full cost recovery. Such steps are being considered for the City's bus company. Other infrastructure services might be appropriate for privatization as well.

The problem of infrastructure financing should also be looked at from the producer side as well. Capital and operating costs can be reduced through systematic efforts to:

1   rationalize the consumption of services through measuring consumption and limiting waste;

2   reduce the costs of services through the introduction of competition (privatization and bidding) and efficiency-enhancing tariff systems; and

3 rationalize budget expenditures by distributing them according to results obtained and not costs incurred, and also distributing them to the truly needy.

With the introduction of instruments and mechanisms to increase efficiency, significant savings in investment outlays and costs can be used to finance the expansion and modernization of the City's infrastructure. There exists a need to create a system for financing municipal investments, which would include, not only traditional sources such as fees, budgetary funds and loans, but also modern sources of funds, like savings in expenditures (from improvements in efficiency), and the procurement of funds through joint ventures with the private sector and foundations.

Making Warsaw more efficient: the role of urban planning

Another enormous opportunity to reduce the cost of infrastructure expansion is to rethink the spatial pattern of urban development in the Warsaw region. If Metropolitan Warsaw can develop in a more compact pattern, making better use of vacant and under-utilized parcels, it can save between $1.0 and 1.6 billion in new infrastructure development costs over the 1992-1997 period.

Beyond these cost savings, there are several other benefits likely to result from compact development. First, with more compact form of development, Metropolitan Warsaw will have a better chance of maintaining a high level of transit usage. Secondly, if financial, producer and consumer services are centralized, it will be easier to generate agglomeration economies. If such economies can be created, businesses will be more productive and profitable. Can Metropolitan Warsaw shift its pattern of urban development? The answer depends on whether the City and surrounding towns can alter their basic urban laws, policies and programs.

For Metropolitan Warsaw to fully exploit the cost and productivity benefits of compact development it must address four key issues:

1 public land ownership;

2 promoting high intensity development;

3 redevelopment of industrial and under-utilized areas; and

4 developing new methods for infrastructure finance.

Virtually all of the land in the central business district of Warsaw is in public ownership. In the remainder of the City, private land ownership ranges from 10 to 46 percent. In contrast, suburban areas are mostly in private ownership. At present, it is extremely difficult, time consuming and risky to try to purchase or obtain the use rights to publicly held land. Titles are uncertain and administrative procedures for disposing of land are complex. As a consequence, private developers and com-